Essays in the Theory of Society

Essays in the Theory of Society

RALF DAHRENDORF

Stanford University Press   Stanford, California

Chapters 1–3 and 6–10 were originally published in German. Chapter 5 is published here for the first time in any language. Chapter 4, copyright 1958 by Ralf Dahrendorf, first appeared in the *American Journal of Sociology*. A substantial portion of Chapter 6 was first published in English under the title "On the Origin of Social Inequality" in *Philosophy, Politics and Society, Second Series*, © 1962 by Basil Blackwell; the essay has been extensively revised and expanded for this volume. All the essays originally written in German have been translated by the author. For details of the essays' printing history, see pp. 281–91.

Preface

The story behind the publication of this volume began when English and American friends suggested publishing a translation of my essay "Homo Sociologicus." My publisher, having asked some expert readers to comment on the piece, had his doubts; at least one of the readers found the essay neither particularly original nor particularly stimulating. Possibly he was right, possibly wrong; what is of interest is that American and European sociologists, at least until very recently, have had strikingly different ideas of what is stimulating. In Germany, "Homo Sociologicus" has gone through six editions and has given rise to more than a dozen critical studies, the most recent of which describes it as "probably the most influential contribution to sociological theory that has appeared in Germany since the war," and "the only one that has led to a full-fledged public controversy." (5: 5.) My publications on class and the theory of conflict have had exactly the opposite fate. Although they were not exactly ignored in Germany, they failed to stimulate discussion, whereas their critical reception both in Britain and in the United States has been very gratifying.

Instead of trying to explain this difference, let me continue the story. My publisher, Mr. Leon E. Seltzer of Stanford University Press (to whom I am greatly indebted for more reasons than the eventual publication of this volume), could not very well discount the judgment of his experts; on the other hand, he did not want to abandon the idea of publishing an English version of "Homo Sociologicus." So he suggested adding a few other pieces written in more or less the same vein and making up a volume of papers under the title of *Essays in the Theory of Society*. This is the volume.

Now one might of course ask what is "the same vein," and why should a whole volume written in this vein be more acceptable than "Homo Sociologicus"? The answer to the question, if there is one, is that these essays as a whole tend to exemplify a view of society that both American and European sociologists may find of interest. In the United States, a certain dissatisfaction with "technical" or "professional" sociology has led many sociologists to take a broader view of their discipline, and in particular to devote more time to what I call para-theoretical interests. The "new sociology" in America, if it is anything at all, is above all a reminder not only of the moral, political, and philosophical implications of technical sociology, but of the potential benefits to theory itself, in the most rigorous sense, of reflection about the nature and course of human society. In Germany, and more generally in Europe, much of the excitement still felt about sociology comes precisely from such para-theoretical reflections. The great debates of European sociology lead to argument rather than empirical testing; they do not exclude the philosopher, or indeed the intelligent outsider, from participation.

Such debates involve, in René König's terms, "the theory of society" rather than "sociological theory": "Whereas sociological theory has to do with detailed problems clearly delimited from each other, with findings that build onto existing knowledge or reject it as the case may be, the theory of society is concerned with the interpretation of the totality of social being." (3: 10.) Robert K. Merton has tried to render the methodological concept intended here more precise. "Much of what is described in textbooks as sociological theory," he writes, "consists of general orientations toward substantive materials," orientations that provide only "the broadest framework for empirical inquiry" but are indispensable to "the process of arriving at determinate hypotheses" (4: 87–88). In other words, though theories of society may be relatively vague and incapable of empirical test, they help us to discover the variables that enter into general explanatory statements capable of empirical test-ing. Theories of society are useful as pointers to sociological theories.

Irving Louis Horowitz has similar ideas. "The forging of a valu-able sociology," he writes, "depends in part on the creation of a social science of values." What is required today is a "new effort to forge a sociology of the big range." "The fourth dimension, history, is missing from our work." (94: 11, 19, 25.) One may doubt whether the concept of a "social *science* of values" makes methodological sense, and whether the notion of small, middle, and big ranges is very illuminating; but the editor of *The New Sociology* certainly has a point in demanding a new look at value-free sociology, a greater readiness to analyze inclusive social units, and an attempt to weave historical awareness into sociological generalizations.

Possibly the most sophisticated attempt so far to clarify the task of sociology thus understood is that of Jürgen Habermas in his defi-nition of critical sociology:

> If, therefore, sociology can be ascribed any task beyond the pragmatic tasks of an empirical-analytical science of planning, it is this: instead of explaining what is *happening* in a given case, to keep us aware of what we are doing, i.e. planning and building, irrespective of whether we are doing it consciously or blindly and without reflection. A critical sociology in this sense should view its subject precisely from an imagined a priori perspective, as a generalized subject of social action; whereas empirical-analytical sociology, which is directly integrated into the system of action, must indeed ignore the point of view of the actor. Only in this *double role* can sociology achieve a consciousness of itself; can it protect itself and society from working uncritically on things as they are, from effecting fixation (and even change) naïvely with scientific means. (1: 228.)

A theory of society, then, not only prepares the way for the formu-lation of sociological theories, but accompanies such theories as a guard against their reification and a reminder of their implications, both theoretical and practical; moreover, it is the basis for making judgments of their value, and in general for understanding the wider context, again both theoretical and practical, in which all

efforts to create a science of sociology stand. "Pro-theory" would describe the aspect emphasized by Merton; "meta-theory" is a term
best reserved for another meaning, namely theories about theories
in the logical sense. I have accordingly used "para-theory" to describe what I have in mind when I speak of the "vein" of these
Essays.

The methodological characterization of this vein, however, lacks
all reference to its substance, which is what really ties these *Essays*
together. From essay to essay, a number of key concepts recur, concepts that I believe add up to a fairly coherent theory of society. In
one of the *Essays,* "Market and Plan," there is a passage in which
most of these concepts play a part:

> The structures of power in which the political process takes
> place offer an explanation not only of how change originates and
> what direction it takes, but also of why it is necessary. Power al-
> ways implies non-power and therefore resistance. The dialectic
> of power and resistance is the motive force of history. From the
> interests of those in power at a given time we can infer the inter-
> ests of the powerless, and with them the direction of change. Here
> is the nexus where norms are laid down, called into question,
> modified, and called into question again. Here is the source of
> initiative, and thus of the historicity—and that means the vitality,
> the openness, the freedom—of human societies. Power produces
> conflict, and conflict between antagonistic interests gives lasting
> expression to the fundamental uncertainty of human existence,
> by ever giving rise to new solutions and ever casting doubt on
> them as soon as they take form.

Power, resistance, conflict, historical change, openness, freedom,
uncertainty—with varying emphasis, these notions pervade the
present volume. Inevitably, the sociological perspective made up
by such notions is a political and philosophical perspective as well.
It is the perspective of a modern liberalism: averse to utopia in sociological theory as in political practice (and in that sense neither
"conservative" nor "radical"), always looking for ways to guarantee
individual liberty in a world of constraints, confident in the ability
of the right social and political institutions to provide the possibility

of free human development, and skeptical of all theories and approaches in social science that ignore or neglect the question of what they have to contribute to bringing about a society in which men may be free.

The publishing history of the ten essays assembled in this volume is described in the notes at the end of the book. Six were originally lectures, and in some of them this is still recognizable. One of them, "Out of Utopia," has been reprinted so often that I confess to a little embarrassment at offering it once again: yet it belongs with the others and cannot be omitted. Between the original version of the earliest ("Values and Social Science") and the most recent of these essays ("Sociology and the Sociologist"), more than ten years elapsed, and while I should not have included any piece to which I no longer subscribe, the difference is bound to tell.

Indeed, these two papers, my *Habilitation* lecture at Saarbrücken in 1957 and my inaugural lecture of 1967 at the new University of Constance (in whose founding I had participated), demonstrate continuities and changes in my thinking in relation to what is basically the same question. The earlier paper, which essentially accepts Max Weber's rigorous distinction of fact and value, betrays only faint traces of a view that has since become my firm conviction: that the sociologist's responsibility extends far beyond the boundaries of his discipline. A similar intellectual development may be seen in some of the other essays, notably the two dedicated to my teacher, the Göttingen philosopher Josef König, one ("Homo Sociologicus") on the occasion of his sixty-fifth birthday in 1958, the other ("Uncertainty, Science, and Democracy") as part of the Festschrift for his seventieth birthday in 1963. All but two of the essays ("Out of Utopia" and "In Praise of Thrasymachus") were originally written in German. Although the basic English versions of all ten are my work, the volume has benefited greatly from the outstanding editing provided by Stanford University Press.

If this volume were just a record of a stage of thought, it might be of little interest. I am glad that it shows movement. Yet it must be said that this volume gathers contributions of a decade that I regard as finished in substantive concern as well as style. I remain, of course, convinced that what these *Essays* say is sound, but I have come to see them as too remote from the needs of present-day sociology. The trouble with theories of society is that the sociological theories they promise, claim to accompany, or criticize are in fact nonexistent. Habermas's point would be much better taken if the "empirical-analytical science of planning" to which he objects were really in existence; it is not, and it is needed. For myself, I intend to turn from the philosophy of *homo sociologicus* to role theory, from reflections on the origin of inequality to the theory of social stratification, from the reorientation of political and sociological theory to the theory of conflict—in short, from praising Thrasymachus to doing what neither he nor his contemporaries did or could do. If the reader should therefore find himself becoming a little impatient in the perusal of this volume, I want him to know that the author shares his feeling.

R. D.

Constance, September 1967

Contents

Essays in the Theory of Society

1

Values and Social Science
The Value Dispute in Perspective

A dramatic chapter in the history of German social science reached its climax on January 5, 1914, in Berlin, at a meeting of the enlarged committee of the Verein für Sozialpolitik.[1] The circumstances of this meeting were strange enough. Before the discussion began, the more than fifty participants passed a number of resolutions that in themselves would have sufficed to ensure their meeting a place in history and legend: they sent the stenographers home, ruled any taking of minutes out of order, formally vowed to disclose nothing about the proceedings to any nonparticipant, and forbade publication of the written papers that had been submitted by eminent scholars as a basis for discussion. The fears that probably gave rise to this secrecy proved justified. The discussion ended in a passionate clash of convictions and personalities, a clash that divided German social scientists into two groups for years and in some respects divides them to the present day. The subject that led to such extraordinary measures and results was precisely the subject of these reflections: values and social science.

Even now it is difficult to reconstruct in detail the prehistory and history of the memorable *Werturteilsstreit* (as the Value Dispute was called at the time), and impossible to do so without taking sides.

---

[1] This "Association for Social Policy," which had been founded in 1872, was in fact the professional organization of social scientists; it subsequently became, and is today, the German Economics Association. In its early years, it was dominated by the intellectuals who originated and supported Bismarck's welfare state policies. For a detailed history of the Verein, see Franz Boese (6).

Whatever one may think about the feasibility and desirability of a value-free social science, the subject of value-free science itself cannot, it appears, be discussed in a value-free, or even dispassionate, manner. So far as the historical Value Dispute is concerned, we know that from the beginning of the century on, the question of the place of "value judgments" in social science arose with increasing frequency and intensity in the debates of the Verein für Sozialpolitik. When in 1904 Edgar Jaffe, Werner Sombart, and Max Weber took over as editors of the *Archiv für Sozialwissenschaft und Sozialpolitik*, they published in their first issue a statement of policy that said, among other things: "Inevitably, problems of social *policy* will . . . find expression in the columns of this journal . . . alongside those of social *science*. But we would not dream of pretending that such discussions can be described as 'science,' and we shall see to it that they are not confused with it." (24: 157.)

This statement was meant to be polemical, and in fact constituted an outright attack on the prevailing mood of the Verein and its then almost undisputed head, Gustav Schmoller. It was Schmoller who had prescribed for the "science of economics" not merely the tasks "of explaining individual phenomena by their causes, of helping us understand the course of economic development, and if possible of predicting the future," but also that of "recommending" certain "economic measures" as "ideals" (23: 77). At the very next meeting of the Verein, the Mannheim meeting of 1905, a violent exchange on this issue took place between Schmoller and Weber, which led to the characterization of Weber and others as a "radical left wing" and had other lasting consequences. A few years later, in 1909, the "radical left wing" founded the German Sociological Society, whose 1910 statutes stated in no uncertain terms: "It is the purpose [of the Society] to advance sociological knowledge by undertaking purely scientific investigations and surveys, and by publishing and supporting purely scientific studies. . . . It rejects all concern with practical (ethical, religious, political, esthetic, etc.) goals of any kind." (8: v.)

In order to make clear the polemical nature of this paragraph, and of the founding of the German Sociological Society as such, the

explicit reference to the Verein in the report of the Society's executive committee at its second meeting in 1912 was hardly needed:
"In contrast to the Verein für Sozialpolitik, whose very purpose is
to make propaganda for certain ideals, our purpose has nothing to
do with propaganda, but is exclusively one of objective research."
(9:78.) Indeed, the founding charter of the Verein für Sozialpolitik
had included such goals as "supporting the prosperous development" of industry, "stimulating timely, well-considered state intervention to protect the just interests of all participants" in the economy, and helping to accomplish "the supreme tasks of our time and
our nation." (6: 248ff.) Despite the controversy, however, the "pure
scientists" remained members of the Verein; indeed, they were the
ones who proposed, in a circular letter of November 12, the explicit
discussion of value judgments that turned into the Value Dispute.
"To lay the groundwork for the meeting, the letter listed four topics for discussion: (1) the position of moral value judgments in scientific economics; (2) the relation of economic development to
value judgments; (3) the determination of the goals of economic
and social policy; and (4) the relation of general methodological
principles to the particular requirements of academic teaching."
(6: 145.)

In accordance with the proposal set forth in the letter, a number
of members wrote "position papers" on the four topics to be discussed. The authors of these statements included Franz Eulenburg,
Wilhelm Oncken, Joseph Schumpeter, Othmar Spann, Eduard
Spranger, Max Weber, and Leopold von Wiese—to mention but
a few of the most important names. At Schmoller's suggestion, the
meeting took place on January 5, 1914, in the conspiratorial atmosphere described above, which was intended (in the words of a partisan, pro-Schmoller report written in 1939 by Franz Boese, then
secretary of the Verein) "to preserve the wholly intimate character
of the discussion, and also to make sure that the expected differences of opinion would not be used by outsiders against the Verein
or against science." (6: 147.) After that, passion held sway: Weber
and Sombart on one side, Karl Grünberg and the majority of those
present on the other, clashed violently, until in the end—to quote

Boese's report again—Weber "once again rose to deliver a weighty statement, which, without mincing words, informed his opponents that they did not understand what he (Weber) was talking about," whereupon he "angrily" left the meeting (6: 147).

If we can trust such reports as we have, the Value Dispute ended with the clear "defeat" of the "pure scientists." Even seven years later, after the First World War and Weber's death, Paul Honigsheim observed somewhat apologetically: "Of all the things Max Weber did, said, and wrote, nothing has been as much talked about, commented on, misunderstood, and laughed off as his doctrine of a value-free approach in sociology." (13: 35.) But the "victory" of the "social politicians" proved ephemeral. The development of social science since the Value Dispute has been, in the words of the German economist Karl Schiller, a continuous "retreat from subjective value-tables to the toolbox" (22: 19). Indeed, it would seem that the relative strengths of the two parties to the debate have been reversed, so that today the defenders of a combination of values and social science feel themselves in the minority, and the "radical left wing" of our own day would be more likely to advance, at least in discussions of methodology, a position nearer Schmoller's.[2] Despite the duration and the undiminished intensity of the dispute, however, many of the questions underlying it have been repressed rather than resolved, with the result that they still require elucidation.

II

It would be wrong to describe the Value Dispute of 1914 as a matter of a few individuals. Yet its course was determined primarily by the one man with whose name it is today inseparably linked and for whom it was more than a scholarly debate: I mean, of

[2] The "conservatism-radicalism" debate is the main concern of American sociologists today; for a balanced, if partisan, discussion, see Jürgen Habermas, "Kritische und konservative Aufgaben der Soziologie" (1). A more general account of the state of the value debate can be found in the proceedings of the German Sociological Society meeting on the occasion of the one hundredth anniversary of Weber's birth, in 1964 (see 10).

course, Max Weber. The polemical statement quoted from the *Archiv für Sozialwissenschaft,* the profound differences with Schmoller, the founding of a German Sociological Society with statutes stressing the need for "pure science," the report of this Society's executive committee at its second meeting, the suggestion that an open debate be held in the Verein für Sozialpolitik—all this was Weber's work. In his essays, collected later under the title *Gesammelte Aufsätze zur Wissenschaftslehre,* and even more vividly in his famous Munich lecture on "Science as a Vocation," the intensity and passion of the bitter struggle to establish a value-free social science come to life. Weber took sides on the question that interests us here; he did so more radically than anyone else. For that very reason it seems useful to relate the following considerations, explicitly or implicitly, above all to Max Weber.

We are concerned here not with reawakening old passions, but with reformulating the relationship between social science and value judgments and essaying a few general propositions. We shall try especially to distinguish between the various aspects of this problem, which were all too often badly confused in the heat of the dispute fifty years ago. In doing so we shall have to distinguish questions that permit of analytic solutions from others that by their very nature allow plausible, perhaps convincing, but in the last analysis only personal answers. Weber called his position paper for the Value Dispute (reworked in 1917 for publication) "The Meaning of 'Value-free' in the Sociological and Economic Sciences." More precisely, we have to ask: What is the legitimate place of value judgments in sociology? Where must they be eliminated from scientific sociology, and how is this to be done? Where, how, and to what extent may value judgments exert their influence without endangering the goals and results of scientific research? Where might it indeed be necessary to abandon Weber's rigid insistence on value-free scholarship?

Even Weber complained that "interminable misunderstandings, and above all terminological (thus wholly sterile) disputes, have arisen over the term 'value judgment,' which obviously do not contribute anything at all to the substance of the problem." (24: 485.)

It seems indeed possible to set out—without extensive discussion—
with the notion that value judgments are statements about what
ought or ought not to happen, what is or is not desired, in the
world of human action. Weber's definition seems useful: "By 'valu-
ation' we shall understand the 'practical' rejection or approval of a
phenomenon capable of being influenced by our actions." (24: 475.)
It seems obvious, moreover, that any such value judgment, any
statement that concerns a practical obligation, includes assumptions that are neither verifiable nor falsifiable by observable facts.
In other words, value judgments cannot be derived from scientific
insights.[3] The assertions of social science and value judgments may
legitimately be seen as two distinct types of statement. We may ask,
therefore, at which points in the sociologist's research he encounters value judgments, and how he should act in these encounters.
If with this question in mind we follow the steps in the process of
acquiring knowledge in social science, it seems to me that we find
six points at which value judgments are an issue. A consideration
of these six points may help to advance the discussion of a value-
free sociology beyond its explosive and unsatisfactory state at the
end of the *Werturteilsstreit*.

III

Scientific inquiry begins, at least in temporal terms, with the
choice of a subject, and it is here that we find the first possible encounter between social science and value judgments. That the process of inquiry begins with the choice of a subject is rather a trivial
statement; but if we advance one step further and ask on what basis
a scholar chooses the themes of his research, we have left the realm
of triviality. A sociologist may be interested in, say, "the position of
the industrial worker in modern society" for many different reasons. Perhaps he merely believes that this is the subject to which
he can contribute most. Perhaps he regards it as a neglected sub-

---

[3] "Critical theorists," i.e., sociologists with a Hegelian bent, prefer to be somewhat
vague on this point, because they do not want to admit the possibility of a positive
science without critical detachment (see Habermas, 1: 244). But even by these theorists
the basic distinction between the "affirmative" and "critical" functions of science is
not really denied.

ject, one whose study may help to close gaps in our knowledge. He may have a research grant from an institute or foundation requiring him to work on the subject. Possibly he hopes to provide materials for political action to remedy a social injustice. Not all these motives (and there may be many others) involve value judgments, but some do; and the example is routine enough to make it clear that value judgments are often a factor in choosing a subject. Can or must such value judgments be eliminated? What is their place at this point in a sociological inquiry?

The first, and broader, of these questions is easily answered. Let us assume that four different scholars, each guided by a different one of the four motives mentioned, begin to investigate "the position of the industrial worker in modern society," and further that this subject has been defined precisely, so that we may reasonably describe the four men as investigating the same thing. Obviously all four may come up with the same results, and so indeed they should if they follow the rules of empirical social science. But in this event the reasons influencing their choice of subject have no effect on their findings. Clearly, then, the choice of subject is made in what may be called the antechamber of science, where the sociologist is still free from the rules of procedure that will later govern his research. It is probably unrealistic to insist that value judgments be eliminated from the choice of subjects; in any case it is quite unnecessary, since the reason why a subject is regarded as worth investigating is irrelevant in principle to its scientific treatment.

This conclusion is by no means new or exciting; long ago Weber rightly dismissed as a "false objection" the claim that the choice of subjects involves a value judgment. But we may still ask whether or not value judgments *should* govern the choice of subjects for sociological research; in other words, whether fruitful scholarship does not in fact require that the choice of subjects be based on certain values. The answer to this question, whether affirmative or negative, does not of course affect our first conclusion. To stay with our metaphor, we are concerned now with the laws, if any, of the antechamber of science, laws that by definition bear no relation to the laws of science itself.

Time and again in the history of sociology, sociologists have been urged to distinguish between "important" and "unimportant" sub-jects for research. Robert Lynd, in his essay "Values and the Social Sciences," describes as the "most prominent characteristic of the well-educated scholar" his ability to make this distinction between "important" and "unimportant" problems intelligently on the ba-sis of what Lynd calls "guiding *values*" (15: 191). And indeed, the fact that there is no objective way of ranking people's motives for choosing subjects does not mean that all subjects are equally rele-vant and important. For example, two "guiding values" that I con-sider both important and defensible in objective terms are that so-ciologists should not be deterred by social taboos from investigat-ing certain "objectionable" subjects, and that sociological research should promote people's understanding of their own society. Per-haps it can even be stated as a general proposition that the quality of scientific research improves to the extent that the choice of sub-ject betrays a personal commitment on the part of the researcher. But we have to realize that such a commitment is in itself a value judgment. It is not part of scientific research; indeed it is in prin-ciple irrelevant to research except as a sort of precondition or moral environment. Its appeal, therefore, is neither to scientific insight nor to critical perception, but to the sense of evidence or possibly to the consensus of scholars.[4]

IV

Our first encounter between science and values, then, proves to be no encounter at all. Our second, which takes place at the stage of theory formation, is equally trivial. In their *Introduction to Soci-ology*, Jay Rumney and Joseph Maier warn their readers: "Sociolo-gy is not an easy subject to study. . . . Our passions and wishes, con-scious and unconscious, too readily enter into the observation, selec-tion, and classification of facts, which are the first steps in all sci-

---

[4] Modern methods of research planning seem to suggest otherwise, but the appear-ance is deceptive. Behind the subject priorities of the research planners we can usually find one or more of the following value judgments: research should be oriented toward government goals; research should be guided by the foreseeable chance of success; and research should be informed by a sense of economy of means.

ences. We see what we want to see and turn a blind eye to things we don't want to see." In order to remedy this alleged evil, the authors urge the sociologist to "train himself in attitudes of scientific objectivity" with the assistance of "psychoanalysis and the sociology of knowledge" (19: 27–28).

Now it is certainly true that many sociologists, in dealing with their subjects, see only what they want to see. Weber, for example, in investigating the genesis of industrial capitalism in Europe, saw the influence of Calvinism but not that of technological innovations. Talcott Parsons confines his analyses of the integration of societies largely to the normative level and neglects problems of institutional organization. The sociologist of our example—a conservative, let us assume—might see the position of the industrial worker in modern society solely as a matter of "adaptation" to industrial conditions and the effects of various adaptations on individual "satisfactions" and social "equilibrium." The things he does not want to see, things he dislikes as a citizen because they go against his political convictions (strikes, labor mobility, and the like), he does not see. Must we prescribe for him—must we prescribe for Parsons and Weber—"psychoanalysis and the sociology of knowledge"? By concentrating on certain aspects of a subject and neglecting others, have they improperly mixed social science and value judgments? Must value judgments be radically eliminated from the formulation of scientific theories?

Popper's argument is convincing:

> All scientific descriptions of facts are highly selective. . . . It is not only impossible to avoid a selective point of view, but also wholly undesirable to attempt to do so; for if we could do so, we should get not a more "objective" description, but only a mere heap of entirely unconnected statements. But, of course, a point of view is inevitable; and the naïve attempt to avoid it can only lead to self-deception, and to the uncritical application of an unconscious point of view. (17: ii, 260–61.)

I think we may go even further and assert that selectivity of this sort, even if based on a value judgment, is not only inevitable but also no threat to scientific inquiry. To see this, we need only distin-

guish between two aspects of scientific inquiry that are often mis-
leadingly confused: the logic and the psychology of scientific discovery.

A selective point of view, such as the conservative bias of the sociologist described above, does cause a scholar to see what he wants
to see and be blind to other things. However, this merely tells us
how the scholar has come to formulate a given hypothesis X; it does
not tell us whether hypothesis X is true or false, tenable or untenable. Neither the values nor the thought processes of a scientist determine the validity of his hypotheses; their validity is determined
only by empirical test. Nor can empirical tests as such affect the
values and thought processes of the scientist in any way. In short,
the psychological motives behind the formulation of any scientific
theory or hypothesis are irrelevant to its truth or validity. It follows
that the encounter between social science and value judgments at
the stage of theory formation cannot have harmful consequences.[5]
Rumney and Maier's exhortation to practice objectivity is just as
misplaced on this point as the often heard criticism that a scholar
systematically undervalues certain aspects of his subject and over-
values others.

This conclusion—that the selective formation of theories is a
pseudo-problem—may at first seem rather too simple. Harmless as
selective theories may be, one might argue, sociologists in particular all too often forget the selective character of their assumptions
once their research is under way, and end up by making excessively
general claims for what are in fact partial theories. Whereas Parsons, for example, begins by trying to examine the normative aspects of social integration, he ends by asserting that the integration of societies occurs exclusively on the normative level. Such
extending of theories beyond the area for which they were designed
is indeed a fault, one that we shall examine below as "ideological
distortion." This problem must not be confused, however, with the
pseudo-problem of value-conditioned selection in the formation of

---

[5] The distinction between the logic and the psychology of science has other uses.
Among other things, it can contribute to clearing up the debate about induction (the
psychological process of discovery) and deduction (the logical structure of discovery).

scientific theories, which is indeed a pseudo-problem so long as "theories" refers to statements that can be conclusively tested by observation.

V

Next we come to still another pseudo-problem that played a highly confusing role in the Value Dispute: the problem of values as subjects of inquiry. At least since Durkheim, Pareto, and Weber, and particularly since Parsons's *Structure of Social Action*, the study of the normative aspects of social action has occupied a prominent place in scientific sociology. This theme has been even more prominent in recent social anthropology. Theorists and researchers alike have devoted much attention to the prevailing values (and deviant values) found in a given social context, i.e., to the value judgments that mold the behavior of people in society by operating as generalized and sanctioned norms.

This is, to be sure, another point of encounter between social science and value judgments, and one, moreover, that is specific to social science. But no extensive argument should be required to demonstrate that this encounter cannot conceivably lead to any serious confusion. When Weber's opponents interpreted his insistence on a value-free sociology as an effort to eliminate the subject matter of social values from sociological research, he was quite justified in charging them with an "almost unbelievably great misunderstanding." Along with Weber we can reply, "If the normatively valid becomes a subject of empirical investigation, it loses, as a subject of investigation, its normative character: it is treated as 'existing,' not as 'valid.'" (24: 517.) Indeed, it is neither necessary nor sensible to renounce the attempt to study the normative elements of social structure with the tools of empirical social science. Although there are numerous difficulties in such research, it involves no serious confusion of science and value judgments.

The three pseudo-problems discussed so far may seem rather far removed from the emotional, if not indeed from the substantive, core of the Value Dispute. But the objection is only partly valid. Even in Weber's statements a certain lack of clarity in posing the

question is apparent, and subsequent writers have repeatedly confused the pseudo-problems of the choice of subjects, the formation
of theories, and the investigation of values with the other, more
serious problems to which we shall now turn. It should be useful,
then, to know which points of encounter between values and a
value-free social science are only seemingly productive of problems.
At the same time, we must not be misled by the relative ease with
which these pseudo-problems are analyzed and dismissed. The problems to be discussed now—ideological distortion, the application of
scientific results to practical problems, and the social role of the scientist—are both considerably more important and much less susceptible to unambiguous solution.

VI

Let us return for a moment to our conservative sociologist and
his study of the industrial worker in modern society. Let us assume
that this gentleman begins by investigating the relation of the worker to his work setting. He finds that workers derive satisfaction from
their membership in small, so-called informal groups. In particular,
he finds that the stronger a worker's ties are to such informal
groups, the greater his output is, and the higher his morale. This
is a relatively precise, testable statement. But now the sociologist
takes a further step, suggested by his conservative outlook, and asserts that membership in informal groups is the *only* factor influencing job satisfaction and productivity. Wages, working conditions, and relations with supervisors and subordinates count for
nothing; everything, he claims, depends on the functioning of informal groups.[6]

This particular way of confusing social science and value judgments—that is, presenting in the guise of scientific propositions
what are demonstrably value statements unsupported by evidence—

[6] The illustration refers vaguely to Elton Mayo's interpretation of the Hawthorne
findings (16). The example is of special interest in our context because a number of
authors with very different temperaments and values have worked on these data.

I shall call ideological distortion.[7] In sociology we encounter time and again two kinds of such ideologically distorted statements. The first is the kind of overextension of specific propositions that is illustrated in our example. All so-called "single-factor theories," theories that assign absolute determining force to a single factor like race, nationality, or the relations of production, belong in this group; so does the familiar contemporary theory that the tendency toward a leveling-in of certain status symbols in present-day Western societies is transforming them into "classless" societies without structurally generated group conflicts.[8] The second is the presenting of untestable and thus speculative propositions as scientific. An example is the thesis of the alienation of the industrial worker. However much sense this thesis may make in philosophical terms, it has no place in empirical social science, since no amount of empirical research can either confirm or refute it.[9]

All distortions of this kind contain implicit value judgments. Moreover, it is evident that if statements are alleged to be based on scientific investigation when they are in fact drawn from other sources, we are faced with a serious confusion of values and social science. But how is the sociologist to avoid ideological distortions, or to perceive and correct them where they have occurred? Three suggested answers to this question are offered in the literature. The first is the one recommended by Rumney and Maier: training in objectivity with the assistance of psychoanalysis and the sociology of knowledge. More than other scholars, the sociologist, himself inseparably a part of the subject of his research, is in danger of confusing his professional statements with his personal value judgments. The only way to avoid this confusion is by instituting a permanent process of self-observation and self-criticism, in which all propositions are systematically scrutinized for traces of ideological

[7] There are many other notions of ideology. This one is best described by Theodor Geiger (12).

[8] One example is the work of Helmut Schelsky (21). See my discussion of the thesis in *Class and Class Conflict in Industrial Society* (7).

[9] I refer here to Georges Friedmann's use of the notion of alienation to explain away overwhelming evidence of job satisfaction (11).

distortion. Another suggestion is that the sociologist explicitly declare the values that have guided him in his research, so that his
readers or listeners will be in a position to analyze any ideological
distortions that he might unwittingly be guilty of.

It seems to me, however, that a third suggestion is considerably
more promising and effective than the first two. Science is always a
concert of many. The progress of science rests at least as much on
the cooperation of scholars as it does on the inspiration of the individual. This cooperation must not be confined to the all too popular "teamwork"; rather, its most indispensable task is mutual criticism. Wherever scientific criticism gives way to a careless or quietis-
tic tolerance, the gate is open to dishonest and worthless research.
Let us not forget that ideologically distorted statements are always
bad scientific statements. And it seems to me that it is the main task
of scientific criticism to expose such statements and correct them.
In the long run, this procedure alone can protect sociology—though
not the individual sociologist—against the danger of ideological
distortion.[10]

VII

The problem of ideological distortion played only a minor part
in the Value Dispute; it was not until the 1920's that Max Scheler
and Karl Mannheim made it a central concern of social scientists.
Another problem seemed much more important to those who at-
tended the meeting of January 5, 1914—the relation between social
science and social policy, or, as we shall put it, the application of
scientific results to practical problems. The desire to relate theories
and propositions to practical life is probably as old as science itself.
Since the beginnings of human thought, technical problems have
time and again stimulated scientific insights. However, our question
here is not whether practical problems may properly inspire scientific research—this is merely an aspect of the problem of choice of
subjects discussed above—but whether the scholar may properly

10 The allusion to Popper in these remarks is evident. For further discussion of the
problem, see the essay "Uncertainty, Science, and Democracy" below.

bridge the gap between the results of his research and practical action. Let us suppose that our conservative sociologist, having discovered the importance of informal groups to workers' morale, systematically sets about fostering the formation of such groups. Is this a legitimate part of his scientific activity or not?

Obviously, the application of scientific results to practical problems involves an encounter between science and value judgments. In order to do what the sociologist of our example does, one must place some value on the workers' morale. Two utterly different ways of thinking meet here: systematic empirical observation leading to insights into what is, and the strictly meta-empirical conviction of what should be. The latter, the value judgment, is in no way implicit in the former, the scientific insight. It is an additional and different matter; it is above all a matter removed from the domain of the social scientist as such. The application of scientific results, involving as it does an implicit or even explicit decision about goals and purposes, cannot be considered part of the social scientist's professional activity. At this point, science and value judgments have to be strictly separated.

Is there such a thing, then, as a scientific social policy? Or does the sociologist have to renounce all intention of intervening in the destiny of the society he investigates? It seems to me that Weber's answer to these questions is just as valid today as it was half a century ago. If by "intervening" (the concept of "social engineering" often used in England and the United States comes to mind here) we mean action related to goals determined by the sociologist himself, then such action lies outside his strictly scientific competence. He can, however, use the scientific knowledge at his disposal to suggest promising ways of realizing goals formulated by someone else. To try to reorganize a company on one's own initiative and on the implicit assumption that the workers' morale is a value is an undertaking beyond the boundaries of science. To express an opinion, however, about how higher morale might best be achieved remains within these boundaries.[11] To quote Weber again: for the

11 The rigor of this statement may be open to dispute. Disentangling means and ends is obviously easier in theory than in practice. But perhaps the discussion of the

scientist, "the purpose of discussing value judgments can be no more than to elaborate the final, inherently 'consistent' value axioms from which . . . contradictory opinions are derived . . . ; to deduce the 'consequences' for certain value positions that would follow from certain ultimate value axioms if they, and only they, provided the basis of value judgments in factual matters"; and above all, "to state the consequences that would necessarily follow from putting a given value judgment into effect." (24: 496.)

VIII

The problem of application leads us immediately to a final aspect of the relationship between social science and value judgments, the problem of the sociologist's social role. Almost certainly this problem was the emotional basis of the Value Dispute of 1914, and it is still controversial today. Social role analysis applies not only to non-sociologists, but to sociologists as well. Like the doctor, the tailor, the accountant, and the party secretary, the sociologist has a social position endowed with certain expectations that its incumbent is expected to fulfill. Perhaps only on this level can the sociologist usefully ask whether his task is exhausted by inquiring into what exists, or whether, as a sociologist, he is obliged to state and defend value judgments as well. When Schmoller held that the social scientist as such was obliged to guide society in the "right" direction, and Weber countered by recommending the relentless separation of what belongs "in the lecture hall" from what belongs "in political programs, offices, and parliaments," the two men were really arguing about the role of the scholar, i.e., about what the scholar as such is called upon to do. Science and value judgments are two different matters. The question is: Should the social scientist profess both of them in his teaching and writing, or does his calling confine him to strictly scientific matters?

There is without doubt a certain internal consistency in Weber's position, which requires a value-free approach not only of sociol-

---

sociologist's social role in the following section will provide an answer to the questions remaining here.

ogy, but also of the sociologist as such. But consistency by itself is no guarantee of truth. Unlike Weber, and at the risk of sounding paradoxical, I want to advance the thesis that whereas sociology as a value-free science in Weber's sense may be desirable, the sociologist as such must always be morally committed if he is to protect himself and others from unintended consequences of his actions.

My main intention in these reflections has been to show that a value-free sociology represents a much less dramatic program than the impassioned disputants of the *Werturteilsstreit* thought it to be. At many points the encounter of social science and value judgments is harmless, and at others the concert of scholarly opinion may exert a corrective influence. A value-free sociology in this sense certainly corresponds to the ethics of scientific research. But the sociologist has to be more than a man who works at sociology. Whatever he does, says, and writes has potentially far-reaching effects on society. It may be true, generally speaking, that sociologists are neither better nor worse than the societies they live in.[12] But even if sociological research merely helps strengthen such tendencies as are already present in society, the sociologist remains responsible for the consequences of his actions. The conservatism of large sections of American sociology is unfortunate in itself. It is also a convincing refutation of Weber's rigorous separation of roles because it is largely unintentional, so that, for example, the conservative implications of structural-functional theory often contradict the functionalists' explicit political convictions. To protect oneself against such unintended consequences of one's actions, to maintain the integrity of one's moral convictions and one's work as a scholar, is thus a requirement that applies to the sociologist *qua* sociologist.

In a strict analytical sense, Karl Jaspers is surely right when he interprets Weber as follows:

> The scientific impulse to discover the truth and the practical impulse to defend one's own ideals are two different things. This does not mean that they can be acted on independently of each

---

12 This thesis has been put forth by Helmut Schelsky (20) in opposition to the claim that empiricism is conservative, theory radical; Schelsky notes that even routine empirical research may be radical in its effect under highly ideological conditions.

other. Weber is simply against confusing the two; only when they are clearly distinguished can they both be acted on efficiently. There is no relation between scientific objectivity and opportunism. The confusion of the two destroys objectivity as well as conviction. (14: 47.)

Indeed, it would probably be unfair to accuse Weber of separating his own scholarly work too rigidly from his political convictions. But the passionate and explosive union of "science as a vocation" and "politics as a vocation" in Weber's personality is so rare, so entirely personal a solution, that it cannot possibly be thought of as a pattern for all sociologists. Perhaps the only difference between my position and Weber's is a slight difference of emphasis. But it seems to me more important today to warn against the radical separation of science and value judgments than to warn against their commingling. Our responsibility as sociologists does not end when we complete the process of scientific inquiry; indeed, it may begin at that very point. It requires no less than the unceasing examination of the political and moral consequences of our scholarly activity. It commits us, therefore, to professing our value convictions in our writings and in the lecture hall as well.

2

Homo Sociologicus
On the History, Significance, and Limits of the Category of Social Role

Ordinarily, we do not much care that the table, the roast, and the wine of the scientist are paradoxically different from the table, the roast, and the wine of our everyday experience. If we want to put down a glass or write a letter, a table seems a suitable support. It is smooth, solid, and even, and a physicist would scarcely disturb us by observing that the table is "in reality" a most unsolid beehive of nuclear particles. Nor can the chemist spoil our enjoyment of the dinner by dissolving roast and wine into elements that we could hardly be tempted to consume as such. As long as we do not approach the paradox of the scientific table and the everyday table with philosophic intent, we solve it in a simple manner. We act as if the table of the physicist and our own table are two different things that have no relevant relation to each other. While we are quite prepared to concede to the physicist that his table is a most important and useful object for him, we are at the same time satisfied with our table precisely because it is not a multiply perforated beehive of moving particles.[1]

The dilemma is less easily solved when we turn to the biological sciences, especially to the biology of man. There is something unsettling about viewing a glass model of a man in an exhibition, or

[1] In an unpublished paper on "Paradox and Discovery," the Cambridge philosopher John Wisdom has discussed the paradox of the two tables at some length. For Wisdom, this paradox and others of its kind are the starting points of a well-considered metaphysics that inquires into the epistemological basis of statements without regard to their logical structure and empirical validity.

standing before an X-ray machine oneself and being "made transparent," or indeed carrying about the X-ray picture of one's own
insides in a large envelope. Does the doctor see something inside me
that I don't know about? Is this photograph me? The closer we come
to ourselves, to man, the more disquieting becomes the difference
between the object of naïve experience and its scientific reconstruction. It is clearly no accident that whereas the terms of physics play
little part in our everyday language and those of chemistry little
more except as they relate to the analysis of foodstuffs, many biological categories have become a part of our direct experience of the
world; that whereas protons and electrons, electromagnetic fields
and the speed of light, are still alien to everyday language and we
only occasionally speak of "acids," "fats," "carbohydrates," and "al-
bumins," we speak all the time of "organs" and their "functions," of
"nerves," "muscles," "veins," and even "brain cells."

But whatever the biologist may reveal to us about ourselves, we
still have the quasi-consolation that our body is not the "real" us,
that biological concepts and theories cannot affect the integrity of
our individuality. We must assimilate biological man to some extent, but it costs us relatively little to identify with him. I am not
aware that biological categories have ever been invoked to dispute
the physical uniqueness of each person. Nobody seems to feel that he
has to defend his moustache, the shape of his nose, or the length of
his arms against scientific references to hair growth, the nasal bones,
or the humerus in order not to be robbed of his individuality and
reduced to a mere illustration of general categories or principles. A
charge of this kind is heard only when science extends the borders
of its artificial world to take in man as an acting, thinking, feeling
creature—when it becomes social science.

Social science has so far presented us with at least two new and
highly problematical creatures whom we are unlikely ever to encounter in our everyday experience. One is the much-debated *homo
oeconomicus* of modern economics: the consumer who carefully
weighs utility and cost before every purchase and compares hun-
dreds of prices before he makes his decision; the entrepreneur who
has the latest information from all markets and stock exchanges and

bases his every decision on this information; the perfectly informed, thoroughly rational man. In our everyday experience this is a strange creature, and yet the concept has proved almost as useful for the economist as the beehive-table for the physicist. By and large, the facts of economic life confirm the economist's theories, and while his assumptions may appear strange and incredible, they enable him to make accurate predictions. And yet, can we still identify light-heartedly with *homo oeconomicus*? Can we, on the other hand, afford to ignore him as we do the table of the physicist?

The paradox of our relation to a second "man" of social science, psychological man (as Philip Rieff called him), is more threatening still. The godfather of psychological man was Sigmund Freud, and with Freud this new creature soon acquired considerable prominence both inside and outside scientific psychology. Psychological man is the man who even if he always does good may always want to do evil—the man of invisible motives who has not become the more familiar for our having made him into a kind of party game. You hate me? That merely means that "in reality" you love me. Nowhere is the impossibility of separating the scientific from the everyday object as overwhelming as in the case of psychological man; nowhere, therefore, is it more obviously necessary, if not to reconcile the two worlds, at least to make their separate existence comprehensible and thus bearable.

In general, economists and psychologists have not been prepared to face the contradiction between their artificial human being and the real one; their critics have usually belonged only marginally to the profession. Perhaps their attitude is right, for we have apparently grown so accustomed to *homo oeconomicus* and psychological man that a protest against these concepts is rarely heard. But our acceptance of the "men" of economics and psychology does not make the dilemma they stand for any less real. Moreover, with the rapid development of social science two new scientific "men" are coming into being: the men of sociology and political science. At a time when the discussion about their elder brothers has hardly died down, it is being revived to cast doubt on the right to existence of *homo sociologicus* and *homo politicus,* or even to prevent their birth at the last moment. Just as a shadow follows the person who casts it, so the protest against the incompatibility of the worlds of common sense and of science (always alive behind the appearance of calm) follows the paths of human inquiry.

Perhaps it is appropriate today to cease our vain and debilitating effort to run away from the shadow, and to turn and face the threat. How does the human being of our everyday experience relate to the glass men of social science? Must we and can we defend our artificial, abstract creatures against real human beings? Are we facing here a paradox analogous to that of the two tables, or is the dilemma of the social scientist's abstraction something different?

Noble and impressive though the definition of sociology as the "science of man" may be, such vague phrases tell us little about the specific subject matter of the discipline. Even the unreconstructed optimist will not claim that sociology enables him to solve the riddle of man for good. Sociology certainly is a science of man, but it is not the only such science, nor can it reasonably aspire to tackle the problem of man in all its depth and breadth. Man in his entirety not only is safely removed from the attack of any single discipline, but may possibly remain forever a nebulous shape in the background of scientific endeavor. Every discipline, if it is to make its statements precise and testable, must reduce its huge subject matter to certain elements from which may be systematically constructed, if not a portrait of the reality of experience, then a structure in whose tissue a segment of reality may be caught.

The problems of sociology all refer us to one fact that is as accessible to our experience as the natural facts of our environment. This is the fact of society, of which we are reminded so often and so intensely that there are good reasons to call it the vexatious fact of society. Mere random probability can hardly explain our behavior toward others and toward ourselves. We obey laws, go to the polls, marry, attend schools and universities, have an occupation, and are members of a church; we look after our children, lift our hats to our superiors, defer to our elders, speak to different people in different tongues, feel that we belong here and are strangers there. We cannot walk a step or speak a sentence without there intervening between us and the world a third element, one that ties us to the world and at the same time mediates between these two concrete abstractions: society.

If there is any explanation for the late birth of a science of society, we may look for it in the omnipresence of the subject matter of that science, which includes even its own description and analysis. Sociology is concerned with man in the face of the vexatious fact of society. Man, every man, encounters this fact, indeed *is* this fact; for society, while it may be conceived independently of particular individuals, would nevertheless be a meaningless fiction without particular individuals.[2] Therefore, for the elements of a science that has as its subject matter man in society, we have to look in the area where man and the fact of society intersect.

There have been many attempts in the history of sociology to find such elements. More than twenty years ago, Talcott Parsons (following Florian Znaniecki) enumerated and discussed four such approaches (52: 30). None of the four, however, satisfies the demands of sociological analysis. It sounds trivial to require that the elements of sociological analysis be sought in the area where the individual and society intersect. Nevertheless, two of Parsons's four approaches did not satisfy this requirement. Among American sociologists especially, it was popular early in our century to seek the unit of sociological analysis in the social group. Society—so Charles Cooley argued, for example—is not composed of individuals, but of groups; the sociologist is not concerned with Mr. Smith, but with the Smith family, with company X, party Y, and church Z. Now it is clearly true that the individual encounters society in social groups; this happens in a very real sense indeed. But possibly this encounter is too real. In the group the individual disappears; if the group is

---

[2] The relation between what I have called here the "vexatious fact of society" and Durkheim's "social facts," facts that force us into their spell, is evident. In the beginning of the first chapter of his *Règles* of 1895, Durkheim described "social facts" as follows: "If I fulfill my obligations as brother, husband, or citizen, if I honor my contracts, I perform duties that are defined without reference to myself and my actions in law and custom. Even if these duties are in accord with my own sentiments and I feel subjectively their reality, such reality is objective, for I have not created it; I have merely inherited it as a result of my education." In this passage Durkheim comes close to the category of role discussed in this essay.

taken as the element of analysis, there is no way left for the sociologist to find the individual as a social animal. If, on the other hand
—as often happens to this day—we take as our elementary unit the
personality, even the social personality, of the individual, it becomes difficult to account for the fact of society. Speaking of groups
means removing the focus of analysis entirely to grounds outside the
individual; speaking of social personalities involves complete concentration on the individual himself. The problem is to find an elementary category in which both the individual and society can be
accommodated.

Most modern sociologists have thought they could satisfy the need
for an elementary analytical category by using as their basis either
(with Leopold von Wiese) the concept of "social relations," or (with
Max Weber) that of "social action." It is not difficult to see, however,
that both of these concepts leave our problem unsolved. Speaking
of "social relations" or "social action" is hardly less general than
speaking of "man" or "society." We still do not know the elements
of which "social relations" and "social action" are composed, the
categories, that is, with which to describe the relations between men
in society or the socially determined action of men.

It is no accident, therefore, that the contemporary proponents of
"social relations" and "social action" introduce in the course of
their analyses, or even in their conceptual considerations, further
categories that come nearer to being the elementary analytical units
that sociology needs. Von Wiese and Parsons refer in related ways
on the one hand to "social formations" or "social systems" as structural units of society, and on the other to "offices" or "roles" as the
individual's crystallized modes of participation in the social process.
Neither pair of categories can in any way be derived from the general concepts "social relations" and "social action"; one is tempted
to suggest that their authors have introduced them almost against
their will. And while this may be rather less than conclusive proof
of sociology's need for such categories, it is at least plausible evidence; and it seems worth reflecting on why the authors found it
necessary to introduce them.

At the point where individual and society intersect stands *homo sociologicus,* man as the bearer of socially predetermined roles. To a sociologist the individual *is* his social roles, but these roles, for their part, are the vexatious fact of society. In solving its problems, sociology necessarily takes social roles as its elements of analysis; its subject matter is the structure of social roles. But by reconstructing man as *homo sociologicus* in this manner, sociology creates for itself once again the moral and philosophical problem of how the artificial man of its theoretical analysis relates to the real man of our everyday experience. If sociology is not to fall victim to an uncritical scientism, the attempt to sketch in some dimensions of the category of social role must not lose sight of the moral problem created by the artificiality of its model. If, on the other hand, philosophical criticism is to go beyond irrelevant generalities, it presupposes a thorough understanding of the uses and abuses of the category of social role.[3]

II

The attempt to reduce man to *homo sociologicus* for the sake of solving certain problems is neither as arbitrary nor as recent as one might think. Like *homo oeconomicus* and psychological man, man as the bearer of social roles is not primarily a description of reality, but a scientific construct. Yet however much scientific activity may resemble a game, it would be wrong to regard it as irrelevant to the reality of experience. The paradoxes of the physicist's table and the everyday table, the sociologist's man and the man on the street, are by no means the end and aim of science; rather they are an entirely unsought and troublesome consequence of the scientist's effort to investigate otherwise inaccessible segments of the world. In an important sense, the atom and the social role, though inventions, are not *merely* inventions. They are categories that at many times and

---

[3] Reflection about the elements of sociological analysis is at any point reflection about sense and nonsense, about the uses and abuses of sociology as a science. However, it takes us beyond the mere exchange of pre-existing opinions. Even though we do not make the defense or critique of sociology our explicit aim, the terms of this essay should enable us to put an end once and for all to the still lingering dispute over the limits and possibilities of a science of society.

places, and under various names, have suggested themselves with an inexplicable necessity to scientists bent on understanding nature, or man in society. Once invented, they are not merely meaningful, i.e. operationally useful, but also plausible. In a certain sense, they are self-evident categories.

Remarkably enough, both the atom and the role were given their present names when the concepts were first invented, and both names have remained the same through the centuries. With respect to the atom, the explanation is evident; the word ἄτομον speaks for itself,[4] and the concept as now used refers consciously to its first use by Democritus. The development of the concept of social role is more complicated and more instructive. It can be shown that in trying to describe the point of contact between the individual and society many writers—poets, scholars, philosophers—have introduced identical or at least related concepts. The words we encounter time and again in this context are *mask, persona, character,* and *role* or *part.* Although there is a conscious terminological tradition here as with the atom, it would seem that many writers have independently come up not merely with the same concept, but with the same name for the concept—as if to prove that names have some content after all.

Role, part, persona, character, and *mask* are words whose basic context, allowing for different stages of the development of language, is the same, namely the theater. We speak of the *dramatis personae* or characters of the play, whose part or role the actor plays; and if nowadays he does not usually wear a mask, the word is no less clearly of theatrical origin. These words have a number of characteristics in common. (1) All of them indicate something that is given to an actor for the occasion, something that is outside himself. (2) This "something" may be described as a complex of modes of behavior, which (3) in turn connects with other such complexes to form a whole, and is in that sense a "part" (as the Latin *pars* and the English "part" for the actor's role still indicate). (4) Since these

---

[4] This example shows, however, that the literal meaning of words must not be overestimated as a clue to their present connotations. In terms of literal meaning, "atom" and "individual" cannot be differentiated; nor does the literal meaning of "individual" tell us that the individual is the basic unit of social science.

modes of behavior are given to the actor, he must learn them in order to be able to play his part. (5) From the point of view of the actor, no role, no *dramatis persona,* is exhaustive; he can learn and play a multitude of roles.

In addition to these five characteristics of theatrical roles, there is a further consideration that takes us to the limits of the stage metaphor. This is that behind all roles, personas, and masks the actor remains a real being, a person in no way affected by the parts he plays.[5] His stage roles are for him superficial, something apart from his inner being. He is "himself" only when he casts them off— or, as John of Salisbury says in his *Policraticus* of 1159 (see 31: 146): "The troupe presents a farce on the stage; one man is called 'Father,' another 'Son,' and the third 'Rich Man.' Soon, when the script-book is shut on these comic roles, the true face returns, the mask vanishes." John of Salisbury's lines are no longer a description of the theater. Indeed, the stage metaphor—as E. R. Curtius has shown by various examples—is a very old device of philosophy and poetry. Among its early uses Curtius mentions Plato's *Laws,* with its notion of living creatures as puppets of divine origin, and his *Philebus,* with its image of the "tragedy and comedy of life" (55: I, 644d–e, 55a: 50b). Seneca uses the same image when he refers to "this drama of human life, wherein we are assigned the parts that we are to play so badly" (60: 80, 7). From St. Paul to John of Salisbury and right up to the present day, the metaphor is frequently found in Christian writings.[6] In time the notion of the *theatrum mundi* becomes almost commonplace. It is used by Luther and Shakespeare, by Calderón and Cervantes. Hofmannsthal's *Great Salzburg World Theater* is but one recent proof that the device is still with us.

Strictly speaking, however, the *theatrum mundi* metaphor is only indirect evidence for the substantive necessity and age-old use of the category of role in the sense of this essay. For insofar as the world is seen as a gigantic play, each player is given just one mask, one persona, one character, one role in it all (by a divine "director,"

[5] This statement is meant in an essential sense. Obviously, an actor may sometimes find it hard, on leaving the stage, to cast off a part that—as we say—he has "lived."
[6] One need but think of the understanding of the trinity as a unity of three "persons," notably in the work of Augustinus.

who has been part of the metaphor since Plato's time). But it was
our intention to go beyond this one-dimensional view of man.
Our aim is to dissolve human action into its components, and by
analyzing these components to arrive at a rational understanding
of the whole. In the circumstances, we do well to turn from the
theatrum mundi to a more manageable use of the theatrical metaphor: its application to the life of the individual, in the sense of attributing to a given person several roles or personas.

This is an old notion, too. It probably found its earliest expression in terms of the Latin word *persona,* or the corresponding Greek
word, πρόσωπον. Cicero gives us a nice illustration for the use of
persona in this sense:

> We must realize also that we are invested by Nature with two
> characters [*personis*], as it were. One of these is universal, arising
> from the fact of our being all alike endowed with reason and with
> that superiority which lifts us above the brute. From this all
> morality and propriety are derived, and upon it depends the
> rational method of ascertaining our duty. The other character is
> the one that is assigned to individuals in particular. (30: I, 107.)

These two natural roles, the result of a general human endowment
and a specific individual endowment, have little in common with
social roles; but Cicero goes on to say:

> To the two above-mentioned characters [*personis*] is added a
> third, which some chance or some circumstance imposes, and a
> fourth also, which we assume by our own deliberate choice. Regal
> powers and military commands, nobility of birth and political
> office, wealth and influence, and their opposites depend upon
> chance and are, therefore, controlled by circumstances. But what
> role we ourselves may choose to sustain is decided by our own free
> choice. And so some turn to philosophy, others to the civil law,
> and still others to oratory, while in the case of the virtues them-
> selves one man prefers to excel in one, another in another. (30:
> I, 115.)

Cicero's reflections presumably echo a lost work of Panaetius
(περὶ τοῦ καθήκοντος), for whom the individual personality was simi-

larly composed of four personas, each to some extent inborn and individual but also to some extent acquired and social. Both Panaetius and Cicero define all four personas as largely inborn or inherent, although the last two may have external causes and limits. From something given to the individual, something outside him, *persona* in Cicero's use has already become a part of the individual; and the same semantic process has consistently led later writers to use "persona" to epitomize the individuality of man. The word "character" (χαρακτήρ: that which is stamped, the impression) has had much the same fate. Similarly, as we shall see, "role," which once meant a predetermined behavior pattern, has increasingly been used by social scientists to refer to an individual's customary or habitual behavior, being thus transformed from a category of sociology into a category of social psychology. Badly as we need a category like "role," "persona," or "character" to describe what happens at the point where the individual and society intersect, it seems difficult to restrict such words to this function.

Not all writers, however, have found it hard to focus on role in our sense of the word. In *As You Like It* Shakespeare puts into Jaques's mouth a speech that eminently anticipates the nature and potential of the category of social role, and thus illuminates many features of the sociological concept of role (II. vii):

> All the world's a stage,
> And all the men and women merely players:
> They have their exits and their entrances;
> And one man in his time plays many parts,
> His acts being seven ages. At first the infant,
> Mewling and puking in the nurse's arms.
> Then the whining schoolboy, with his satchel
> And shining morning face, creeping like snail
> Unwillingly to school. And then the lover,
> Sighing like furnace, with a woeful ballad
> Made to his mistress' eyebrow. Then a soldier,
> Full of strange oaths, and bearded like the pard,
> Jealous in honor, sudden and quick in quarrel,
> Seeking the bubble reputation

Even in the cannon's mouth. And then the justice,
In fair round belly with good capon lin'd,
With eyes severe and beard of formal cut,
Full of wise saws and modern instances;
And so he plays his part. The sixth age shifts
Into the lean and slipper'd pantaloon,
With spectacles on nose and pouch on side,
His youthful hose, well sav'd, a world too wide
For his shrunk shank; and his big manly voice,
Turning again toward childish treble, pipes
And whistles in his sound. Last scene of all,
That ends this strange eventful history,
Is second childishness and mere oblivion,
Sans teeth, sans eyes, sans taste, sans everything.

Shakespeare's main concern here is with age roles, which are only one class of social roles, but the speech at least hints at occupational and other roles. "The world" is a stage, which players enter and leave. But each player makes more than one appearance, and every one in a different mask. The same player enters the stage as a child and leaves it to return as a young man, a grown man, and an old man. Only when he dies does he have his last exit; but by then new and different players are on the stage playing "his" parts.

Today, Shakespeare's metaphor has become the central principle of the science of society. From the sociological point of view, the idea that relates the individual meaningfully to society is the idea of the individual as a bearer of socially predetermined attributes and modes of behavior. Jack Smith as a schoolboy, with a satchel and a shining morning face, creeps unwillingly to school; as a lover, he sighs and sings a ballad to his beloved; as a soldier, he wears a beard, curses, is quarrelsome and jealous of his honor; as a judge, he dresses carefully and is full of wise saws. "Schoolboy," "lover," "soldier," "judge," and "old man" are in a strange way both this particular individual, Jack Smith, and something that can be separated from him and spoken of without reference to him. Shakespeare's judge may no longer be appropriate for the stage of our time, but we too can say what a judge is like, whether his name is Jack Smith or John O'Connor. In our time as in Shakespeare's, it is the vexatious fact of society that wrests the individual out of his individuality and defines his being by the alien categories of the world outside himself.

The fact of society is vexatious because we cannot escape it. There may be lovers who neither sigh nor make a woeful ballad to their mistress's eyebrow, but such lovers do not play their role; in the language of modern American sociology, they are deviants. For every position a person can occupy—whether it is described in terms of age, family, occupation, nationality, class membership, or what have you—"society" has defined certain personal qualities and modes of behavior as acceptable. The incumbent of such a position must decide whether or not to behave as society says he must. If he yields to society's demands, he abandons his virgin individuality but gains society's approval. If he resists society's demands, he may preserve an abstract and bootless independence, but only at the expense of incurring society's wrath and painful sanctions. It is with this decision that *homo sociologicus* is born, along with man as a social being. With this decision begins that "appearance as" on the stage of life which Cicero tries to catch in the concept of *persona*, Marx in the concept of "character mask,"[7] and Shakespeare, along with most modern sociologists, in the concept of "part" or "role."

It is understandable that the idea of social role has repeatedly been described in theatrical terms. What could be more plausible than an analogy between prescribed behavior patterns for actors in given parts and socially defined behavior norms for persons in given positions? And yet such an analogy may be misleading. Whereas the unreality of events is assumed in the theater, it cannot be assumed with respect to society. Despite the theatrical connotations of "role," it would be wrong to see the role-playing social personality as an unreal person who has merely to drop his mask to appear

[7] Marx refers at several points to the "character mask" of the capitalist or the bourgeois. In a similar sense he distinguishes at one point (45: 8) between (1) the "persons of the capitalist and the landowner" and (2) capitalist and landowner as "personifications of economic categories," i.e. as social roles. For examples of the use of "character mask" and other concepts, see section VII below.

as his true self. *Homo sociologicus* and the undivided individual of our experience stand in a dangerous and paradoxical relationship, one that it would be wrong to ignore or minimize. The characterization of man as a social being is more than a metaphor. His roles are more than masks that can be cast off, his social behavior more than a play from which audience and actors alike can return to the "true" reality.

III

Perhaps it is a little unfair to stress the vexation of *homo sociologicus*, inevitable though it is, before this new man has had the chance to prove himself. We have introduced the forefathers of sociological man, we have discussed the problems with which he confronts us, but so far we have not asked precisely who he is and what his capacities are. To be sure, we could simply point out that *homo sociologicus* figures prominently in the works of contemporary social scientists, and suggest that these works be consulted for a summary of his properties. Such a course, however, would lead us into difficulties. For agreed though many sociologists are on the name of their creature, they have very different ideas of his nature. Let us therefore ignore the contradictory literature on our subject, and address ourselves to it directly. We shall begin with the context of observation and theory in which *homo sociologicus* emerges, and only afterward measure our findings against those of other sociologists.[8]

Let us assume that at a party we are introduced to a Herr Doktor Hans Schmidt.[9] We are curious to find out more about our new acquaintance. Who is Hans Schmidt? Some of the answers to this question we can see right away. Hans Schmidt is (1) a man; more

---

[8] The following analysis is nonetheless oriented throughout to the sociological discussion of the categories in question. We are forgoing an explicit critical discussion at this point in the hope of taking in stride certain hurdles that the conceptual debate has so far been unable to get past. Where the following discussion is directly dependent on the work of others, the usual acknowledgments are made.

[9] It would have been easy to give Herr Schmidt an English name, but not so easy to translate all his roles, every one of which has clear cultural connotations. Since it is useful for the subsequent argument if these cultural connotations stand out clearly, I have left Herr Schmidt his original German name.

precisely, (2) an adult man about 35 years of age. He is wearing a wedding ring, and is therefore (3) married. The context of his introduction tells us further that Hans Schmidt is (4) a citizen, (5) a German, (6) an inhabitant of town X, and, since he has the title of Doktor, (7) a professional man. Everything else we have to find out from mutual acquaintances. They may tell us that Herr Schmidt is (8) a grammar school teacher by profession, (9) the father of two children, (10) a Protestant in the predominantly Catholic population of X, and (11) a former refugee who came to X after the war; that he has made a good name for himself by becoming (12) vice-chairman of the local organization of the Y party and (13) treasurer of the local soccer club; and finally that he is (14) a passionate and excellent card player, and (15) an equally passionate, though less excellent, driver. His friends, colleagues, and acquaintances have much more to tell us about Herr Schmidt, but with the information we have acquired, our curiosity is satisfied for the time being. Among other things, we feel that Herr Schmidt is no longer a stranger to us now. What is behind this feeling?

It might be argued that what we have found out about Herr Schmidt does not really distinguish him from other men. Not only Herr Schmidt but many other men are Germans, fathers, Protestants, and grammar school teachers; and if there is only one treasurer of the local soccer club at any given time, there were others before him, so that this office, too, is not unique to Herr Schmidt. Indeed, our information about Herr Schmidt refers without exception to certain places that he occupies, i.e., to points in a coordinate system of social relations. For the informed, every position implies a net of other positions connected with it, a position field. As a father, Herr Schmidt stands in one position field with his wife, his son, and his daughter; as a schoolmaster, he is related to his pupils, their parents, his colleagues, and the officials of the school administration; as vice-chairman of the Y party, he is related to his colleagues on the party committee, to higher party officials, to other party members, and to the voting public. Some of these position fields overlap, but no two are identical. Every one of the fifteen positions of Herr Schmidt that we know about has its own position field.

The term *social position* designates every place in a field of social relations, if we extend the concept of social relations to include not merely positions like grammar school teacher and vice-chairman of the Y party, but also father, German, and card player. Positions may in principle be thought of independently of their incumbents. Just as the mayor's office and the professor's chair do not cease to exist when they become vacant, the positions of Herr Schmidt do not depend on his personality or even his existence. A man not only can, but as a rule must, assume a number of positions, and it may be supposed that the number grows with the complexity of the society. Moreover, the position field corresponding to a given position may consist of a multitude of distinct referents, as with Herr Schmidt's positions of grammar school teacher and treasurer of the local soccer club; that is, positions may themselves be complex. It may accordingly prove useful to see social positions as sets of *position segments,* i.e., to see the position of teacher as made up of the position segments teacher-pupils, teacher-parents, teacher-colleagues, and teacher-administrators, each standing for a different direction of relationship.

However, these conceptual distinctions and definitions cannot explain why Herr Schmidt is no longer a stranger to us once we know what positions he holds. For it hardly makes sense to assume that Herr Schmidt is nothing but the aggregate of his positions, that his individuality consists, if not in any one position, in the constellation of the whole. Many of his characteristics cannot conceivably be inferred from his positions: whether he is a good or bad teacher, a strict or lenient father; whether or not he can control his emotions; whether or not he is satisfied with his life; what he thinks about his fellowmen when he is all by himself; where he would like to spend his vacation.[10] Herr Schmidt is more than an incumbent of social positions, and much that his friends know about him neither the casual acquaintance nor the sociologist knows or wants to know.

If Herr Schmidt's positions do not tell us everything about his personality, however, it is astonishing how much they do tell us.

---

[10] As these remarks suggest, in learning that Herr Schmidt is an excellent card player but not an excellent driver, we learn more than we need to know for defining his social positions.

The positions themselves, of course, provide us merely with the most formal sort of knowledge. They tell us what Herr Schmidt's social fields of reference are and with whom he has social relations, but they tell us nothing about the substance of these relations. And yet no further questions are needed for us to find out what this substance is: i.e., what Herr Schmidt does in his numerous positions— or in any case what he should do, and therefore probably does. As a father, Herr Schmidt looks after his children, helps them, protects them, and loves them. As a grammar school teacher, he imparts knowledge to his pupils, judges them fairly, advises their parents, shows deference to the school principal, and behaves in an exemplary fashion. As a party functionary, he attends meetings, gives speeches, and tries to sign up new members. Not only what Herr Schmidt does, but what he is like, can be derived to some extent from his positions—indeed, a man's appearance often reveals "who he is," i.e., what positions he holds. As a grammar school teacher Herr Schmidt wears a teacher's "decent" but not too expensive clothes, including shiny trousers and coats with leather elbows; as a husband he wears a wedding ring; one can probably see in his demeanor whether the Y party is a radical party; his appearance is sporty; he is probably above average in intelligence and energy. This list shows that *homo sociologicus,* like psychological man, can be turned into an amusing party game with serious overtones.[11] Every position carries with it certain expected modes of behavior; every position a person occupies requires him to do certain things and exhibit certain characteristics; to every social position there belongs a *social role.* By assuming a social position, the individual becomes a character in the drama written by the society he is living in. With every position he assumes, society hands him a role to play. It is by positions and roles that two conceptually distinguishable facts, the individual and society, are mediated; and it is in terms of these two concepts that we describe *homo sociologicus,* sociological man, the basic unit of sociological analysis.

Of the two concepts, position and role, role is by far the more

---

11 Indeed, *homo sociologicus* has become a television game, notably on those quiz programs that feature efforts to "guess" a person's occupation from his appearance and demeanor. Without the fact of society, such programs would make no sense.

important. Positions merely identify places in fields of reference; roles tell us about how people in given positions relate to people in other positions in the same field. Social roles represent society's demands on the incumbents of social positions. These demands may be of two kinds: demands affecting behavior (*role behavior*) and demands affecting appearance and "character" (*role attributes*). Because Herr Schmidt is a grammar school teacher, certain attributes and a certain kind of behavior are required of him; the same holds for each of his other fourteen positions. Although the social role associated with a given position cannot tell us how a person in this position will actually behave, we do know, if we are familiar with the society that defines this role, what is expected of one who is assigned it. Social roles, then, are bundles of expectations directed at the incumbents of positions in a given society.

Like positions, roles are in principle conceivable without reference to particular persons. The behavior and attributes expected from the father, the grammar school teacher, the party functionary, or the card player can be described without reference to any particular father, teacher, party functionary, or card player. Finally, each of a man's social roles potentially comprises a number of *role segments*. The expectations associated with the role of grammar school teacher may be subdivided into expectations with respect to the role segments teacher-pupils, teacher-parents, and so on. Thus every role is a complex or set of behavior expectations.[12]

All too frequently, logical differences between various kinds of statements about behavior are overlooked. "Herr Schmidt went to church yesterday," "Herr Schmidt regularly goes to church on Sundays," and "Herr Schmidt as a practicing Protestant should go to church regularly on Sundays" are all statements about social be-

---

[12] The terms introduced in this section—"position," "position segment" ("positional sector"), "role," "role behavior," "role attributes," and "role segment" ("role sector")—may all be found in the study by Neal Gross *et al.* (36), chap. iv, "A Language for Role Analysis." Apart from the definition of terms, what is new in Gross's treatment is the distinction between role behavior and role attributes, and the subdivision of positions and roles into segments or sectors. Such a subdivision has been suggested also, with different terms, by Robert K. Merton in his essay "The Role-Set" (4); and the distinction between "roles" and "tasks" introduced by Talcott Parsons seems to serve a similar purpose. For more on terminological issues, see section VII below.

havior; yet they are distinguishable by more than the form of the verb. The first statement refers to something Herr Schmidt has in fact done at a specific time, a particular instance of behavior. The second sentence refers to something Herr Schmidt is doing regularly, a regular mode of behavior. The third statement refers to something Herr Schmidt should do regularly, an expected mode of behavior. Without doubt all three statements are in some sense sociologically relevant, since going to church is a form of behavior that can tell us something about a society. But only the third statement is relevant to sociological analysis; only in this statement do the individual and society appear to be related in a definite way. Both the particular behavior and the regular behavior of Herr Schmidt remain in some sense his private property. Although both help to create a social reality, and although both may serve, in surveys for example, as data for impressive tabulations, the fact of society does not appear in them as an independent and active force.

In speaking of social roles, then, we invariably refer to expected behavior; our concern is invariably with the individual as confronted with demands generated outside himself, or with society as it confronts the individual with such demands. The mediation of the individual and society is not accomplished by action in itself, or even by the establishing of social relations; it is accomplished only in the individual's active encounter with socially prescribed patterns of action. The first concern of sociology, therefore, is always with these patterns or roles; the further question of how particular individuals actually come to terms with role expectations makes sense only if we know what to make of these expectations.

Three features characterize the category of social role as an element of sociological analysis. (1) Like positions, social roles are quasi-objective complexes of prescriptions for behavior which are in principle independent of the individual. (2) Their particular content is defined and redefined not by any individual, but by society. (3) The behavior expectations associated with roles are binding on the individual, in the sense that he cannot ignore or reject them without harm to himself. These three features give rise to three recurrent questions of role theory, which we must try to answer if we are to present the case of *homo sociologicus* with any degree of precision. (1) How in detail does the encounter of individual and society occur? How do predetermined roles become a part of people's social behavior? What is the relation between *homo sociologicus* and psychological man? (2) Who or what is this "society" that serves as the defining agency of roles? Can the process of defining and redefining social roles be rendered so precise that such irritating personifications can be dispensed with? (3) How is the force of role expectations made binding? What mechanisms or institutions prevent the individual from simply dismissing the behavior prescriptions that he encounters as irrelevant and arbitrary?

IV

Clearly, it makes sense to speak of a mediation of the individual and society only where the two do not merely exist side by side, but are connected in definite ways. The statement that there is a grammar school teacher named Hans Schmidt, and that thus-and-such modes of behavior and attributes are associated with the social role of grammar school teacher, is without analytical value unless it can be shown that Herr Schmidt's relationship to his social role is neither purely accidental nor alterable by his own free decision, but a matter of necessity and constraint. It must therefore be shown that society is not merely a fact but a vexatious fact, one that we cannot ignore or flout without punishment. Social roles are a constraining force on the individual, whether he experiences them as an obstacle to his private wishes or a support that gives him security. The constraining force of role expectations is due to the availability of *sanctions,* measures by which society can enforce conformity with its prescriptions. The man who does not play his role is punished; the man who plays his role is rewarded, or at least not punished. Social pressure to conform to prescribed role expectations is by no means peculiar to certain modern societies, but a universal feature of all social forms.[13]

---

[13] Certain American "nonconformists" mistakenly believe that "keeping up with the Joneses" is an American invention. The undeniable variations from one society to another in the degree of open and hidden constraint brought to bear on their

The concept of sanction is often applied exclusively to punishments and reproofs; however, in keeping with sociological usage we shall apply it here in a wider sense. There are positive as well as negative sanctions: society may bestow decorations as well as impose prison sentences, acknowledge prestige as well as expose unacceptable behavior. Still, it seems best in the present context to think chiefly in terms of negative sanctions. Not only is it often difficult to characterize positive sanctions in precise and operational terms,[14] but they do little to explain the pressure to which *homo sociologicus* is steadily exposed. One can renounce rewards and decline decorations, but to escape the force of the law or even of social disapproval is difficult in all societies. It is not only kings that go to Canossa. Like role expectations themselves, the sanctions attached to them are subject to change; but also like role expectations, they are ubiquitous and inescapable.

The effect of sanctions is most immediately clear in the case of role expectations supported by the force of law and legal institutions. Most social roles include such elements, certain *must-expectations*[15] that can be ignored or flouted only at the risk of legal prosecution. As a man, Herr Schmidt must not have sexual relations with other men; as a husband, he must not have extramarital sexual relations. As a grammar school teacher, he is expected to educate at least his older pupils without using the cane. If, as treasurer of the local soccer club, he uses the club's money to pay his card-playing debts, he incurs the negative sanctions laid down by law. So far as the law applies to people as incumbents of positions, as to a large extent it does, it may be understood as an aggregate of sanc-

individual members cannot be expressed in terms of conformism. Rather, they refer to the range of choice left to the individual by a given society's social role definitions. Such definitions in themselves imply a pressure to conform on all points covered.

[14] This is a difficult problem, with which theorists of stratification in particular have been struggling. One can of course develop scales of rewards such as income and prestige, but so far the necessary connection between such rewards and role expectations has not been conclusively demonstrated. In the absence of such a connection, there is no way of classifying role expectations by the positive sanctions associated with them.

[15] The term is chosen by analogy to the German legal term "must-prescriptions." This holds correspondingly for the terms "shall-expectations" and "can-expectations" introduced below.

tions by which society guarantees conformity with its role expectations. Must-expectations are the hard core of any social role. Not only is it possible to formulate them, but they are in fact formulated, or codified; and their compulsory character is nearly absolute. It may further be observed that the sanctions associated with them are almost exclusively negative. Perhaps Herr Schmidt may someday be awarded a plaque for "25 years' driving without an accident"; otherwise compliance with the law yields no positive profit.

But laws and law courts are by no means the only manifestations of role expectations and sanctions. To be sure, it can be argued that the range of legally regulated behavior increases with social development;[16] in any case this range is much larger in contemporary developed societies than in historical or underdeveloped societies. Nevertheless, even in present-day Germany, France, England, and America there is a wide range of social behavior which is beyond the reach of courts and laws (except in a metaphorical sense), and which most citizens consider more important than the range subject to legal sanctions. If Herr Schmidt, as vice-chairman of the local organization of the Y party, insists on proselytizing for the Z party among his colleagues, they are unlikely to accord him much approval even though no court of law could try him for this offense. More precisely, no official court of law could try him. In fact, many organizations today have developed quasi-legal institutions of their own to enforce conformity with their behavior prescriptions. And surely it is hardly less painful for a man to be excommunicated by his church, expelled by his party, dismissed by his firm, or stricken from the register of his professional organization, than to be sentenced to prison by a court of law. These are extreme sanctions, but there are also milder penalties—from silent disapproval to reproofs, compulsory transfers, and delays in promotion—whose effects must not be underestimated. Apart from must-expectations, then, most social roles include certain *shall-expectations,* which are scarcely less compulsory than must-expectations. With shall-expectations

---

[16] This was one of the theses of the evolutionary theorists of the turn of the century; see, for example, L. T. Hobhouse's *Morals in Evolution.* The thesis clearly has a proven core, but the borderline between custom and law is often hard to define, especially where common law and precedent dominate.

negative sanctions still prevail, although the man who complies with them punctiliously can be sure of the esteem of his fellowmen. Such a man "is a model of behavior"; he always "does the right thing," and therefore "can be relied on."

By contrast, a third group of role expectations, *can-expectations,* carry mostly positive sanctions. If Herr Schmidt spends a great deal of his leisure time collecting funds for his party, if as a teacher he volunteers to conduct the school orchestra or as a father he spends every free minute with his children, he gains esteem by doing "more than he needs to," more than his fair share. Even can-expectations do not yet bring us to the domain of unregulated social behavior. The man who never does more than what is absolutely necessary must have very effective alternative sources of gratification to remain unaffected by the disapproval of his fellowmen. This is true above all in the occupational sphere, but also in political parties, voluntary organizations, and educational institutions, where compliance with can-expectations is frequently a condition of advancement. Difficult as it may be to formulate the precise substance of can-expectations and the sanctions associated with them, they play no less a part than must- and shall-expectations in the roles that fall to us, whether we want them or not, on the stage of society.[17]

[17] Herr Schmidt's position as treasurer of the soccer club may be used to exemplify the classes of role expectations and their sanctions:

Kind of Expectation	Kind of Sanction		Example of Behavior
	Positive	Negative	
must-expectations	——	punishment by court of law	honest financial demeanor
shall-expectations	(popularity)	social exclusion	active participation in club meetings
can-expectations	esteem	(unpopularity)	voluntary collection of funds

A similar classification of role expectations by degrees of compulsoriness is introduced by Gross *et al.* (36: 58ff), using the terms "permissive" (can-), "preferential" (shall-), and "mandatory" (must-) expectations; but the absence of a reference to legal sanctions deprives their analysis of much of its potential strength.

In classifying and defining the sanctions that enforce conformity with social role behavior, we enter the field of the sociology of law. Between must-, shall-, and can-expectations on the one hand, and law, custom, and habit on the other, there is more than an analogy; the two sets of concepts apply to identical phenomena. Just as laws can be seen as the result of an ongoing historical process by which habits crystallize into customs, customs into laws, so social roles are subject to permanent changes in this sense. And just as laws may lose validity as their social background changes, so must-expectations may lose their force. For example, whereas it was once a must-expectation in Western society that a husband would take care of his parents and his wife's parents as well, today a man gains at most a certain additional prestige by interpreting the expectation that he will love his parents as an obligation to take care of them.[18] The subtle problem of the social foundations of the legal system cannot be considered in detail here, since not all of its aspects contribute to an understanding of the category of social role. But it is useful to keep in mind that the mediation of the individual and society by social roles links the individual, *inter alia,* to the world of law and custom. Herr Schmidt plays his roles because law and custom force him to do so; but only by playing his roles does he come to perceive law and custom as definite realities, and thus become a part of the normative structure of society. The category of role, then, is a meaningful starting point also for the sociological analysis of legal norms and institutions.

It would be hard to formulate role expectations clearly were it not for the fact of sanctions, which make it possible to classify roles by the degree to which their associated expectations are compulsory. Some of Herr Schmidt's social roles involve many and far-reaching must-expectations—notably citizen, but also husband and father. Others involve no legal sanctions whatever—notably card player, but also Protestant and German. The degree of institutionalization of social roles, i.e., the extent to which the associated ex-

---

[18] The intimate connections of law and custom, and the ways in which actual behavior influences behavior expectations, may also be illustrated by the debate in many countries over the penalties attached to homosexuality and abortion.

pectations are enforced by legal sanctions, provides us with a standard for judging how significant a given role is not only to society, but to the individual as well. If we can succeed in quantifying the weight of sanctions, we shall have a means of ordering, characterizing, and distinguishing all known roles in a given society.[19]

However, just as *homo sociologicus* does not exhaust the human personality, so no one of Herr Schmidt's roles can prescribe his entire behavior in the corresponding social position. There is a range in which the individual is free to behave as he chooses. In view of our emphasis on society's vexatiousness, it becomes especially important to define this range of freedom. Clearly, it is up to father Schmidt whether he wants to play ball or electric trains with his children, and no social agency prescribes whether teacher Schmidt will gain his pupils' attention by his wit or his intellectual competence. But these areas of free decision are small in comparison to the broad areas of constraint associated with sanctioned role expectations. Indeed, the more precise we render the category of social role, the more threatening becomes the problem of *homo sociologicus,* sociological man, whose every move expresses a role imposed on him by the impersonal agency of society. Is *homo sociologicus* a totally alienated man, given into the hands of man-made powers and yet with no chance of escaping them?

We cannot yet give a precise answer to this question, which is in some ways central to these reflections. But it is worth repeating here that social roles and the associated sanctions are not merely a vexation. To be sure, people do get worried and anxious when society forces them to do things that they would not have chosen to do on their own. But society at the same time supports people and gives them security, even people who do their best to throw off their roles whenever they possibly can. It is an entirely speculative question whether anyone would be capable of shaping his entire behavior on his own, without the assistance of society. Since complete freedom has its drawbacks, as was clear long before Jean-Paul Sartre

[19] A beginning effort to this end has been made in an as yet unpublished dissertation by Karl F. Schumann on the theory and techniques of measuring social sanctions (59).

wrote *La Nausée,* it is at least conceivable that a human being stripped of all roles would find it very difficult indeed to make his behavior meaningful. What is more, it seems certain that many of the gratifications we experience come from our roles themselves, which is to say from constraints not of our own making. The problem of man's freedom as a social being is a problem of the balance between role-determined behavior and autonomy, and in this respect at least the analysis of *homo sociologicus* seems to confirm the dialectical paradox of freedom and necessity.

V

The parts of the actor are specified in overt ways: they are originally written by an author, and later supervised by a director, both of whom can be identified as persons. But who defines social roles and watches over their acting out? Although many recent writers would answer "society," just as we have so far, the term is hard to justify. Society is patently not a person, and any personification of it obscures its nature and weakens what is said about it. Although society is a fact, one that can cause people to stumble like a stone or a tree stump, the author and director of the social drama cannot be identified by simply pointing to the fact of society. To be sure, society consists of individuals and is in this sense created by individuals, though Herr Schmidt's particular society is perhaps more his predecessors' work than his own. On the other hand, experience suggests that in some sense society is not only more than the sum of its individual members, but something significantly different in kind. Society is the alienated persona of the individual, *homo sociologicus,* a shadow that has escaped the man to return as his master. Even if we renounce for the moment the attempt to sound the depths of this paradoxical condition, as sociologists we must still seek some way, not only of identifying the agency responsible for social rules, but of describing this agency with operational precision. In the literature, this problem has rarely been considered and never been solved; yet modern sociology has assembled all the tools for its solution.

The meaning of expressions like "social norms," "role expectations defined by society," and "sanctions imposed by society" cannot be explained in general terms except by metaphors or demonstrably unsatisfactory statements.[20] Does "society" in such expressions mean all people in a given society? This interpretation is obviously too broad. Most people in any given society play no part whatever, direct or indirect, in formulating the expectations that make up such roles as father, grammar school teacher, and citizen (to say nothing of treasurer of the X-town soccer club or vice-chairman of the local branch of the Y party). They are not asked, and even if they were, their opinion would have little binding force for others. Whatever the significance of opinion surveys may be, no one claims that they are the source of norms. Is it then perhaps a country's parliament or government that specifies role expectations and sanctions on behalf of "society"? Clearly this assumption is not altogether wrong, but it is too narrow. Even in a totalitarian state, at least shall- and can-expectations defy administrative commands; and in any state many norms of social behavior are unknown, and indeed of no interest, to the government. Where approaches of this sort go wrong is in trying to relate the singular noun "society" to a single agency or collectivity, and thus ignoring the possibility that society might conceal a multitude of forces of similar character but diverse origins.

In defining position and role, we observed that it is sometimes useful to regard both categories as sets of segments. Most positions involve not merely a single relation to another person (such as husband-wife), but a field of relations to other persons and to categories or aggregates of persons. The grammar school teacher is linked to his pupils, their parents, his colleagues, and his superiors, and he recognizes a separate, identifiable set of expectations for each of these groups. He is supposed to impart knowledge to his pupils but not to his superiors, to decide on his pupils' marks with colleagues but not with parents. If he is unfriendly to his colleagues, he incurs

---

[20] The same holds for expressions in which "social" and "society" do not explicitly appear, such as "institutionalized expectations" and "culture patterns." All such expressions require precise definition, at least with respect to social roles.

their sanctions, not those of his pupils; and whether he shows deference to his superiors is a matter of little concern to his pupils' parents. It seems plausible to think of "society" with respect to this position in terms of the groups that make up its relational field: i.e., to explore the connection between the norms of these groups and the role expectations of the positions defined by them.

In interpreting the data gathered in the United States by Samuel A. Stouffer and others about the American soldier in the Second World War, Robert K. Merton developed the category of "reference group," which several social scientists have since found useful for defining the notion of role.[21] This category, which originated in social psychology and is used by Merton primarily in a social-psychology sense, derives from the observation that people orient their behavior according to the approval or disapproval of groups to which they do not themselves belong. Reference groups are outgroups functioning as value standards; they constitute the frame of reference within which a person evaluates his own behavior and that of others. With only a slight narrowing and shift of meaning the concept may be interpreted sociologically and applied to our present problems. If we define a reference group not as an arbitrarily chosen out-group, but as a group to which a person has a necessary relation by virtue of one of his social positions, we can state that every position segment establishes a relation between the position's incumbent and one or more reference groups. Thus understood, reference groups are of course not necessarily out-groups; the incumbent may be a member of such a group by virtue of his position. In these terms, the position field of teacher Schmidt may be described as an aggregate of reference groups every one of which imposes prescriptions on him and is capable of sanctioning his behavior either positively or negatively. The question of the nature of "society" turns into another question: How do reference groups

21 Merton first developed this category in his essay "Contributions to the Theory of Reference Group Behavior," written with Alice S. Rossi. He later elaborated it in a longer essay, "Continuities in the Theory of Reference Groups and Social Structure" (see 4). The theory of reference groups has been related to role analysis by Merton himself, as well as by Joseph Ben-David, David Mandelbaum, Siegfried F. Nadel, and others.

formulate and sanction the expectations of the positions they define?[22]

To my knowledge, a similar question has been raised only once in the literature, in Neal Gross *et al., Explorations in Role Analysis* (36). The answer offered by Gross and his coauthors warrants a brief departure from our strategy of deferring a critical examination of the literature. Gross distinguishes as we do between positions and roles, and conceives them both as aggregates of segments. For Gross as for us, every position segment and role segment refers to a group of other positions and roles (he does not use the term "reference group"). As a way of discovering exactly how these reference groups influence the positions and roles that they define, Gross suggests asking the members of a given position's reference groups what expectations they associate with the position's incumbent. Gross himself applied this suggestion to the position of school superintendent. In a series of interviews, he asked superintendents' superiors, teachers, superintendents themselves, and others what they expected from a school superintendent. Gross believed that their answers would help him to arrive at a clear definition of role expectations, and at the same time would indicate to what extent the members of a reference group agree with respect to such expectations. Unsurprisingly, on many points Gross found no consensus at all, or at best a weak majority. He is accordingly moved to ask:

> How much consensus on what behaviors is required for a society to maintain itself? How much disagreement can a society tolerate in what areas? To what extent do different sets of role definers hold the same role definitions of key positions in a society? On what aspects of role definitions do members of different "subcultures" in a society agree and disagree? To what extent is deviant behavior a function of deviant role definitions?

---

[22] Obviously the concept of "group" is used in a very loose sense when one speaks of reference groups. At least in the modified meaning that we have given the concept here, reference groups are not only groups proper, i.e. identifiable formal units, but also, among other things, mere categories like "inhabitants of town X." It is rarely a good idea to extend a term's meaning this way. If Merton had not reserved the term "role-set" for a slightly (although not entirely) different meaning (see 4), we might consider using "reference sets" rather than "reference groups."

Why do members of society differ in their role definitions? (36: 31.)

In more than one respect, the study by Gross and his coauthors represents an advance over earlier discussions of role. It is conceptually clear and plausible; above all, it makes a serious attempt to replace "society" by more precise and operationally useful categories. But in seeking to relate his concepts to empirical research, Gross abandons one of the essential elements of the category of social role. By attributing the force of social norms to the uncertain basis of majority opinions, he makes the fact of society subject to the arbitrariness of questionnaire responses. If six out of ten parents interviewed think that a school superintendent should not smoke and should be married, these expected attributes or actions are for Gross constituents of the role of school superintendent; if, on the other hand—Gross does not go this far, but nothing in his approach rules out such absurdities—thirty-five out of forty pupils think that none of them should ever get bad marks, this too is an expectation, associated in the first instance with the role of teacher but applying also to the school superintendent as the teacher's superior.

One suspects that Gross has taken the word "expectation" too literally, and has forgotten that laws also involve expectations by which people's behavior is guided into certain channels, indeed that laws and law courts are outstanding examples of what is meant by role expectations and sanctions. Role expectations are not modes of behavior about whose desirability there is a more or less impressive consensus; they are modes of behavior that are binding for the individual and whose binding character is institutionalized, i.e., valid independently of his own or anybody else's opinion.[23] It follows that if we are to connect the categories of role and reference group, it will not be by ascertaining the opinions of reference group

[23] In this respect Gross misunderstands earlier role definitions when he imputes to them a "postulate of role consensus" (36: chap. iii). Imprecise as it may be to speak of "culture patterns" and "expectations defined by society," such phrases clearly imply quasi-objective, institutionalized norms, not a consensus of opinions or conceptions. What must be rendered precise, therefore, is norms and not opinions.

members. If there is any point in interviews of this sort, it is to find out what prescriptions and sanctions are in fact valid in these groups, and constitute, so to speak, their "positive law."

Our thesis here is that the agency which defines a given position's role expectations and sanctions may be found in the norms and sanctions of that position's reference groups, and specifically in such of these norms and sanctions as refer to the position in question. Grammar school teacher Schmidt is a state official, and is therefore subject to the general statutes pertaining to officials and the special regulations of his department; he is a teacher, and is thus subject to the rules and prescriptions of his professional organization; but on a less formal level his pupils and their parents also constitute reference groups with defined norms and sanctions aimed at teachers' behavior. Generally speaking, it is possible to identify in any human group those rules and sanctions by which it influences the behavior of its members and of those non-members with whom it establishes relations. These rules and sanctions, which can in principle be separated from the opinions of both members and non-members, are the origin of role expectations and of their binding character. It follows that to articulate these expectations for a given position, we must first identify the position's reference groups and then find out what norms obtain in these groups with respect to that particular position.

Obviously, such a procedure works best with organized reference groups. All must- and most shall-expectations of social positions are the work of such groups. Must-expectations are found only where society as a whole, through its legal system, is the relevant reference group, i.e., where certain demands on the incumbent of a position are enforced by law. Shall-expectations often have their origin in public organizations or institutions, professional associations, business enterprises, political parties, or clubs, many of which have by-laws, or clearly established customs or precedents, that spell out their norms and sanctions. But when we come to a reference group like "pupils' parents," and in general to the whole range of un-codified can-expectations, documents and precedents do not help us much. Is it not, after all, essential in this case to interview mem-

bers of reference groups and seek a consensus? Sensible and realistic
as this method may seem, it is nevertheless fallacious. If we want to
preserve the concept of role from the arbitrariness of individual
opinions, to keep it at the point of intersection of the individual and
society, it is far better to forget about can-expectations for the time
being than to substitute the behavioral pseudo-precision of opinion
research for the structural fruitfulness of the category of role. Since
adequate methods for identifying unfixed role expectations have
not yet been found, we shall accordingly confine ourselves to formulating the accessible elements of social roles in terms of known
norms, customs, and precedents.[24]

The opinions of the members of reference groups and the degree
of consensus in these groups are obviously significant both for socio-
metric purposes and for role analysis. But their significance is not
where Gross presumed to find it. So far we have taken the norms
and sanctions of the reference groups of social positions as given;
but it remains to ask how these norms came into being as such in
the first place, or—what is the same thing—how they can be changed
or repealed. Possibly there is an analogy between consensus and
norms on the one hand, and custom and law on the other. A norm
that is not supported or at least tolerated by a majority of group
members is on weak ground. If, for example, a teachers' association
requires all teachers to arrange weekly parents' meetings but most
teachers consider it pointless to hold meetings so frequently, we
can safely predict that in due course this norm will be modified, or
at least that it will not be enforced and will thus be converted from
a shall- into a can-expectation. It is not the validity of norms but
their legitimacy that is affected by the opinions of those concerned:
thus if Gross had weighed the findings of his study against the institutionalized role expectations of the position of school superintendent, he might have come up with some interesting findings

[24] In informal groupings, such as the parents of a given teacher's pupils, norms
often become visible only if challenged (and then, of course, in intimate contact with
the opinions of those involved). A teacher tells his pupils obvious nonsense, which
they relay to their parents; the parents decide to do something about it. Such precedents then live on as norms; where they are present, we can identify can-expectations.
For a possible alternative way of identifying can-expectations, as for the whole problem of the empirical analysis of role expectations, see section VIII below.

about the future of this role and the legitimacy of the associated expectations. In a theoretical discussion, then, we must distinguish clearly between (1) fixed norms of reference groups, which are assigned to the incumbent of a position as role expectations; (2) the opinions of members of reference groups about these norms, which determine their legitimacy and likelihood of change; and (3) the actual behavior of role players. For the concept of social role, norms are relevant only in the first sense, as expectations; questions about their legitimacy and the actual behavior of the persons to whom they apply presuppose the role concept and are significant only in terms of that concept.

Among the reference groups that have us all, as incumbents of social positions, in their sway, society as a whole with its legal system is of particular interest, among other things because of its apparent resemblance to the "society" that we have dismissed as too imprecise a concept for sociological analysis. We have defined must-expectations as expectations supported by the force of law and the sanctions of law courts. Wherever these expectations apply, it is clear that no subdivision of society can be identified as the appropriate reference group. Although not all parts of the legal system are applicable to us in every one of our roles—although civil-service law is irrelevant to father Schmidt, and maritime law to Herr Schmidt in all his roles—neither the legal system as a whole nor any of its parts may be described as a norm instituted for others by a particular reference group. As a set of latent expectations, or more frequently prohibitions, the law applies to us in most of our social roles. Insofar as teacher Schmidt is subject to civil-service law and father Schmidt to family law, we must assume that the whole society of which Herr Schmidt is a part measures his behavior in terms of these norms. Here "the whole society" means all members of society to the extent that they are represented by legislative and judiciary institutions. In this limited sense, society as a whole constitutes a reference group, and functions like other reference groups in defining and controlling role expectations.[25]

---

25 This raises difficult problems that cannot be explored here. Their core is the fact that maritime law, for example, although applicable only to a limited set of persons and institutions, involves as law the claim to universality. In empirical analy-

Unless appearances deceive, applying reference group theory to the category of social role can help us to replace the personification "society" by more precise categories. With respect to social roles, the vexatious fact of society proves to be a conglomeration of more or less binding, more or less particular group norms. Every group contributes to determining the patterns of many roles; conversely, every role may be the result of influences from many groups. The resulting pattern is not always a unified, well-balanced whole; indeed, it may be characterized by various forms of social conflict, among them conflict within roles, which we shall consider below. What happens when the norms of teacher Schmidt's colleagues and those of his superiors prescribe contradictory behavior for him, so that whatever he does will disappoint one group or the other and incur its sanctions? Some conflicts of this kind are notorious in modern societies. One thinks of the university professor, torn between the demands of research, teaching, and administration; of the doctor, torn between doing his best to help his patients and charging as little as possible to the public health insurance; of the labor manager in a co-determination enterprise, torn between cooperating with his managerial colleagues and serving the workers he represents. These examples suggest how conceptual clarification, by enabling us to ask more precise questions, may contribute to the solution of empirical problems.

VI

In the last two sections we tried to elucidate the "binding character" and "social definition" of role expectations. Another idea that needs explaining takes the form of statements such as "Roles are assigned to the individual," or "In roles, the individual and society are mediated." How does a person acquire his positions and roles, and how does he relate to them? Since sociologists have de-

---

sis, this double aspect of laws is further obscured by special-interest legislation, laws pushed through parliaments by particular groups who seek to give their norms the appearance of universality. In terms of logic, it is important to recognize that as a reference group "society as a whole" need not be regarded as comprising all other groups, but may in given contexts stand alongside other reference groups as a subset of itself.

voted considerable attention to these questions, our discussion here becomes to a great extent a summary of familiar research. At the same time, this discussion will bring us very close to the initial problem of this essay: the problem of how to state clearly, and how to make bearable, the paradoxical relationship between the human being of our experience and role-playing *homo sociologicus*. For the relationship of the individual to his social roles involves the creation of *homo sociologicus* out of his human counterpart, the transformation of man into an actor on the stage of society.

The encounter of individual and society can be clarified by an intellectual experiment which, though clearly unrealistic, offers insights of considerable value. Since positions can be conceived and related to each other independently of their occupants, the structure of society can be thought of as a giant organization chart in which millions of positions are centered in their fields like suns with their planet systems. Grammar school teacher, father, German, and treasurer of the X-town soccer club are all places on this chart that can be identified without so much as thinking of Herr Schmidt. Next, let us imagine that Herr Schmidt and all his contemporaries are as yet devoid of any social position, that they represent pure social potential. The intellectual experiment consists in devising ways of joining the two, the positions on the chart and the position-less people, in such a way that every position on the chart is occupied by at least one person and every person is given at least one position. The latter requirement is easier to satisfy than the former, for the number of positions far exceeds the number of available people; but nearly random combinations of positions should be permitted.[26] Less schematically, but analogously in the points that concern us, every society is faced with the task of bringing together positions and men; this is one basic function of the social process.[27] Mathe-

[26] In social reality, of course, the possibilities of combining positions and people are by no means random. Rather, it would seem possible to develop a classification of positions so that every person can have but one position in every class (e.g., the classes of sex, age, family, national, and occupational positions). This is the difference between the fact of society and purely random conditions.

[27] The process of position allocation is often described by English and American sociologists as one of role allocation. If one accepts the distinction between positions and roles suggested here, the expression is imprecise; for what is allocated is in the first place positions (although each position has an associated role).

matically speaking, the problem of coordinating a great many "persons" with even more "positions" has a huge number of possible solutions. With respect to individual positions and persons, the same holds for society. But among these solutions, groups may be distinguished by certain criteria, and social mechanisms may be indicated that lead to certain solutions. Just as the behavior of *homo sociologicus* does not simply follow the laws of random probability, so the process of position allocation is not a matter of unrestricted mathematical permutations.

With respect to allocation, social positions are of two broad types: those that a person can do nothing about one way or the other, and those that he acquires by his own activity. All positions based on biological characteristics, for example, are of the first type: Herr Schmidt's sex and age positions (the fact that he is a man and an adult) are no more within his power to alter than his position as son in his family of origin. That he is a German and a citizen also follows automatically from the fact that he was born in a certain place and has reached a certain age. In addition to these *ascribed positions*, however, Herr Schmidt as a German in the middle of the twentieth century has a number of *achieved positions*, i.e., positions that he occupies at least to some extent by his own effort. In becoming a grammar school teacher, treasurer of the soccer club, and a driver, he has asserted an element of choice; these positions have not fallen to him without effort on his part. The distinction between ascribed and achieved positions is valid for all societies; but positions may change from ascribed to achieved, and (more rarely) vice versa. The "occupational" position of king in a hereditary monarchy is not achieved, and the same was true of many other occupations in preindustrial societies. Indeed, the distinction between these ascribed and achieved positions is not always clear. Is "Catholic" for the child of Catholic parents in a Catholic country an achieved position? Is "father" for Herr Schmidt an ascribed position? If we take the realistic possiblity of choice as our standard, we must answer no in both cases; but even this criterion cannot exclude marginal cases.[28]

---

[28] The distinction between ascribed and achieved positions was introduced in this meaning by Ralph Linton (42: 115): "Ascribed statuses are those which are assigned

Ascribed positions are like the prescriptions of a totally planned economy; society need not concern itself with their destiny. Indeed, to be quite rigorous we should have to exclude these positions from our intellectual experiment as being not generally available. With achieved positions, by contrast, where individual choice is involved, some social mechanism is necessary to decide who acquires which positions. Not everybody can become prime minister, president of a company, or treasurer of the X-town soccer club. In industrial societies the educational system tends to be the decisive social mechanism for assigning achieved positions (if the paradox is permitted), at least insofar as these may be broadly described as occupations. In schools and universities the individual's choice is brought into line with society's various needs for achievement; the diploma translates the resulting performance into a claim to a certain kind or level of achieved position. Within social organizations, too, the principle of achievement (activity, success) serves as a criterion for allocating positions. But as a result of these institutional mechanisms for evaluating achievement, the allocation of positions becomes a process of permanently decreasing possibilities, and further constants are introduced into our mathematical experiment. Even the ascribed position "man" limits the sum of all further possible positions; such positions as adult, professional man, and inhabitant of town X are further restrictions. Eventually, such restrictions reduce Herr Schmidt's range of choice to such an extent that only a very limited number of positions remain open for him. Here again it is but a step from experiencing society as a support and a source of security to experiencing it as an obstacle and a vexation.

In any case, social positions are a Danaän gift from society to the individual. Even if he has not acquired them by his own effort, even if they have been ascribed to him from birth, they demand something from him; for every position carries with it a social role, a set

---

to individuals without reference to their innate differences or abilities. They can be predicted and trained for from the moment of birth. The achieved statuses are, as a minimum, those requiring special qualities, although they are not necessarily limited to these. They are not assigned to individuals from birth, but are left open to be filled through competition and individual effort." Even apart from the term "status" (on which see section VII), this definition contains a number of obscure features that have only recently been cleared up along the lines indicated in the text.

56 ESSAYS IN THE THEORY OF SOCIETY

of expectations addressed to the behavior of its incumbent and sanctioned by the reference groups of its field. But before the individual can play his roles, he must know them; like an actor, man as a social being must learn his roles, become familiar with their substance and the sanctions that enforce them. Here we encounter a second basic mechanism of society, the process of socialization by the internalizing of behavior patterns. The individual must somehow take into himself the prescriptions of society and make them the basis of his behavior; it is by this means that the individual and society are mediated and man is reborn as *homo sociologicus*. Position allocation and role internalization are complementary, and it is thus no accident that industrial societies have assigned primary responsibility for both processes to a single institutional order—the educational system. Even in modern societies, however, the family, the church, and other institutions support the educational system in its task of allocating positions and socializing the young.

The two concepts generally used to describe the process of mediation between the totally unsocial individual and a completely individuated society—socialization and internalization—clearly belong to the point of intersection between the individual and society; and the category of role accordingly falls on the borderline of sociology and psychology.[29] From the point of view of society and sociology, it is by learning role expectations, by being transformed into *homo sociologicus*, that man becomes a part of society and accessible to sociological analysis. Man devoid of roles is a nonentity for society and sociology. To become a part of society and a subject of sociological analysis, man must be socialized, chained to the fact of society

[29] The intermediate position of role between sociology and psychology is often emphasized, and is indeed an important characteristic of role. A remark by Bertrand Russell is apposite here: "Every account of structure is relative to certain units which are, for the time being, treated as if they were devoid of structure, but it must never be assumed that these units will not, in another context, have a structure which it is important to recognize." (57: 269.) For the sociologist, roles are irreducible elements of analysis. The psychologist, by contrast, is concerned with their other, inner side, the side facing the individual, and he is accordingly led to dissolve roles into their psychologically relevant components. A systematic delimitation of the two disciplines in these terms would be conceivable, but like other such delimitations it would be of doubtful utility.

and made its creature. By observation, imitation, indoctrination, and conscious learning, he must grow into the forms that society holds in readiness for him as an incumbent of positions. His parents, friends, teachers, priests, and superiors are important to society above all as agents who cut into his social *tabula rasa* the plan of his life in society. If society is interested in the family, the school, and the church, it is only partly because they help the individual to develop his talents fully; it is primarily because they prepare him effectively and economically for carrying out all the tasks that society has set him.

For society and sociology, socialization invariably means depersonalization, the yielding up of man's absolute individuality and liberty to the constraint and generality of social roles. Man become *homo sociologicus* is exposed without protection to the laws of society and the hypotheses of sociology. The process occurs wherever society exists. Only Robinson Crusoe can hope to prevent his alienated rebirth as *homo sociologicus*.

For the individual and for psychology this process has a different aspect. From this perspective human beings are not transformed into something alien, are not socialized; rather, they take something that exists outside them into themselves, internalize it, and make it a part of their personality. By learning to play social roles, then, we not only lose ourselves to the alien otherness of a world we never made, but regain ourselves as personalities given unique shape by that world's vexations. At least for the psychology of personality, the internalization of role expectations is one of the significant formative processes of human life; as we know from recent research, it simultaneously affects many levels of the personality. It may increase our knowledge, or it may lead to repressions and conflicts; in any case, it affects us very deeply. Socially, the most important corollary of the internalization of social roles is the concurrent internalization of the sanctions which, as custom and law, control our behavior. Since Freud, it has been clear that the norms of society and other reference groups can be to some extent internalized in the conscience or superego, with the result that the warning and sentencing voice of society is capable of sanctioning our behavior through ourselves. At least for some roles and role expectations, we can assume that external agencies are not necessary to remind us of the binding character of social statutes. It is by no means unimportant that society can judge our behavior by our own conscience even where we succeed in deceiving the policeman or the judge.

Beyond all psychology and sociology, the vexation of society is a question of how much freedom of choice is left to man by the all-pervading constraints of society, or—to put the question more actively—how much he can arrogate to himself. In its most frightening aspect the world of *homo sociologicus* is a "brave new world" or a "1984," a society in which all human behavior has become calculable, predictable, and subject to permanent control. In reality, however, although we are in fact unable to separate Herr Schmidt from the role player Schmidt, after all his roles are taken into account he retains a residual range of choice that escapes calculation and control. It is not easy to define this range of choice, but it appears to have at least three components. There is not only the freedom that every role leaves its player by not pronouncing on certain matters (for example, father Schmidt's free choice of playing ball or playing electric trains), but also a freedom *within* role expectations arising from the fact that they are largely defined by exclusion rather than determined positively. Few role expectations are all-encompassing prescriptions; most take the form of a range of permitted deviations. Expectations associated with negative sanctions, in particular, are essentially privative; we are not supposed to do certain things, but are otherwise free to do as we please. Finally, the individual's alienated relationship to society implies that he both is and is not society; if society shapes his personality, he can help shape society. Role expectations and sanctions are not unalterably fixed for all time; like everything social they can be changed by changes in people's behavior and opinions. However, much as such considerations may do toward reconciling us to the paradox of *homo sociologicus*, they scarcely help to render *homo sociologicus* more compatible with the man of our everyday experience.

VII

Only in a meaninglessly general sense can we say that *homo sociologicus,* as we have sketched him here, is at the basis of all theoretical and empirical research in contemporary sociology. There has been an unmistakable trend toward agreement on the meaning and importance of social position and role, and on the use of these specific terms; but there remain astonishing differences between sociologists with respect to these and other elements of sociological analysis, as the merest glance through any sociological journal will confirm. This is one of the reasons why we have put off discussing earlier attempts to describe the man of sociology. At last, however, we are in a position not only to summarize recent work on roles and deride it as full of contradictions, as is usually done,[30] but to resolve the contradictions by considered critical decisions. In doing so, we shall confine ourselves to a few main aspects of the conceptual dispute, and a few of the leading disputants. We can accordingly claim only representativeness, and not completeness, for the positions and problems discussed.

The terminologically strict use of the elementary categories in question here can be traced to Ralph Linton's discussion of "Status and Role" in his *Study of Man,* which first appeared in 1936. Nearly all later attempts at definition cite this discussion, and although Linton himself later modified his views—whether intentionally or unintentionally is not clear—it seems sensible to start with what he originally wrote.[31] Linton first speaks of "status," which is what we have called "position" here: "A status, in the abstract, is a position in a particular pattern." (42: 113.) This definition, which is similar to ours but less precise, Linton immediately elaborates as follows: "A status, as distinct from the individual who may occupy

---

30 Such summaries have been published at regular intervals; see, for example, those by L. J. Neiman and J. W. Hughes (51), Theodore R. Sarbin (58), and Neal Gross *et al.* (36).

31 On Linton's later changes, see Gross *et al.* (36: 12–13), and note 36 below.

it, is simply a collection of rights and duties." (42: 113.) By way of illustration Linton uses the much-quoted image of the driver's seat in a car: the car's equipment—steering wheel, gearshift, accelerator, brakes, clutch—is given to the individual driver as a constant with equal potential for all drivers. How then are roles defined? "A role represents the dynamic aspect of a status. The individual is socially assigned to a status and occupies it with relation to other statuses. When he puts the rights and duties which constitute the status into effect, he is performing a role. Role and status are quite inseparable, and the distinction between them is of only academic interest." (42: 114.)

Few statements by sociologists have been quoted as often as these sentences, and yet all the ambiguities of the categories "role" and "status" (or "position") are present in this, their classic definition. The first ambiguity is terminological: we must establish terms for the two elementary categories that are not only adequate but reasonably unlikely to be misunderstood. Like all terminological questions, this is of but moderate substantive significance. The second ambiguity is in the delimitation of the two categories, if indeed (considering Linton's last remark) two categories are necessary at all. This ambiguity is rather more significant than the first. If status describes a "collection of rights and duties," what remains for role? Is there a substantively justified, formulable difference between the "static" and "dynamic" aspects of places in a field of social relations?[32] These questions consistently lead to a third ambiguity both in Linton's definition and in most later ones, an ambiguity that has occupied us before and requires special attention. Are roles what the individual does with patterns given to him by society, or are they as much a part of society as they are of the individual? Are they objective data, separable from the individual, or subjective ones, inseparably part of his personal life?

[32] "Static" and "dynamic" are expressions that sociologists use often and with pleasure; yet they rarely have an unambiguous meaning. In the present context they seem to me entirely out of place. In what sense are my "rights" more static than my "actions"? Why is my position more static than my "rights"? Unfortunately, as some of the following quotations show, not only Linton's definition but his distinction between "static" and "dynamic" roles has survived for a generation.

This last ambiguity raises the most important problems, as we shall see. Linton himself seems to understand by roles not complexes of expected modes of behavior (which he ascribes instead to "status" as "rights and duties"), but actual behavior with respect to such expectations. Seen this way, "role" is not a quasi-objective elementary category of sociology, a category in principle independent of specific individuals, but a variable of social psychology. How teacher Schmidt in fact behaves to his pupils or his superiors is by no means without social interest, but it tells us less about the fact of society than about Herr Schmidt's personality. This error, which is not fully articulated by Linton, is carried to its logical conclusion by Kingsley Davis when he says:

> How an individual actually performs in a given position, as distinct from how he is supposed to perform, we call his role. The role, then, is the manner in which a person actually carries out the requirements of his position. It is the dynamic aspect of status or office and as such is always influenced by factors other than the stipulations of the position itself. (32: 89–90.)

Here, the category of role is almost deliberately removed from the area of intersection between the individual and society and handed over to the social psychologist. So defined, role fails to incorporate precisely what we had regarded as central to it, namely behavior expectations. The approach of Hans H. Gerth and C. Wright Mills is very similar: "More technically, the concept of 'role' refers to units of conduct (1) which by their recurrence stand out as regularities and (2) which are oriented to the conduct of other actors." (35: 10.) If sociologists define role in this way, one can hardly blame social psychologists for distinguishing with H. A. Murray between "individual roles" and "social roles" (47: 450–51), or for agreeing with P. R. Hofstätter: "As a role one may define a coherent behavior sequence which is geared to the behavior sequences of other persons." (37: 36.) (In fact Hofstätter, who speaks a little later of the "separability of roles from their particular bearer," is more sociological than the sociologists quoted.) People's regular behavior toward other people gains sociological meaning only insofar as it may be understood as behavior with respect to predetermined patterns that are assigned to the incumbent of a social position irrespective of his individual identity. It is these patterns, and not (as with Linton, Davis, Gerth and Mills, and many social psychologists) the behavior itself, that we have called social roles.

Psychologizing definitions characterize one line of thinking about the category of role. A second, which surprisingly never conflicts openly with the first, has been much more fruitful. It is especially surprising that George C. Homans and Talcott Parsons, both of whom explicitly refer to Linton's definition, do not apparently see it as conflicting with their own much less ambiguous and indeed very different formulations: "A norm that states the expected relationship of a person in a certain position to others he comes into contact with is often called the role of this person." (Homans, 39: 124.) "The role is that organized sector of an actor's orientation which constitutes and defines his participation in an interactive process. It involves a set of complementary expectations concerning his own actions and those of others with whom he interacts." (Parsons, 45: 23.) Similarly, John W. Bennett and Melvin M. Tumin understand by roles "the expected behavior which goes along with the occupancy of a status" (29: 96), and Merton speaks of "structurally defined expectations assigned to each role" (4: 110). All these characterizations of role are based on the objectivated, sociological notion of complexes of expected behavior, as opposed to actual regularities of behavior.

These two concepts of role are clearly incompatible. The first defines Herr Schmidt's father role as the way he regularly behaves toward his children; the second finds it in the norms that his society has generally adopted and laid down for fathers. T. H. Marshall, perceiving the difficulty, has proposed that the two approaches be reconciled by leaving the category of role entirely to social psychology and making status, purged of its psychological elements, the basis of sociological analysis: "Status emphasizes the position as conceived by the group or society that sustains it. . . . Status emphasizes the fact that expectations (of a normative kind) exist in the relevant social groups." (44: 13.) To support his proposal, Marshall cites the legal definition of status as a "condition of belonging to a particular class of persons to whom the law assigns peculiar legal capacities or incapacities, or both" (44: 15). Siegfried F. Nadel also invokes the legal concept of status: "By status I shall mean the rights and obligations of any individual relative both to those of others and to the scale of worthwhileness valid in the group." (49: 171.) However, contrary to Marshall's proposal and following A. R. Radcliffe-Brown, Nadel introduces the parallel concept of "person," a term that we have encountered in a similar meaning in the "persona" of the drama.[33] As a last example of the attempt to achieve terminological clarity by extending the concept of status, we offer Chester I. Barnard's definition of status as "that condition of the individual that is defined by a statement of his rights, privileges, immunities, duties, obligations . . . and, obversely, by a statement of the restrictions, limitations, and prohibitions governing his behavior, both determining the expectations of others in reference thereto" (27: 47–48).

Confusing as the abundance of definitions may appear, they clearly have a common core very near the assumptions of our earlier discussion. All the authors cited assume an elementary category of sociological analysis that is defined by expected patterns of behavior ("rights and duties"); apart from Continental European sociology, which in this respect as in others is still hampered by a provincialism stemming from its older but outdated traditions,[34] there are hardly

---

[33] Cf. Radcliffe-Brown: "The components or units of social structure are persons, and a person is a human being considered not as an organism but as occupying a position in a social structure." (56: 9-10.) "Within an organization each person may be said to have a role. . . ." (56: 11.) Nadel: "We might here speak of different 'aspects' of a person, or of different 'roles' assumed by it, or simply of different 'persons.' Though this is a question of words, the last-named usage seems to me the most consistent as well as convenient one. Understood in this sense, the person is more than the individual; it is the individual with certain recognized, or institutionalized, tasks and relationships, and is all the individuals who act in this way." (50: 93.) In a footnote to this remark Nadel refers to the close connection of the concepts "person" and "status" in legal language. But it is clear both from Nadel's formulations and from Radcliffe-Brown's that the category of "person" is too inclusive to replace that of position or of role; their concept of "person" corresponds rather to our *homo sociologicus*.

[34] This statement was truer when this essay was written (in 1957) than it is today. After becoming familiar with the work of sociologists in other countries, European

any differences of opinion on this point. Most of the authors cited propose a pair of such categories: either "status" and "role" (following Linton); or "position" or "office" and "role" (Homans, Davis); or "status" and "person" (Nadel). Even those authors who propose only the single category of "status" seem in effect to recognize two categories. Marshall, for example, in defining status simultaneously as position and as a complex of normative expectations, ascribes to one concept two quite distinct meanings. Marshall's definition shows at least the possibility, if not the necessity, of distinguishing between a place in a field of social relations and the expectations associated with occupying this place. Quite apart from the question of which terms may prove most suitable, the definitions quoted suggest that we need not one concept, but two.

Finally, a psychological element appears in some definitions, namely, the actual behavior of the individual incumbents of positions. Now it is indeed one of the tasks of sociology "to provide the link between the structural study of social systems and the psychological study of personality and motivation" (Marshall, 44: 11), but precisely this connecting-link function makes it necessary to guard jealously the intermediate position of sociology's basic categories. There is no way to get from what the individual does, or even does regularly, to the fact of society, which in principle is independent of the individual. The sum and the average of individual actions are as incapable of explaining the reality of law and custom as a consensus ascertained by interviews. Society is a fact, and a vexatious one at that, precisely because it is created neither by our impulses nor by our habitual behavior. I can break the rules of my reference groups, and I can break a long-standing habit; but the two kinds of action are essentially incommensurate. The first puts me into a tangible conflict with the fact of society, a force outside myself; the second involves only myself. The behavior of *homo sociologicus,* of man at the point of intersection between the individual and society, cannot be determined by "factors other than those given with the position," as Davis rightly states in discussing the effects of actual

_____
sociologists have at last begun again to contribute actively to the theoretical discussion in the discipline.

behavior, without recognizing that by this standard his own role concept becomes sociologically useless. The person of our everyday experience expresses himself by individual variations of behavior; not so *homo sociologicus*.

Leaving aside all psychological elements, then, we may summarize the present state of the problem as follows. Some authors use a single term, usually "status," to describe both a place in a field of relations and the expectations associated with this place; with these authors, as with Linton, "status" oscillates in meaning between "position" and "rights and duties." Other authors use two terms, often "status" and "role," to express these two meanings. (Interestingly enough, some authors have tended to fuse both meanings in the term "role"; thus Parsons, for example, who used the term "status-role-bundle" in his writings before 1951, has since spoken mostly of "roles.") Reduced to these terms, the old conceptual dispute turns largely into a terminological question, which is to say a matter to be determined by considerations of convenience. We need only make a simple critical decision to escape the maze of definitions and counterdefinitions without injury to the basic ideas of any of the conflicting parties.

Fortunately, terminological clarification requires only a short step in a familiar direction. As the term for a place in a field of social relations, "status" and "position" compete for recognition. But "status" is losing ground, and for good reason. In general usage, "status" refers primarily to one particular kind of position, namely, position in a hierarchical scale of social prestige, a meaning that differs significantly from the one in question here.[35] The same holds for the word's legal meaning. Legal status means more than merely a place in a network of relations; indeed, it includes certain rights and duties that we specifically want to separate from the simple concept of place. "Position," by contrast, is a neutral word, unburdened by misleading connotations, which is exactly what we

---

[35] Strictly speaking, "social status" in this sense describes not only a special kind of position, but a position of positions. Not a human being, but a position (e.g. an occupation) has prestige and in that sense a "status." This meaning of "status," which is important in many contexts, must be distinguished clearly from our much more neutral concept of position.

need. In using "position" we have followed the lead of Gross and his colleagues.[36]

As for "role," the term itself is generally accepted; the problem, as we have seen, is that social psychologists and sociologists assign it different meanings. If neither discipline is prepared to renounce the term, a definitive solution may be impossible in the foreseeable future. And yet it appears that the divergence of definitions may be more apparent than real. As it happens, social psychologists have succeeded in rendering the notion of habitual behavior precise, whereas sociologists have so far failed to do the same with their notion of expected behavior. Once this deficiency is remedied, I see no reason why the concept and term "social role" should not be accepted by social scientists in the sense indicated in this essay.

Our critical survey of the literature in this section has been rather more general and vague than the discussions of previous sections. Unfortunately, this corresponds to the state of the problem. Only in the works of Gross and Merton do we find impressive advances in rendering the fundamental categories of sociological analysis more precise. With their distinction between roles and role segments, or role sets and roles, these authors have cleared the way for connecting role theory and reference group theory, and have helped prepare the way for the empirical investigation of roles.[37]

[36] Linton's arguments against this use of "position" are incomprehensible to me. They are nonetheless of interest as illustrating Linton's later thoughts on the elementary categories in question: "The place in a particular system which a certain individual occupies at a particular time will be referred to as his status with respect to that system. The term position has been used by some other students of social structure in much the same sense, but without clear recognition of the time factor or of the existence of simultaneous systems of organization within the society. Status has long been used with reference to the position of an individual in the prestige system of a society. In the present usage this is extended to apply to his position in each of the other systems. The second term, role, will be used to designate the sum total of the culture patterns associated with a particular status. It thus includes the attitudes, values, and behavior ascribed by the society to any and all persons occupying this status. It can even be extended to include the legitimate expectations of such persons with respect to the behavior toward them of persons in other statuses within the same system.... Insofar as it represents overt behavior, a role is the dynamic aspect of a status: what the individual has to do in order to validate his occupation of the status." (43: 368.)

[37] Since this was written, some good work has been done along these lines, notably by Michael Banton (25), Siegfried F. Nadel (50), and Heinrich Popitz (5).

Although *homo sociologicus* was until recently a mere postulate, an idea whose usefulness many suspected but no one had conclusively demonstrated, there would seem to be a chance today of testing the postulate by applying it to empirical problems. Only after such a test proves successful will *homo sociologicus* change from a mere paradox of thought into a true doppelgänger, a disturbing approximation to the man of our experience. Only then will the alienated rebirth of man as *homo sociologicus* become an inescapable philosophical problem for sociologists.

VIII

The inventors of *homo oeconomicus* and psychological man did not conceive of them as embodying philosophies of human nature, although critics of these concepts have seen them as carrying this implication. If, as we have tried to show here, the critics' claim is not as easily dismissed as economists and psychologists would have us believe, still it has nothing to do with why these artificial men of social science were originally created. *Homo sociologicus* poses a dilemma that we can escape only by dogmatism; but it is not dogmatism that has led us to postulate the rebirth of man as a role-playing creature. Rather, it is the hope of making the fact of society accessible to statements whose validity can be decided by controlled observations. First of all, and above all else, *homo sociologicus* is a tool for rationalizing and explaining certain aspects of the world we live in. Scientific method in this sense has its own moral and philosophical problems. Very possibly tomorrow's sociologist will face as difficult a conflict of conscience as today's nuclear physicist.[38] But that must be as it will. To make a future Galileo of sociology publicly recant his insights would no more hold up the progress of sociology than Galileo's perjury held up the progress of physics. Obscurantism and suppression are always the worst means of deal-

---

[38] One need but think of the none too distant possibility of keeping totalitarian governments in power with the assistance of sociological insights—or of "human relations in industry," as the current phrase goes, whose implicit goal is often to prevent strikes and wage demands without regard to their legitimacy.

ing with imminent conflicts. Here as elsewhere it is better to face the dilemma boldly than to run away from it.

In our discussion so far, the empirical or scientific usefulness of *homo sociologicus,* the understanding we gain by his invention, has been little more than an assertion, a promise. So far, published research bears out the promise only to a very limited extent.[39] At several points, we have hinted at possible applications of the role concept; we shall now incorporate these hints in a more systematic argument for the usefulness of this concept in analyzing particular sociological problems.

Categories like position, role, reference group, and sanction can be applied to research problems only if they are operationally precise. We have referred several times to the difficulty of describing particular social roles. Nearly everything remains to be done in this respect. Ideally, the sociologist would have a kind of sociological periodic table of elements at his disposal, i.e., an inventory or chart showing all known positions with their associated role expectations and sanctions (to begin with, perhaps, in one society). In fact, we do not even have the beginnings of such an inventory; no strict description of a social role has ever been attempted.[40] It is not so much that sociologists are indolent; it is rather that partial descriptions of roles suffice for most problems of sociological analysis, and that any description of social roles involves considerable methodological and technical problems. Neither of these considerations, however, relieves us of the necessity of developing adequate methods of describing social roles; for even partial descriptions, to be valid, presuppose such methods.

The first step in identifying social roles empirically is classificatory. It seems sensible to begin by sorting out the classes of social

[39] Much as the concept of role has been discussed by sociologists, it is not used as often in empirical research as one might expect; and where it is used, it is often defined *ad hoc.* This disappointing situation is probably due in part to technical difficulties (discussed below) in the way of rendering role and other categories empirically precise.

[40] Gross and his collaborators did of course intend to describe the role of the school superintendent precisely (36). But their misleading definition of roles (by majority opinions in reference groups) makes their description of little practical use.

positions that are applicable to everyone, or nearly everyone: e.g., the classes of family, occupational, national, class, age, and sex positions. Even if it should not make sense in the end to classify all known social positions, it seems possible and profitable (for example, in describing the positions held by a given person) to establish subdivisions for the most important classes of positions. We must also classify role expectations. Here we have made a beginning by distinguishing must-, shall-, and can-expectations; but more refined gradations are clearly desirable, perhaps even quantitative distinctions in the case of certain negative sanctions. A scale assigning numerical values to all possible negative sanctions from prison terms to disapproval by members of reference groups might be very useful in classifying role expectations.[41]

The next step is to identify the reference groups that define particular social positions. It is hard to say whether there is a determinate and determinable number of reference groups for any given position, but it would probably suffice to identify the most important reference groups for each position; often this information is readily inferrable from a position's place in an organizational or quasi-organizational context. What is hardest to assess is the relative weight of different reference groups for given positions. Who is more important for the role behavior of the teacher, his superiors or his colleagues?[42] Wherever two or more reference groups associate different expectations with a position, this question obviously becomes crucial. Perhaps it could be answered, and a rank order of reference groups established, on the basis of the severity of the negative sanctions at the disposal of the relevant reference groups.

The most important and most difficult step is to identify and define role expectations and sanctions. This is the difficulty on

[41] All standards are originally arbitrary; there is thus no reason why one should not try to classify sanctions, say, on a scale from 10 (long prison term) to 1 (disapproval by members of reference groups), or 0 (sanctionless role range). Such measures might also serve to distinguish groups of roles. For example, only a few roles extend into the range of severe sanctions (citizen, political positions); for this very reason these may well be of special significance.

[42] This question, too, must of course be understood as a structural question, i.e., a question of the importance of various reference groups in the institutional context, not of the personal preferences of a teacher or an average of teachers.

which all efforts to make the role concept operationally precise have foundered. We have already indicated one way of overcoming this difficulty, namely, by ascertaining all the laws, rules, and customs of reference groups that are applicable to a given position, since all such rules and customs are role expectations associated with this position. For can-expectations, which cannot be ascertained by this method, we can perhaps make use of the social psychologist's trick of "placing" a person by inferring his main social positions from his appearance, language, and demeanor. This trick can be reversed. Random groups of people[43] might be asked what appearance and demeanor they think is expected of the incumbent of a given position. Such replicable "experiments in definition"[44] would give us guidelines at least for those can-expectations which are not laid down in any law or statute and yet shape so much of the behavior of *homo sociologicus.* Although it would be dangerous to rely entirely on experiments in definition, they promise a welcome addition to our ways of ascertaining must- and shall-expectations.

In these technical remarks, we are thinking of role descriptions only as elements in a larger analysis, as data to be used in dealing with specific problems. But such descriptions themselves may furnish telling insights; indeed, literary descriptions of particular roles historically preceded not only their strict definition, but the very concept of role. Even in the sociological literature there are many informative (if methodologically uncertain) descriptions of particular roles. Margaret Mead has investigated the specific features of sex roles (46); S. N. Eisenstadt has done the same for age roles (34). A small library might be filled with sociologists' descriptions of occupational roles: railwayman and manager, druggist and boxer,

[43] The word "random" requires two qualifications here. First, it would not be advisable to ask members of reference groups about positions determined by their group, because that would make it difficult to distinguish between institutionalized expectations and personal opinions. Second, it is necessary to choose respondents with some knowledge of the positions in question; unskilled workers will be hard put to pronounce on the position of accountant. Given these requirements, it makes good sense (and methodologically it seems unobjectionable) to choose students or even sociologists as respondents.

[44] The notion of experiments in definition and their application in social psychology is due to P. R. Hofstätter (37: 35ff) (38).

salesgirl and unskilled worker. Many studies of the characteristic behavior of certain social strata or classes (e.g. 26), as well as most works on the problematic subject of national character (e.g. 40), are essentially descriptions of roles. In all these cases, the comparative description of roles across historical and geographical boundaries has proved very fruitful.

A concern with particular roles leads to a concern with specific problems of sociological analysis, since it involves the confrontation of role expectations with actual behavior. We have already noted two aspects of this confrontation: the difference between roles and the actual behavior of their incumbents; and the difference between the norms of reference groups, insofar as these define role expectations, and their members' opinions of these norms. In both cases the role concept yields insights into the regularities of social change. Consider, for example, the role of Assistant in German universities, which is defined strictly in terms of learning and research; if in fact a majority of Assistants have teaching and administrative duties, it may be presumed that a change of role definitions is imminent. The extent of agreement between roles and actual behavior, between norms and opinions, is an index of social stability; disagreement indicates the presence of conflict, and thus the possibility and the likely direction of change.

The study of intra-role conflict is particularly important for the investigation of social structure. Thus Joseph Ben-David (28) has examined the role of the physician in bureaucratized medicine, who is expected to do his best by his patients while at the same time complying with administrative obligations that may run counter to his patients' interests. Such conflicts are usual in professional positions today; the so-called liberal professions are a thing of the past. Since the conflicting expectations of the two reference groups in this situation—clients or patients, and superordinate agencies—cannot both be met, some change in the social structure is imperative. So long as no such change occurs, the professional man must either break the law or act in a manner quite unintended by the reference groups (for example, a doctor may neglect his patients, whose sanctions are less severe than those of government agencies or insurance companies). Many problems of social behavior can be explained in terms of a conflict of expectations within roles.

The study of conflicts *within* roles became possible only with the concept of role segments; before that, however, there was some study of conflicts *between* roles, i.e., of the problems that arose when a person was obliged to play two or more roles with contradictory expectations. Some such inter-role conflicts are created and resolved by people's arbitrary choices; others, of far greater structural importance, are built into the process of position allocation. The man who cannot reconcile his simultaneous membership in two hostile political parties can leave one of them; but the member of parliament who must function as a businessman as well, or the worker's son who as a lawyer must comply with the expectations of his new and higher social level, finds himself in a conflict that he cannot escape by sheer choice. The familiar problem of the reduced significance of the family in industrial society has been successfully tackled with the help of these concepts. Neil Smelser, in his study of the Lancashire cotton industry during industrialization (61), has shown how the shift of production from the home to the factory led to a separation of familial and occupational roles and ultimately to a conflict between them. Whereas formerly a father combined his work and the education of his children, a father working in a factory had to separate the two functions and reduce the time and energy spent on one of them. The conflict between occupational and familial roles, and its gradual resolution by the reduction of the expectations associated with familial positions, can be documented in historical detail, and accordingly makes a good paradigm for many other processes of the social division of labor.

The role concept is clearly useful in analyzing how a single individual is affected by the conflict of expectations within and between his roles; but its usefulness does not stop there. Consider, for example, the problem of industrial conflict. Why is there a conflict between employers and workers? Is it because there is some inherent hostility between these groups? Are workers and employers, as people, irreconcilable foes? Obviously, such an assumption makes little sense; and yet it is at least implicit in many discussions of the subject. With the categories developed here we can clarify the problem. Workers and employers are the incumbents of two types of roles which are defined, among other things, by contradictory role expectations. The conflict between the two role types is structural, i.e., essentially independent of the feelings and views of the role players themselves; it exists only insofar as Messrs. A, B, C are incumbents of the position "employer" and Messrs. X, Y, Z incumbents of the position "worker." In other positions—for example, as members of a soccer club—A, B, C and X, Y, Z may be good friends. All sociological statements about their relationship leave them unaffected as human beings; they are strictly statements about people as incumbents of positions and players of roles.[45]

The example of industrial conflict is but one of many. There certainly are sociological problems that can be solved without direct reference to social roles as there are sociological publications in which the word "role" neither occurs nor needs to occur.[46] But even such works, insofar as they are sociological, are nowhere concerned

[45] This approach to the explanation of industrial and political conflicts is elaborated in my book *Class and Class Conflict* (7). In outlining the empirical applications of the category of role, I have deliberately given precedence here to problems of social conflict. Structural-functional theorists, by contrast, tend to relate the elementary categories of position and role to the so-called integration theory of society, a demonstrably one-sided analytical position. According to the integration theory, units of social structure may be understood as systems; all the elements of a system contribute to its functioning in a definable manner, and any element that does not so contribute is eliminated from the analysis as "dysfunctional." Sensible as this approach may be in certain cases, it would be wrong to generalize it and misleading to define role and position in this restricted manner. We have defined roles as complexes of behavior expectations adhering to social positions. This does not imply an exclusive focus on behavior patterns that contribute to the functioning of an existing system. Behavior that the integration theory would consider "dysfunctional" is equally subject to norms, i.e., to being crystallized into role expectations. Thus even if the functioning of the existing "system" is jeopardized by labor's wholesale rejection of the distribution of power in industry, there is every reason to regard labor's attitude as a behavior expectation associated with the position "worker."

[46] Analogies to natural science are objectionable to many social scientists, but one seems worth proposing here. Even in physics by no means all problems directly involve the atom. Entire branches of physics—e.g., classical mechanics—have been developed without a single reference to atoms. Nevertheless it would be correct to describe the atom as a fundamental element of the physical sciences. Possibly role sociology, i.e., the scientific concern with roles as such, will one day be a special field like nuclear physics; such a development would not affect the fundamental character of the role concept.

with the full human being, his feelings and desires, his idiosyncrasies and peculiarities. The assumptions and theories of sociology
refer not to man but to *homo sociologicus,* man in the alienated
aspect of an incumbent of positions and a player of roles. It is not
Schmidt the man but Schmidt the grammar school teacher who has
a relatively low income despite high social prestige; not Schmidt
the man but Schmidt the party official who asks questions from the
floor at meetings of the opposition party; not Schmidt the man but
Schmidt the driver who defends himself before the traffic judge
against the charge of speeding; not Schmidt the man but Schmidt
the husband and father who takes out an expensive life insurance
policy as protection for his family. And Schmidt the man? What
does he do? What can he do without being robbed of his individuality and converted into an incumbent of positions and a player of
roles? Does the man Schmidt begin where his roles end? Does he
live in his roles? Or is his a world in which roles and positions exist as little as neutrons and protons in the world of the housewife
who sets the table for dinner? This is the insistent paradox of *homo
sociologicus.* Our discussion of it will take us next to the region
where sociology and philosophy meet.

IX

"The inhabitant of a country," Robert Musil remarks, "has at
least nine characters: an occupational character, a national character, a civic character, a class character, a geographical character, a
sex character, a conscious character, and an unconscious character,
and perhaps a private character as well. He combines them all in
himself, but they dissolve him, and he is really nothing but a small
channel washed out by these trickling streams, which they flow into
and leave again to join other little streams and fill another channel. This is why every inhabitant of the earth has a tenth character as well, which is nothing more nor less than the passive fantasy
of unfilled spaces. It permits man everything except one thing: to
take seriously what his nine or more other characters do and what
happens to them. In other words, then, it forbids him precisely that

which would fulfill him." (48: 35.) Like the village chemist who outdid the BBC Meteorological Service with his "forecasts," the poet here anticipates the sociologist's insight into his subject matter. Musil does even more. His observation, which is equally remarkable for the richness of its substance and the irony of its form, establishes for the sociologist not merely the subject of his science, but also the limits of his method. Musil sees the paradox of the two human beings, and solves it in the irony of his reflection.

The inhabitant of a country is man in relation to society; he is not simply man, but man in a "country," living along with others within certain political boundaries on which he depends. As such, he has a number of characters, masks, personas, roles. Among these are his occupational, national, civic, class, regional, and sex characters; Musil might have added age, family, and others. Moreover, the inhabitant of a country is not merely *homo sociologicus,* but also psychological man; there are two souls in his breast, one his conscious Ego, the other his unconscious Id, and both are colors in the spectrum on which his figure oscillates. His characters, which are yet not his, leave him a small range of freedom, which, if he has the desire and ability, he may perhaps use for matters that are his and his alone. This private character stands alongside the other characters. Man "has" these characters, they are thoroughly his, and yet he has not made them. They have their reality outside him, and by taking them on he loses himself. They dissolve him. What remains is man as a "small channel washed out by these trickling streams," a player of roles that are no more of his devising than the laws of the country he lives in. His roles are conferred on him, and he is shaped by them; but when he dies, the impersonal force of society takes his roles away and confers them on somebody else in new combinations. From the unique, man has turned into the exemplar, from the individual into the member, from a free and autonomous creature into the sum of his alien characters.

But man, this particular human being Hans Schmidt whom we encounter at a party, is not merely the sum of his characters. We sense and know that there is something else about him, that he is not merely the inhabitant of a country but an inhabitant of the earth, and as such free of all ties to society. His tenth character is more than a mere supplement to the other nine; it rules an entire world in which it tolerates no other characters beside itself; it encompasses all other characters and thus makes them disappear. Man the inhabitant of a country is merely an object of ironical protest for man the inhabitant of the earth. The claim to exclusiveness on the part of the inhabitant of a country is nothing but a distant piece of presumptuousness for the inhabitant of the earth, to which he listens and about which he smiles without its ever penetrating the spaces of his imagination. His tenth character dies with the inhabitant of the earth; it is entirely his and is administered by him alone.

Musil's ironic withdrawal to "the passive fantasy of unfilled spaces" may not be the most satisfactory response to the paradox of the two human beings; but his words make that paradox dramatically clear. However we turn and twist *homo sociologicus*, he will never be the particular person who is our friend, colleague, father, or brother. *Homo sociologicus* can neither love nor hate, laugh nor cry. He remains a pale, incomplete, strange, artificial man. Yet he is more than the showpiece of an exhibit. He provides the standard by which our world—and indeed our friend, our colleague, our father, our brother—becomes comprehensible for us. The world of *homo sociologicus* may not be the world of our experience, but the two are strikingly similar. If we identify with *homo sociologicus* and his predetermined ways, our "tenth character" rises in protest; but we are nonetheless constrained to follow his paths as they appear on the maps of sociology.

Two intentions were the godparents of sociology. The new discipline was supposed to make the fact of society accessible to rational understanding by means of testable assumptions and theories, and to help the individual toward freedom and self-fulfillment.[47] To-

47 It seems to me that the origins of sociology may be traced to four social and intellectual constellations, each containing both moral and scientific impulses (though in different mixtures). (1) Scotland in the late eighteenth century (after Hume), when men like Adam Smith and Adam Ferguson, Sir John Sinclair and John Millar, were concerned with understanding the breaking up of feudal society and the incipient problem of industrialization. (2) France in the early nineteenth century, when men like Saint-Simon and Comte were concerned with mastering the meaning of the French Revolution. (3) Germany in the 1830's and 1840's (after Hegel), when David

day, Alfred Weber says what many feel when he mourns the "abundance of sociologies" which "no longer have as their focus man and
his destiny as a whole," and maintains that "sociology is concerned
with the structure and dynamics of human existence" (63: 13, 12).
But Weber's formulation is not altogether fortunate, for it conceals
a fundamental objection behind the appearance of a straightfor-
ward definition of the subject matter of sociology. According to
Weber, whereas sociology after some decades of rapid development
has come considerably closer to a rational understanding of the fact
of society, the autonomous human being and his freedom have been
lost sight of in the process. By constructing *homo sociologicus,* sociologists have let Herr Schmidt, with his unique individuality and
his personal claim to respect and freedom, slip through their fin-
gers. Sociology has paid for the exactness of its propositions with
the humanity of its intentions, and has become a thoroughly inhuman, amoral science.

Alfred Weber and the many who share this view are mistaken in
one important respect. It was no accident that in the course of time
sociology lost sight of people as human beings; rather, this development was inevitable from the moment that sociology emerged as a
science. The two intentions with which sociology began are incompatible.[48] As long as sociologists interpret their task in moral terms,
they must renounce the analysis of social reality; as soon as they
strive for scientific insight, they must forgo their moral concern
with the individual and his liberty. What makes the paradox of
moral and alienated man so urgent is not that sociology has strayed
from its proper task, but that it has become a true science. The former process would be reversible, but the latter leads to an inescap-

---

Friedrich Strauss, Ludwig Feuerbach, Bruno and Edgar Bauer, Arnold Ruge, Moses
Hess, Friedrich Engels, and Karl Marx took two steps simultaneously: from criticizing
religion to criticizing society, and from theory to practice. (4) England in the late
1880's (1889 saw the publication of the first *Fabian Essays* and the organization of the
great trade unions of the unskilled), when George Bernard Shaw, Beatrice and Sidney
Webb, Charles Booth, and other social politicians perceived that they could realize
their goals only if they thoroughly understood the workings of society. It is with this
background in mind that I speak of the two intentions of sociology.

[48] Max Weber's notion of "value-free social science" is relevant here. This notion
is discussed in the first and last essays of this volume, and in section X below.

able question. Is man a social being whose behavior, being predetermined, is calculable and controllable? Or is he an autonomous
individual, with some irreducible measure of freedom to act as he
chooses?

So far we have referred to the paradox of the two human beings
as if it were beyond theoretical or practical resolution. At this
point, we shall have to see whether this is really so. Is there a necessary contradiction between the moral image of man as an integral,
unique, and free creature and his scientific image as a differentiated, exemplary aggregate of predetermined roles? Must we assume
that man is either one or the other, so that either our moral experience or our scientific reconstruction is wrong? At least one aspect
of this question, that of the free or conditioned character of human
action, has been dealt with extensively by Kant in his third antinomy of pure reason; and since Kant was concerned with the same
paradox that concerns us, we may do well to follow his argument.
The paradox has two motifs or aspects, which we have made no
effort to connect. One is that the man of our experience is free,
whereas *homo sociologicus* is determined; the other is that the inhabitant of the earth is an undivided whole, whereas the inhabitant of a country appears to us as a mere sum, or set, of impersonal
elements. Kant's discussion can be applied to both aspects.

In the language of Kant, *homo sociologicus* is man under the
spell of natural "laws";[49] his every move is merely a link in a chain
of recognizable relations. The integral individual, by contrast, cannot be linked to such a chain; he is free. Each of these two versions
of man can be justified by a logically conclusive argument; they are
thesis and antithesis of an argument that defies immanent resolution:

> Thus nature and transcendental freedom differ in the same
> way as lawfulness and lawlessness. The former may burden our

---

[49] Kant himself occasionally, and especially in his *Anthropology*, touches on the
borders of social science, but essentially "lawfulness" and "lawfulness according to
the laws of nature" are the same to him. Today the notion of "natural laws" appears
dubious to natural scientists and even more dubious to social scientists. It suggests the
idea of an immanent necessity behind scientific theories, which (as we know thanks
in large part to Kant) remain always hypothetical.

reason with the difficulty of seeking the origin of events ever higher in the chain of causation, because all causality is determined; but it offers as a reward the all-pervading unity of experience in accordance with laws. By contrast, the deceptive glitter of freedom[50] promises calm to the searching mind in the chain of causation by leading it to an uncaused first cause that acts of itself; but this first cause, being blind, shrugs off the guiding light of rules, by which alone a completely coherent experience is possible. (41: 463.)

According to Kant, each of the two—nature and freedom, *homo sociologicus* and the integral human being—has its charms and deficiencies. The thesis of freedom may be "dogmatic" and "speculative," but it is no less popular for these drawbacks, especially since it accords with our "practical interest." In the antithesis of lawfulness "moral ideals and principles lose all validity" (41: 474), but by way of compensation we are given a reliable and orderly "empirical" means of comprehending the world. Both sides are given to a certain "lack of modesty" (41: 477). The sociologist describes man as an aggregate of roles, and unthinkingly goes on to claim that he has discovered the nature of man. His opponent, in the name of the integral human being, disputes the sociologist's very right to dissect man into his components and reconstruct him scientifically.

If and only if we assume—so Kant goes on to argue—that outside our experience but accessible to it there is a being in itself, a *Ding an sich*, the contradiction between the two theses is indeed an unresolvable antinomy. But there is no evidence to support such an assumption. Rather, the transcendental critique shows that thesis and antithesis, inhabitant of the earth and inhabitant of a country, do not contradict each other but are simply different ways of comprehending the same subject, ways that derive from different sources of knowledge. Kant makes this point in a metaphor so strik-

<hr>

50 The quotation is taken from Kant's argument for the antithesis ("There is no freedom, but everything in the world happens merely by the laws of nature"), and therefore does not do justice to the argument for the thesis of freedom. This context explains the expression "deceptive glitter of freedom."

ingly like Musil's observation (not to mention our stage metaphors) that one is almost tempted to wonder whether Musil has translated Kant into his freer language:

> But every efficient cause must have a *character,* i.e., a law governing its causality, without which it would not be a cause at all. And so we should find in a subject of the world of the senses first of all an *empirical character,* by which its actions, as phenomena, are connected with other phenomena by permanent laws of nature in such a way that these actions can be derived from the other phenomena, so that the two together constitute a single row of the order of nature. Second, we should have to allow it an *intelligible character,* by which it is the cause of those actions as phenomena, but which is not itself in any way accessible to the senses, not a phenomenon. One might call the first the character of the thing as a phenomenon, the second the character of the thing in itself. (41: 527–28.)

Musil dissolves Kant's empirical character into a series of characters; but Kant's intelligible character is precisely Musil's "tenth character," a unit of an utterly different kind from the others. As a phenomenon, i.e., in his observable behavior, man is a role-playing, determinate creature. But he has in addition a character of freedom and integrity, which is completely unaffected by his phenomenal character and its laws. "Thus freedom and nature, each in its complete meaning, would in the same actions, depending on whether one considers their intelligible or their sensible cause, be encountered simultaneously and without any contradiction." (41: 529.)

Kant states explicitly that man is one of the phenomena of the world of the senses to which these considerations apply; from the discussion of this "example" he derives his distinction between understanding (*Verstand*) and reason (*Vernunft*) (41: 533). Every man has an empirical character, and this character is strictly determined; in studying it, "we are simply observing [man], and in the manner of anthropology seeking to explore the motive cause of his actions physiologically" (41: 536). In addition, and at the same time, every man has an intelligible character, a practical reason that makes him a free and moral being. The antinomy of human knowledge is thus revealed as merely apparent; there is no plausible reason to reject Kant's conclusion that the two characters "may exist independently of each other and undisturbed by each other" (41: 541). Although the free, integral individual is not accessible to empirical research and cannot be, we know about him in ourselves and in others. And although the constructed, conditioned exemplar is based on the systematic study of phenomena, all the study in the world cannot make it more than a construction of the mind. The paradox of the two human beings, if it exists at all, is different in kind from the paradox of the two tables. Whereas the latter opposes two genuinely contradictory ways of seeing the same phenomena, the former is dispelled by a critical review of its epistemological basis. The two shapes of the table are competing theories in the same sphere of knowledge; the two characters of man are an expression of essentially different possibilities of knowledge.

Although Kant's arguments fully apply to our context, the paradox of the two human beings is by no means a mirage. We never claimed that it was identical with the paradox of the two tables; instead we have described it from the outset as more urgent, more inescapable, more important to come to terms with, than the paradox of the tables. The difference in urgency can now be made explicit. If we speak of the physicist's table and the table of our experience, we assert a paradox consisting of the statements "This table is smooth and solid" and "This table is (not smooth and solid, but) a beehive of nuclear particles." But the paradox of the two human beings involves more than the apparent difference between the statements "Man is indivisible and free" and "Man is an aggregate of roles and conditioned." With respect to our knowledge of man these two statements are not even contradictory. They become contradictory only when we translate them from the transcendental into the empirical sphere, and relate them to the practical problems of ethics. Here the conditioned man poses a moral problem as the nuclear table does not and cannot. Whenever we deal with human beings, we must consider not only pure knowledge but the practical realm of morality; and in this realm our paradox changes from a question of knowledge that can be examined (or evaded) into a problem that must be faced before any meaningful progress can be made. We do not have to decide whether man is an "inhabitant of a country" or an "inhabitant of the earth." We do have to decide whether sociology, by transforming man into *homo sociologicus,* has gone against its original intentions and become a promoter, or at least an unprotecting supporter, of unfreedom and inhumanity.

X

Historians were the first social scientists to see the conflict between integral man and his sociological shadow, and to resolve it, precariously, for their own discipline. At least since history's claim to scientific status was asserted in the nineteenth century, it has been debated whether a systematic concern with history can stop at science, or whether it must not always include a measure of art.[51] Not all historians have been advocates of an artistically inspired historiography; Clio is one of many victims of the nineteenth century. But every historian worth the name knows that even the best scientific theories of economics, psychology, and sociology can hardly help him re-create the past. As soon as he gets beyond testing abstract assumptions against specific situations, as soon as he tries to catch a single historical situation in its human richness and tragic depth, the theories of science desert him, leaving him with integral man and the passive fantasy of unfilled spaces. The historian cannot reconstruct Herr Schmidt from his roles. If historiography were merely a testing ground for the more rigorous social sciences, there would be no need to worry about it. But it is clearly more than a testing ground. The historian's purposes, artistic and pragmatic alike, demand more immediate access to the actors of past dramas than sociology can offer.

The historian's problem is not a problem of scientific knowledge.

---

[51] Fritz Stern's anthology *The Varieties of History* (62) follows this discussion through two centuries; the following remarks are stimulated by this volume.

Rather, it stems from the fact that once science deals with man, the logical separation between the man of science and the man of our everyday experience becomes insignificant for all practical purposes. With respect to our actions, the "inhabitant of the earth" and the "inhabitant of a country" are not two spheres that exist side by side wihout ever disturbing each other. Musil is quite right in saying that the inhabitant of the earth fails to take seriously the very things that would fulfill him. What is more, he opposes the inhabitant of a country on principle for trying to fill his unfilled spaces with alien laws. Insofar as *homo sociologicus* is more than the private toy of hermits pursuing their exercises of contemplation on distant mountains, he becomes a challenge to moral man and his goals.

The paradox that Kant's transcendental critique cannot resolve arises from the moral effect of the notion of *homo sociologicus* in a society that is only too ready to replace its common sense by scientific theories.[52] Already our courts of law are finding it difficult to reconcile the expert opinions of social scientists with the guilt of the accused. For the sociologically schooled journalist and his readers, even the most inhuman political movement becomes a "necessary" consequence of identifiable causes and conditions. We may not be far from the point at which *homo sociologicus,* man without individuality or moral responsibility, replaces the completely autonomous integral individual as the basis of men's self-perception and thus of their actions. It is this practical competition between *homo sociologicus* and the human being of our experience that has produced our dilemma. Because *homo sociologicus* as a product of science has the advantage in our century, it is urgent that some effort be made to resolve this paradox, or at least to clarify it.

[52] The problem in question here was not unfamiliar to Kant; but its solution in the *Critique of Practical Reason* misses the core of the dilemma. What Kant—for good reason—treats as an intellectual problem is today above all a social problem. To put this another way, the dilemma of the two human beings comes neither from the incompatibility of statements about the two nor from a doubt in principle about which of the two should serve as the practical basis of morals. Rather, it comes from the social influence of sociology and the spreading of sociological assumptions in hypostatized form, which logical criticism has proved powerless to stop.

We may note, not without irony, that the fault of sociology in creating this dilemma is not the fault of sociologists. The old saw *tout comprendre c'est tout pardonner* holds here, as it does for any practical application of science. As it happens, it now seems clear that sociology, being concerned solely with the empirical character of man, had to enter a sphere in which, as Kant says, "moral ideals and principles lose all validity"; while at the same time, owing to its concern with man and the necessity of making its findings public and teaching them in the university, it had to become a moral force in society. In terms of sociology's two original intentions, the sociologist has an unresolvable role conflict. On the one hand, he is expected to proceed scientifically, and thus, if necessary for analytic purposes, to deal with man as *homo sociologicus*; on the other hand, he is expected to help liberate man from his subservience to external purposes, and thus to deal with Herr Schmidt as an autonomous, free individual. Here, however, an element of choice and of possible guilt in sociologists' behavior becomes apparent after all. Like the doctor who decides to neglect his patients rather than lose favor with officials in the public health insurance organization, sociologists have been too ready to give up their moral mandate for the cool precision of scientific method. This choice brings few recriminations. Generally speaking, people have as little hold over the sociologists who investigate them as patients have over their doctors,[53] whereas bureaucratized organizations and the community of scholars are always ready to subject their aberrant members to the sanction of expulsion. Nevertheless the choice is a bad one, and its consequences in the large seem likely to be incomparably more severe (if they are not already) than the consequences of the alternative decision.

It is ironic, almost tragic, that the man who made sociology's decision in favor of science, and thus against its moral mandate, was perhaps more aware than any other sociologist of the paradox of

[53] This assertion requires two qualifications. On the one hand, there is at least a remote chance (increasingly exploited in the United States) for patients to bring suit against physicians for malpractice. On the other hand, the hypostatized society of the sociologist—the total state—constitutes an indirect sanction whose severity is beyond doubt.

the two human beings. Nevertheless, there can be little doubt that Max Weber's rigid separation of science and value judgments, his insistence on a value-free social science, has led to the abandonment of sociology's moral intention. Without doubt, this was not Weber's purpose. In demanding that value judgments and moral impulses be punctiliously kept separate from scientific concerns, he sought to restore both science and values to their proper dignity. His great error lay in his failure to see that social science and its findings themselves constitute a great moral force, which, if it is not deliberately harnessed, works so strongly against liberty and individuality that a morality independent of science cannot withstand it. What Weber's powerful if explosive personality could unite—the rigor of value-free science and the passion of a moral position—his successors could not. A value-free sociology became established, but the concern with man's freedom and autonomy disappeared.[54]

Weber's error is not in the logic of his distinction, which is unassailable. He is right to warn against confusing values and scientific insights; indeed, his distinction between the two is a legitimate application of Kant's distinction between the empirical and the intelligible character. Weber's error is one of emphasis. This, too, is historically and biographically understandable. The discussions in the Verein für Sozialpolitik left him no choice but to emphasize in his arguments the points at which mixing science and value judgments would lead to harmful consequences for both.[55] But today Weber's opponents in these discussions are forgotten, whereas his arguments (backed by his prestige) are very much alive, with the result that they are often taken out of context and through no fault of Weber's do more harm than good. Many sociologists are still hardly aware of the hypothetical character of their artificial

[54] For a further discussion of Weber's position, see the preceding essay, "Values and Social Science."

[55] If there is any fault to be found here, it is first of all in the Value Dispute itself, which continues to cast its shadow over German social science. The aspect of the Dispute that has caused the most trouble is the unlikely combination of political conservatism and value-laden science in the thought of Weber's opponents, and political criticism and value-free science in Weber's own thought. Many of the effects of Weber's thesis can be better understood in the light of this "false" confrontation.

man. When they speak of the human personality as an aggregate
of roles, they ignore man's "tenth character," his intelligible, moral
character, without which he becomes a horrible phantom of the
totalitarian imagination. If even sociologists exhibit confusion on
this point, one can hardly blame their students and others for following them. And it is only a step from seeing man as a mere role
player to the alienated world of "1984," where all loving and hat-
ing, all dreaming and acting, all individuality beyond the grasp of
roles, becomes a crime against society—society in this sense being
sociology hypostatized.

Since Weber's time, the pragmatic problem of the two human
beings has gained rather than lost in urgency, and the time has
accordingly come for us to revise our position toward it. In doing
so, to repeat, we are not challenging the logical validity of the distinction between science and value judgments. Nobody wants an
ideologized science, a science that consciously or unconsciously offers scientific theories as moral precepts or vice versa. Here, Weber
is as far from being superseded as Karl Mannheim, Theodor Geiger, and other critics of ideology. But to require the sociologist to
select projects that seem likely to benefit the cause of the individual
and his liberty is not to reestablish ideology. The sociologist does
not endanger the purity of his scientific activity by preferring to
work with testable theories that recognize the individual's rights
and the richness of his life. It is methodologically quite above suspicion for a social scientist to keep an eye out for ways of making
his own findings further individual freedom and self-fulfillment.

Behind these specific demands there is something else, something
even more important. No amount of critical analysis can finally resolve the dilemma of the two human beings; we can at best hope
to master it satisfactorily in our actions. Both *homo sociologicus*
and the free individual are part of our world and the way we interpret that world. It follows that the sociologist must first of all recognize the dilemma and keep its urgency in mind. Anyone who
cannot bear the melancholy insufficiency of a sociological science
of man should renounce the discipline, for a dogmatic sociology is
worse than no sociology at all. The sociologist has every reason to
envy historians their opportunity to merge the person Hans Schmidt

and his role-playing shadow in a single work—their opportunity, that is, to combine science and art. He himself does not have this opportunity. It is the more difficult for him to keep in mind the dilemma of the two human beings, and not to lose sight of the autonomous individual in his concern with *homo sociologicus*. In sociological investigations Herr Schmidt the person has no place, yet he must never be forgotten. Awareness of the autonomous individual and his claim to liberty must inform every sentence the sociologist speaks and writes; society must constantly be present to him not only as a fact, but as a vexation; the moral insufficiency of his discipline must always appear as a passionate undertone in his work. Only by replacing the unintended practical effects of a seemingly pure sociological science with effects that are consciously intended to be advantageous to the individual and his freedom can we hope to translate the dilemma of the two human beings into fruitful action.

The sociologist as such is not, and should not be, a politician. But even worse is the sociologist who sees the career of a scientist as requiring him to renounce all critical concern with his own actions and his society. The abstention of the non-voter always favors the stronger party; and in practical matters in general, no abstention is without consequences. It is but a weak consolation for the sociologist, therefore, that Kant's transcendental critique finds *homo sociologicus* compatible with the free individual. The practical dilemma remains. Only if the sociologist selects his research projects with an eye to what may help liberate the individual from the vexations of society, if he formulates his hypotheses with a view to extending men's range of free choice, if he does not shy away from supporting political changes designed to increase individual freedom, and if he never forgets the superior rights of Herr Schmidt the person over his role-playing shadow—only then can he hope to use the insights of sociology to protect man the inhabitant of the earth from the boundless demands of man the inhabitant of a country. Only then can the sociologist cease being a brake and become a motor of a society of free men, a society whose vexatiousness, along with the all too passive fantasy of unfilled spaces, is swallowed up in the active reality of freely filled time.

3

Sociology and Human Nature
A Postscript to Homo Sociologicus

That sociology is a science of man is one of those dangerously imprecise formulations that stand in the way of scientific understanding, and not for the layman alone. Of course, a theory of social classes, an analysis of the social structure of a city or an office, an investigation of authority in the family, and an explanation of political revolution are all concerned with things human. But so are the theories of human biology and psychology, of economics and anthropology. And so also, after all, are historiography and pedagogy, jurisprudence and philology, medicine and art history; yet to describe these last as sciences of man would be to say nothing significant about them.

Nor would it be correct to say that each of these disciplines (along with others not mentioned) deals with but one aspect of the total problem of man, so that man is, as it were, the synthetic subject matter of them all. Indeed, the error in speaking of sciences of man (and, for that matter, of natural sciences) lies precisely in the implication that scientific disciplines can be defined in terms of their so-called subject matter. It would be very daring even to assume that our encyclopedia of scientific subjects and disciplines represents in any meaningful way the articulation of the world. It seems proper, therefore, to acknowledge that the range of problems dealt with under the name of a given scientific discipline is determined by basically arbitrary traditions, and is therefore potentially subject at any time to expansion or contraction. Thus it can happen that matters which a decade ago were regarded by men in a given discipline as a suitable subject of research are today indignantly rejected by those in the same discipline.[1] Probably academic recognition of a new discipline always betokens the fragmentation or redefinition of these arbitrary traditions.

Now it would obviously be an exaggeration to claim that sociology has attained as firm a consensus as older disciplines on the matter of what problems to investigate and how to approach them. What sociologists call sociology is still a mixed bag of many different problems, modes of statement, and claims to knowledge—to say nothing of what non-sociologists hold to be sociology. Anyone who knows the tendency among American sociologists to define the mandate of their discipline prematurely on the basis of a consensus that at times seems rather forced, will not regret the presence in Europe of a lively debate on this subject; here as elsewhere, conflict generates progress. In recent years, however, there has unmistakably been increasing agreement among European sociologists about the place of human behavior in what are generally described as sociological theories. One symptom of this agreement is the increasing use of a certain set of categories, notably position, role, role expectation, and sanction.

It is widely agreed, and attested to by the poetry of all ages, that people invariably perceive each other as the possessors of certain attributes or the incumbents of certain *positions*: father and son, colleague and colleague, superior and subordinate, German and Frenchman, etc. Every such social position—and there must always be more than one, because society is not conceivable without a degree of internal differentiation[2]—defines a field of social relations. In saying "teacher," we are saying (not of course analytically, but

[1] A proof and at the same time a further illustration of this thesis may be found in the fact that definitions of disciplines with identical names—among them sociology, psychology, and social policy—vary considerably from country to country.

[2] Aristotle's statement "When all are equal, there can be no state" (97: 1261a) may also be correctly interpreted to mean that at least some division of labor and social stratification, or differentiation of kind and of rank, is always implied when we speak of society. To the sociologists, in contrast to Aristotle, it is not people who are distinguished by kind and rank, but their social positions.

synthetically) "teacher-pupil," "teacher-teacher," "teacher–school administration," "teacher-parents"—i.e., we are establishing a field of positions around the central position in question. Theoretically, every society may be represented as a huge, multidimensional structure of such relations.[3] This concept of society is the basis of recent attempts to simulate social processes with the help of electronic computers.

What makes the structure of social positions come to life is role behavior. By virtue of being a certain someone, we do certain things; more precisely, our social position not merely places us into a field with other positions, but also gives other people more or less specific *expectations* of us. For every position, then, there is a *social role,* a set of modes of behavior that is ascribed to the incumbent. American sociologists like to describe roles as the "dynamic aspect of positions"; it would probably be better to describe them as what lends substance to the empty form of social positions.

A great many conceptual and theoretical questions (which will not be considered here) arise from this approach.[4] But for our argument it is important to remember that even if we can strive for social positions and roles, that is, even if they are attainable by our efforts, they are of course not subject to our defining. The field of relations in which a position places us, and the set of expectations associated with it, are binding on us as soon as we become the incumbent of that position and the player of the associated role. The system of social *sanctions,* i.e., of rewards for conforming and punishments for deviant behavior, guarantees that we will not evade this binding character of roles.

With the assistance of these few categories (explained here very inadequately), we may formulate the proposition that implicitly or explicitly underlies all research and theoretical work in modern sociology: *Man behaves in accordance with his roles.* Thus man basically figures in sociological analyses only to the extent that he com-

---

[3] What is meant by multidimensional is that Mr. X stands as "teacher" in one field, as "father" in a second, as "German" in a third, etc. A "society" is a highly complex structure consisting of all such position fields for all its members.

[4] Some of them have been discussed in the foregoing essay, "Homo Sociologicus."

plies with all the expectations associated with his social positions. This abstraction, the scientific unit of sociology, may be called *homo sociologicus*. In an angry and critical mood, one might say that sociology is the science, and thus the instrument, of conformism; to put the same point less angrily and more precisely, sociological theories equate the playing of social roles with the whole of human behavior.

To discuss the scientific implications of this statement would require little less than an encyclopedia of the social sciences. We would have to ask how the categories I have mentioned, "role" and "position," relate to the other basic categories of sociology, "norm" and "power." We would have to investigate the interaction of individual personality (in the sense of recent psychological theory) and social role. Finally, we would have to consider the great problems of role theory itself. For example, are there typical "role-sets" (Merton) that fall to individuals in given societies? What is the structural significance of the distinction between achieved and ascribed positions? How can incompatible role expectations or roles be reconciled? Under what conditions and in what ways do social roles change? With such questions, role theory soon blends into general sociology, a field whose every question has to do with the concept, empirical identification, and analysis of social roles, and with man as *homo sociologicus*.

II

That the category of role and especially the postulate of role-conforming behavior have significance beyond their sociological applications is clear even to sociologists (although it is probably no accident that European sociologists make more of this point than American sociologists). What this extra-sociological significance involves can hardly be illuminated more ironically than by comparing the opening sentences of two very different essays on this subject. Helmuth Plessner, in whose work it is hard to separate sociology from philosophy, writes: "In defining sociology as a science, it seems perfectly plausible at first to require that it be con-

cerned exclusively with social phenomena that are strictly capable
of being experienced, and that as an empirical discipline it detach
itself once and for all from philosophical speculation." (74: 150.)
In contrast, a critical representative of the empirical sociology Plessner is describing, Hans Paul Bahrdt, begins: "At first glance it seems
almost a matter of course that sociology must have an 'image of
man'; it even seems reasonable that sociology should have a special
'sociological image of man' determined by the peculiar nature of
its subject and its secular role." (64: 1.) It is clear from their choice
of words ("at first," "at first glance") that both Plessner and Bahrdt
intend to reject the arguments they describe as "perfectly plausible"
and "a matter of course"; but the conflict between the two positions as described is enough to indicate how far the significance of
homo sociologicus transcends the borders of the discipline.

Clearly the assumption that all men behave in accordance with
their roles at all times is demonstrably false. At one time or another,
almost everyone violates the expectations associated with his positions. One might infer, therefore, that all sociological theories, insofar as they operate on this assumption, are bad theories; and in
fact this point is occasionally made by laymen, and even scholars,
who do not understand the logic of scientific discovery. Actually,
misunderstandings of this kind cause little trouble. In economic
theory the protracted argument over whether a *homo oeconomicus*
who permanently weighs profits and losses is a realistic image of
man's economic behavior has been decided: literal realism is quite
unnecessary so long as the theories based on this model provide
powerful explanations and useful predictions. Extreme advocates
of the modern deductive-logic school of science—notably its founder, Karl Popper—at times go so far as to say that the less realistic
the assumptions, the better the theory. What this statement means
obviously depends on what we mean by a "good" theory, and thus
by a "better" one. Since this question is important in our context,
let us consider it in the light of an example.

It has been widely observed in German universities that students
of working-class origin are the most inclined to join dueling fra-
ternities. It has also been observed that upwardly mobile people

are more inclined to vote for conservative political parties than people who have not risen above their parents' social position. How can we explain such observations? In both cases we encounter a version of role conflict, namely the conflict between what is expected of the people concerned as children of their parents and what is expected of them in their new positions, acquired by upward mobility. A young man's parents may vote for a radical party, but in his new social stratum he votes conservative. Now the assumption that man behaves as *homo sociologicus* makes possible a general explanatory proposition: that a person in a situation of role conflict will always choose the role with which the stronger sanctions are associated. In our two cases, it seems clear that for the working-class student, and even more for the person whose career is well under way, the parents' sanctions are relatively mild compared with those of their new peers. This is why people go against their parents in these cases. It follows as a prediction that the working-class child who rises socially will in due course deny and betray his origins many times.

This is an example of a "good" sociological theory. It allows us to derive from a general statement definite, precise, and unrestricted predictions, and it has considerable explanatory power with respect, say, to the voting behavior of people who have risen socially from working-class origins. All this is true even though the role conformity assumed by the theory is obviously "unrealistic," in the sense that there are many people who do not behave in the manner postulated here. If we should now try to make our assumption "realistic," the entire theory would fall to pieces. The following statement would clearly be more "realistic": "In the face of role conflict, many people (perhaps 60 per cent) are inclined to prefer the role with which the stronger sanctions are associated; others (say 25 per cent) behave in accordance with moral principles without regard to social sanctions; and some (say 15 per cent) react to role conflicts with complete resignation or passivity."[5] Such a statement is all very well, but it can no longer be used to explain anything. To the extent that the assumptions underlying scientific

[5] The percentages in this statement are entirely fictitious.

theories become "realistic," they also become differentiated, restricted, ambiguous, unconducive to definite explanations or predictions. In this sense, then, the less realistic and more stylized, definite, and unambiguous the assumptions underlying a theory are, the better the theory is.[6]

With this methodological excursus behind us, we can now turn to the question of the meta-sociological significance of *homo sociologicus*, or sociology's image of man. If one assigns to sociology—as by no means all sociologists do—the task of formulating precise theories in the sense indicated above, and if one sees the construct *homo sociologicus* in this context, then this construct in no way implies an image of man. F. H. Tenbruck would then be quite right in substance (though his formulation is a little unfortunate) when he describes social role as "a construct by which, within the limits indicated, we can calculate the behavior of man as a social creature, without making any claim to describe this behavior as it occurs in reality" (76: 29).[7]

Indeed, as a stylized and empirically almost arbitrary construct, *homo sociologicus* explicitly renounces a sociological image of man: it proclaims the intention of finding powerful explanatory theories of social action rather than describing the nature of man accurately and realistically. The reason why sociology in this sense has no image of man is not (as Plessner repeatedly seems to suggest) that sociology "renounces" certain questions and kinds of statements,[8] but that scientific theories yield statements that are entirely different in range and purpose from statements about the nature of man. To put the matter paradoxically, at the risk of being misunderstood: even if sociology asks questions about man, it is in substance

---

[6] It hardly need be mentioned that the point of view defended here is very rigorous; it implies, among other things, that even very precise probability statements cannot be accepted as theories. For the everyday requirements of science, this rigor would undoubtedly have to be mitigated.

[7] The formulation is unfortunate because a mere "calculation" does not suffice to justify a reliance on "unrealistic" assumptions.

[8] See, for example, 74: 150: "[Sociology's] renunciation of the questions of universal history and the psychological analysis of motives is offset by an anticipated gain in insight into the internal mechanisms that condition the social life of men and thus make their socialization possible."

concerned not with man but with ways of reducing man's actions to rational terms. Not only is sociology improperly defined as a science of man, but it is fundamentally indifferent to man as such, since it can reach much further with *homo sociologicus* than with statements that aim at an accurate description of man's nature.

III

This radical distinction between scientific sociology and philosophical anthropology is necessary if we are to avoid minimizing, by one facile formulation or another, the seriousness of the problem that concerns us here. For although the conclusion that sociology as a science neither has nor needs an image of man, and in particular that *homo sociologicus* cannot provide such an image, may be the last word on our problem in terms of the logic of science, we must remember that the logic of science is only one aspect of methodology. We must also deal with certain other aspects, aspects that are not logical but moral and even political. In recent discussions of sociology's image of man, there have been repeated references to the "reification" of *homo sociologicus* (although not always using this term, which is preeminently Tenbruck's). By reification is meant the reinterpretation or misinterpretation of a deliberately unrealistic assumption, made in the interests of good scientific theory, as a realistic description of the nature of man.[9] Of course, it is both easy and necessary to guard against this kind of reification of postulates. But first one should ask whether there might not be certain peculiarities of social science, and of sociology in particular, that at least encourage the reification of categories and postulates, and perhaps make it empirically almost unavoidable. In my opinion there are, and it is only from the perspective of these peculiarities that the real problem of a sociological image of man becomes apparent.

Earlier we observed that if sociology is defined as an empirical science, *homo sociologicus* has no implications for the nature of

[9] I confess to a certain amusement at Tenbruck's charging me, of all people, with reification; see section IV below.

96   ESSAYS IN THE THEORY OF SOCIETY

man. As we have seen, however, this view of sociology is by no means generally accepted. Indeed, so many people see sociology's domain and methodology in so many different ways that logical arguments alone do not suffice to counter the tendency to reification. There are several kinds of sociologists who do not see sociology as an empirical science: those who, in pursuing Wilhelm Dilthey's tradition of irrationalism, deny in principle the possibility of rigorous theories in the so-called sciences of the mind (*Geisteswissenschaften*); those who, while they admit this possibility, nevertheless see the task of sociology as interpretative analysis on the model of history, that is, as striving for the highest possible degree of descriptive "realism"; and those who are indifferent to the distinction between testable and speculative statements, and thus between the statements of sociology and those of philosophical anthropology. To all such sociologists, the idea of inventing *homo sociologicus* as a deliberately "unrealistic" fiction for the sole purpose of formulating powerful explanatory theories must seem meaningless, or at least incomprehensible. Since they do not recognize the epistemological basis of the postulate of role-conforming behavior, *homo sociologicus* to them is not even an example of reification, but simply anthropological speculation masquerading as science. As long, then, as scientists of the mind and philosophical sociologists are as numerous as they are in European sociology (a situation, if I may say so without unduly confusing the issue, that is by no means to its detriment), the objective reification of sociological postulates will not be halted simply by repeating *ad nauseam* the claims of a nominalist epistemology and the associated logic of science.

A second reason for the inadequacy of the purely logical argument is even more significant, for it is inescapable. Science is not possible without publicity; the notion of a "secret science" contains a *contradictio in adiecto*.[10] Now in the traditional sciences (including economics) publicity means essentially professional pub-

10 This statement, made dogmatically here, is by no means a matter of course—especially in the country that invented the absurdity of "inner freedom." On the contrary, it expresses a logic of scientific research that is specifically predicated on the fundamental uncertainty of human knowledge. See the essay "Uncertainty, Science, and Democracy" below.

licity: i.e., discussion by a circle of people who agree on basic principles, or, more precisely, by a circle of people who have all accepted the second life of science and its moral conventions. But in the newer social sciences, as well as in psychology, the situation is different. Here publicity frequently means "general publicity"; publications in sociology, social psychology, and psychology are read by many people who have never seriously considered becoming scientists. It would be unrealistic for a social scientist to ignore this public effect of his research—an effect, by the way, that may be measured partly, though by no means solely, by the circulation figures of professional publications. The "general public" has no understanding at all of the subtle distinction between statements meant "realistically" and deliberately "unrealistic" postulates; indeed such postulates involve a fundamental deviation from the world of common sense which is at the very heart of the first contradiction between science and common sense.[11] Instead, the wider public sees *homo sociologicus* as the scientific truth about man.[12]

Nothing could demonstrate more clearly how misleading it is to speak of the "scientific orientation" of our world. Possibly the number of people who try to orient themselves by scientific theories or research findings is greater today than ever before; but an understanding of the peculiar nature of scientific statements is as rare today as it ever was. That science is knowledge based on logical supposition, that many scientific statements can by no means be taken literally, and above all that science does not impart certainty, is even today known at best to those who are personally engaged in the effort to catch the world of experience in the net of their theories. It follows that the public, which cannot and must not be denied access to scientific research, is bound to make the mistake of reifying *homo sociologicus* to some extent, and hence that the sociologist must address himself to this misunderstanding.

---

[11] This statement is not intended to express a value judgment, and is certainly not meant as a depreciation of common sense.

[12] Even the expression "scientific truth" can be defended only ironically. That science is capable of providing irrefutable truths is one of the serious errors of common sense.

It is an old question whether people may be held responsible for the unintended consequences of their actions. In terms of motivation, many a great teacher would have to be acquitted of the errors of his disciples, but in other cases things are not so clear. Who can say whether the Soviet Union is Marx's fault? Perhaps an attitude of legal positivism is best in such cases. From this point of view we may impute guilt by omission to the sociologist who, in full awareness of the damage done by his theories, washes his innocent hands in the pure logic of scientific discovery. To repeat, because the postulates of sociological analysis are likely (if not certain) to be misunderstood both inside and outside the discipline, the sociologist must leave the comfortable refuge of his logical righteousness and take a moral stand for or against the anthropological interpretations of his misunderstood theories.

Obviously the need for such a clarification does not in any way dictate its substance. To be sure, the sociologist's statement must specify that he never intended *homo sociologicus* as an image of man; but we have seen that this logical statement is not enough. What is needed next is itself anthropological and thus valuational, and—if one wants to call it that—moral. For the sociologist will have to state whether he accepts or rejects the anthropological statements that are erroneously, and more or less accidentally, derived by reification from his similar-sounding theoretical postulates. If only for the sake of making his efforts logically unassailable, the sociologist has to make it clear whether he subscribes to an image of man corresponding closely to the reified *homo sociologicus,* or whether he regards it as a caricature of man in his moral (as epistemologically distinct from his scientific) existence. Thus sociology, or more precisely the individual sociologist, in fact needs at least the rudimentary image of man that comes from taking an anthropological rather than a logical view of *homo sociologicus.*

IV

Partly implicitly, partly explicitly, the preceding argument also underlies the concluding parts of my essay "Homo Sociologicus."

This essay has happily found many thorough and incisive critics in the profession, most of whom have attacked the particular anthropological position that I take in response to the demand discussed here. This is especially true of Tenbruck's critique, which is largely based on the completely erroneous suspicion that I myself reify *homo sociologicus*: "There is thus in Dahrendorf a crass reification of the nominal concept of role. . . . His entire essay is based on the assumption that his definition of role is a definition of something real." (76: 29.)[13] As for Bahrdt, he is preaching to the converted when he argues, in criticizing my essay, "It would seem that [sociology's] long-standing semi-dependence on the mother discipline of philosophy cannot be ended so quickly. Even the methodological pluralism that prevents the inner consolidation of sociology will be with us for a long time." (64: 16.)

One important objection to the demand that the sociologist take a stand on his construct *homo sociologicus*—i.e., to make this quite clear, not the concept of role but the postulate of role-conforming behavior—has been made by Arnold Gehlen (69: 368ff.). Gehlen rightly sees this demand as calling for a "political" statement (as he calls it). Invoking Max Weber, Gehlen rejects any such statement as "unscientific," especially if it is to have a " 'propagandist' effect, that is encouraging, affirming, promoting, etc.," for "at that moment it becomes agitation masquerading as science, even if it is for a worthy purpose. It is necessary that the scientist live in a given society, that he approve of its orders and political principles [*sic!*], but that he not actively support these principles." This is why the sociologist cannot legitimately be invited to try to protect himself from the possible reification of *homo sociologicus* by taking a value position, especially since "at the level of reflection reached today," a "wholesome political decision in matters of freedom" remains possible despite the extent to which scientific theories make human behavior appear determined. Schelsky probably means

---

13 Fruitful as Tenbruck's criticism is in many details, it is based, strictly speaking, on two fundamental misunderstandings: first, that "Homo Sociologicus" is an attempt to secure the "acceptance of role theory"; second, that I subscribe to a methodological realism. These avoidable misunderstandings make an extensive rebuttal difficult.

much the same thing in his criticism of "Homo Sociologicus" for its attitude toward the image of man and the reified *homo sociologicus*; he ends with the statement, "Moralizing has at all times been the greatest enemy of theory, especially in sociology." (20: 108.)

Here we are faced with basic differences in scientific attitude, differences (with one apparent exception) that cannot be resolved unambiguously. Only the reference to the "level of reflection reached today" (Schelsky's "scientificated world"), as an argument that science is harmless even if it is liable to be misunderstood, seems capable of being tested. Even here, however, closer consideration reveals that Gehlen is relatively indifferent to the measurable degree of people's understanding of the substance and methods of scientific research; his concern is with more abstract secular structures. Thus it is still an open question whether the sociologist regards the "wholesome political decision in matters of freedom" as a private affair, and thus lets things take their course even if they follow from misinterpretations of his own theories; or whether he is one of those anachronistic "happy few" who "can think and act 'in one cast'" (whatever this means) and who, according to Gehlen, are unqualified to be scholars.[14] Faced with the terrible picture of a world of hypostatized *homines sociologici*, I prefer the anachronism of enlightened moralizing, even if the authority of Max Weber seems to justify the detachment of Gehlen and Schelsky. There is perhaps little point in quarreling over such dogmatic statements; it would be equally possible to claim that moralizing has at all times been the stimulus that advanced theory, especially in sociology.

V

Obviously the objections of Gehlen and Schelsky go beyond my belief that sociologists should decide what they think about the

---

[14] According to Gehlen, "In the twentieth century, the happy few who can think and act 'in one cast' are best suited to be politicians and not scholars." And again, "This is not a scientific question; *homo sociologicus* ... is a camouflaged *homo politicus orientalis*."

probable distortions of their logically unassailable constructs, to attack the particular point of view that I proposed in "Homo Sociologicus." Since this proposal has met with intense resistance elsewhere as well, it may be worthwhile to recapitulate it briefly here.

Unfortunately a society populated by *homines sociologici,* i.e., the massive reification of the basic assumptions of sociological theories, is only too easily conceivable today. America's "lonely crowd" comes as close to being such a society as Russia's "democracy without liberty." It is by no means difficult to argue that misunderstood sociological theory serves not only as an instrument of Soviet terror, but as the ideology of American suburbia. As a science, sociology is still in its infancy; but already—contrary to the wishes, although often not the practice, of sociologists—it has developed capacities for curtailing freedom that as recently as half a century ago were conceived of only in utopian fantasy. In view of such dangers it seems to me necessary not only that the sociologist speak out in the matter of reification, but that he clearly dissociate his image of man from *homo sociologicus.* The sociologist should make it clear that for him human nature is not accurately described by the principle of role conformity, that indeed the difference between this theoretically fruitful construct and his idea of human nature amounts almost to a contradiction.

This image of man, which is so far merely privative, may be filled in in several ways. Here, I should think, is the place to return critically to the greatest thinker of the real, i.e. pre-Hegelian, enlightenment.[15] In any case, what sociological theory does not tell us about man is his moral quality; it does not show us man as we recognize him in the world of action. This moral quality of man detaches him in principle from all claims of society; it is what enables him to throw off the hypostatized regularities of sociological theory. Scientifically it may be plausible and useful to interpret the educational process as the socialization of the individual, but morally it is crucial that the individual be capable of holding his own against

[15] Certain prejudices of intellectual history ("One cannot understand Kant without Hegel") make such a step difficult in Germany; for this reason Germans would do well to remember the broader Western tradition of the Enlightenment.

the claims of society. If the assumption of role conformity has proved extraordinarily fruitful in scientific terms, in moral terms the assumption of a permanent protest against the demands of society is much more fruitful. This is why an image of man may be developed that stresses man's inexhaustible capacity for overcoming all the forces for alienation that are inherent in the conception and reality of society. It need scarcely be added that this, too, would be the outline rather than the substance of an image of man; in this formulation, too, the privative element is dominant. But such a sketchy image seems good enough if one is primarily interested in sociological analysis. Although the sociologist must not evade the obligation to say what he thinks about the reified versions of his constructs, he need go no further than is strictly necessary to dissociate himself from misinterpretations of his views.[16]

Critics of this argument for a privative view of the nature of man object most of all to its direct identification of role playing with constraint. Thus Bahrdt argues plausibly, in terms of both the theory and its reified misinterpretation, that people are often free to put their individual stamp on their roles.[17] This is certainly true: "Freedom in the sense of absence of constraint does not stand in contradiction to the fact of social role playing. The very peculiarity of defining roles by expectations is that expectations only very rarely assume the character of constraint." (71: 468.) Not only do roles always leave their incumbents a range of individual choice, but also there is the phenomenon of successful deviance from expectations, a phenomenon that Merton describes as "rebellion" (in contrast to "retreatism") because it leads to changes in social structure. But it is probably no accident that Bahrdt develops this argument to support his thesis that man is not a "fully adaptable

16 This is a formal objection to Judith Janoska-Bendl's argument that the notions of "individual" and "freedom" in my "Homo Sociologicus" suffer from "indefiniteness" (71: 467, 470). Substantively, of course, there can be little doubt about the importance of rendering these concepts more precise; Mrs. Janoska-Bendl has made a beginning here.

17 Elsewhere (64: *passim*) Bahrdt refers time and again to the individual's "personal achievement in translating role expectations into concrete terms."

creature": this, too, is a privative view of man in terms of socio-logical analysis, and thus complies with the logical and moral re-quirements set forth here.

We are taken one step further by Tenbruck and Armand Cuvil-lier, who maintain that speaking of man apart from his social per-sonality is either misleading or nonsensical. Cuvillier sees in such formulations a confusion of "individuality" and "personality," and refers to Durkheim's thesis that the personality can be realized only in society (67: 664–65). Tenbruck, somewhat rashly, goes even further: "Sociology and social psychology have shown, indepen-dently of each other, that man without roles does not and cannot exist." (76: 31.) This (though I deplore the echo of *tu quoque*) is reification,[18] or sociologism—that is, the uncritically realistic inter-pretation of scientific assumptions! The fact that in sociology and social psychology the idea of role helps explain human behavior implies absolutely nothing about the real existence of men with or without roles; it is therefore in principle irrelevant to the premises and conclusions of a philosophical theory of man. (Conversely, if such a theory refers to sociological, social psychological, or anthro-pological research in order to establish itself as "scientific," it is guilty of either a deliberate or an ignorant effort to deceive.) The statement that the human personality can realize itself only in so-ciety does not follow from role analysis, and does not make it any the less necessary to hold up against a hypostatized *homo sociologi-cus* a moral image of the human person.

There remains, however, one serious objection to consider, a point first raised by Plessner, adopted by Tenbruck at one point in his critique, and at least implied by Judith Janoska-Bendl. This objection is apposite because it makes its appeal to precisely the level of pragmatic logic that I have invoked earlier in this essay. Plessner argues that by contrasting the moral personality of man with the significance of society for the individual, we not only revive the unhappy distinction between a public and a private

---

[18] There is some danger that sociologists today will keep on charging one another with "reification" just as the thinkers of the Hegelian Left once kept on accusing each other of being "theologians."

existence, but actually imply a preference for the private existence, and thus lend support to the "unpolitical German":

> If sociology finds itself prepared in principle to separate being in a role from the real being of the self, and to uphold the real being against the vexation of society (as Dahrendorf has recently done with his *homo sociologicus*), then it gives new support to the antisocial affect, whether it intends to or not. If in order to make the sphere of freedom unassailable we identify it with that of privacy (and privacy, we should note, in an extra-social sense), freedom loses all contact with reality, all possibility of social realization. (74: 114–15.)

More emphatically still, and with reference to another of Plessner's writings, Tenbruck refers to the German "tradition that distinguishes society from the individual and sees the social being as alienated—a tradition to which the history of literature, of philosophy, of politics, bears telling testimony. On this point, social traditions and the intellectual approach to social questions lead to the same misunderstanding: sociological concepts are turned upside down." (76: 37.) Very reservedly and yet with unmistakable intent, Janoska-Bendl asks "why, with respect to the role-playing (because socialized) man, the Hegelian—or Marxian—dialectical solution is not even considered." Earlier, she mentions Plessner's and Tenbruck's point that the individual, "as a mature social ego, is capable of reshaping his role, determining himself what it shall be, and thus—dialectically—going beyond it" (71: 473, 469).

These objections are too serious and too important to be dismissed with a few quick remarks. It is quite true that few things illustrate the lack of a bourgeois revolution in German history more clearly than the unpolitical German. But it is important here to distinguish clearly between two attitudes which only superficially resemble each other: that of the "inner emigrant," and that of the liberal. Plessner and Tenbruck claim that in a theory of man in which society functions as a vexation, the individual must necessarily be seen as turning away from social and political affairs and thus as becoming irresponsible; such a theory is analogous to Heidegger's "theory of human decadence in the deficient mood of the 'one,' " which as Plessner rightly remarks "is spoken right out of the soul of German 'inwardness' " (74: 140). But both Plessner and Tenbruck forget that there is another confrontation of the two—society and the individual—in which the motive of protest is dominant. The individual as a moral being, as a living protest against the vexation of society; Riesman's "inner-directed man"; the political resistance to society's claim to dictate man's every move—these are the liberal conceptions that have led me to make the statements to which Plessner and Tenbruck object. Perhaps such statements are especially likely to be misunderstood in Germany; for in fact I was aiming at something quite different from the "transcendental reflection" that Schelsky believes in and at times imputes to me, and on which Janoska-Bendl considers my views and hers identical.[19] The possibility of this misunderstanding seems to justify Plessner's objections. But that an unresigned political protest against the alienating forces of society is possible seems to me one of the great lessons of the Anglo-Saxon liberal tradition.

Janoska-Bendl is right in her assumption that a view of this kind involves an irreconcilable antinomy (to associate in her sense Kant and Kierkegaard). The search for conciliation, from which German moral philosophy has been suffering ever since Fichte, does not seem to me a path to liberty even under the colorful name of dialectics. Janoska-Bendl cautiously suggests that "freedom as insight into necessity" also permits "using force to accomplish liberty" (71: 486). There is a strange dialectic of dialectics in the fact that this "also" is the regular consequence of the attempt to apply dialectics to reality. Why do so many find it so hard to discover freedom in the antinomic existence of man?

Bahrdt concludes his essay on images of man in sociology with the somewhat disappointed observation that there probably is no compelling image of this kind after all. In substance I should agree with him, but without sharing his disappointment. With respect to our knowledge of human nature, sociology is in a difficult and contradictory position. Its theories basically have nothing to do

---

[19] Cf. Schelsky (20: 108): "Dahrendorf comes ... closest to the kind of transcendental theory of sociology we have sketched."

with the essence of man. But since these theories are based on assumptions that may be misinterpreted by those who do not know or accept the conventions of scientific research, sociology is obliged to pronounce on such misinterpretations. In the nature of the case, any such pronouncement is compelling only in its logical substance. Beyond that there is no sociological view of human nature, as there is no generally compelling image of man, but only more or less convincing attacks on the problem. Perhaps philosophy is always definable as thought with a moral intention. In any event, differences in the philosophic realm cannot harm the development of sociology. Images of man, too, belong in that sphere of para-theory where the most fruitful stimuli for new theories may originate, even if the stimuli themselves are personal rather than testable by experience.

4

Out of Utopia
Toward a Reorientation of Sociological Analysis

> "Then I may now proceed to tell you how I feel about the society we have just described. My feelings are much like those of a man who has beheld superb animals in a drawing, or, it may be, in real life, but at rest, and finds himself longing to behold them in motion, executing some feat commensurate with their physique. That is just how I feel about the city we have described."
>
> *Socrates, in Plato's* Timæus

All utopias from Plato's Republic to George Orwell's brave new world of 1984 have one element in common: they are all societies from which change is absent. Whether conceived as a final state and climax of historical development, as an intellectual's nightmare, or as a romantic dream, the social fabric of utopias does not, and perhaps cannot, recognize the unending flow of the historical process.[1] For the sociologist it would be an intellectual experiment both rewarding and entertaining to examine, say, the totalitarian universe of 1984 for potential sources of conflict and change and to predict the directions of change in Big Brother's society. Its originator, of course, did not do this: his utopia would not make sense unless it was more than a passing phase of social development.

It is no accident that the catchwords of Huxley's Brave New World—"Community, Identity, Stability"—can be applied with equal justice to most other utopias. Utopian societies have (to use

---

[1] There have been many utopian constructions, particularly in recent decades. Since these vary considerably, it is doubtful whether any generalization can apply to all of them. I have tried to be careful in my generalizations on this account, and to generalize without reservation only where I feel this course can be defended. Thus I am prepared to argue the initial thesis of this essay even against such assertions as H. G. Wells's: "The Modern Utopia must not be static but kinetic, must shape not as a permanent state but as a hopeful stage, leading to a long ascent of stages." (87: ch. 1, sec. i.) It seems to me that the crucial distinction to make here is the distinction between intra-system processes, i.e., changes that are actually part of the design of utopia, and historical change, the direction and outcome of which are not predetermined.

a term popular in contemporary sociological analysis) certain structural requisites; they must display certain features in order to be
what they purport to be. First, utopias do not grow out of familiar
reality following realistic patterns of development. For most authors, utopias have but a nebulous past and no future; they are
suddenly there, and there to stay, suspended in mid-time or rather
somewhere beyond the ordinary notions of time. For the citizens
of 1984, our own society is hardly more than a fading memory.
Moreover, there is an unexplained gap, a kind of mutation somewhere between 1948 and 1984, which must be interpreted in the
light of arbitrary and permanently adapted "documents" prepared
by the Ministry of Truth.

The case of Marx is even more pertinent. It is well known how
much time and energy Lenin spent in trying to link the realistically
possible event of the proletarian revolution with the image of a
Communist society in which there are no classes, no conflicts, no
state, and, indeed, no division of labor. Lenin, as we know, failed,
in theory as in practice, to get beyond the "dictatorship of the proletariat," and somehow we are not surprised at his failure. Whether
by rational argument or empirical analysis, it is hard to link the
wide river of history—flowing more rapidly at some points, more
slowly at others, but always moving—with the tranquil village pond
of utopia. Nor are we surprised that in social reality the "dictatorship of the proletariat" soon turned out to involve more and more
of the former, and less and less of the latter.

A second structural characteristic of utopias seems to be the uniformity of such societies, or, to use more technical language, the
existence of a universal consensus on prevailing values and institutional arrangements. This, too, will prove relevant to any explanation of the impressive stability of all utopias. Consensus on values
and institutions does not necessarily mean that utopias cannot in
some ways be democratic. Consensus can be enforced, as it is for
Orwell; or it can be spontaneous, a kind of *contrat social,* as it is
for some eighteenth-century utopian writers, and later (in a per-
verted way, i.e. by conditioned spontaneity) for Huxley. One might
suspect, on closer inspection, that from the point of view of politi-

cal organization the results in the two cases would turn out to be rather similar. But this line of analysis involves critical interpretation and will be postponed for the moment. Suffice it to note that the assumption of universal consensus seems to be built into most utopian constructions and is apparently one of the factors explaining their stability.

Universal consensus means, by implication, the absence of structurally generated conflict. In fact, many builders of utopias go to considerable lengths to make it clear that in their societies conflict over values or institutional arrangements is either impossible or simply unnecessary. Utopias are perfect—be it perfectly agreeable or perfectly disagreeable—and consequently there is nothing to quarrel about. Strikes and revolutions are as conspicuously absent from utopian societies as are parliaments in which organized groups advance their conflicting claims for power. Utopian societies may be and indeed often are caste societies; but they are not class societies in which the oppressed revolt against their oppressors. We may note, third, that social harmony seems to be one of the factors adduced to account for utopian stability.[2]

Some writers add to their constructions a particularly clever touch of realism: they invent an individual who does not conform to the accepted values and ways of life, Orwell's Winston Smith or Huxley's Savage. It is not difficult to imagine a surviving capitalist in Communist society or similar disturbers of the peace in other utopias, and indeed utopias usually have various effective means at their disposal for doing away with such disrupters of unity. But how did they emerge in the first place? That question is rather more difficult to answer. Characteristically, utopian writers take refuge in chance to carry off this paradox. Their "outsiders" are not (and cannot be) products of the social structure of utopia; they are deviants, pathological cases infected with some unique disease.

In order to make utopia at all plausible, utopians must of course allow for some social activities and processes. The difference be-

[2] Richard Gerber states, in his study of *Utopian Fantasy* (80: 68): "The most admirably constructed Utopia fails to convince if we are not led to believe that the danger of revolt is excluded."

tween utopia and a cemetery is that occasionally some things do happen in utopia. But—and this is the fourth point—all processes going on in utopian societies follow recurrent patterns and occur within, and as part of, the design of the whole. Not only do they not upset the status quo; they affirm and sustain it, and it is for this reason that most utopians allow them to happen at all. For example, most writers have retained the idea that men are mortal, even in utopia.[3] Therefore, some provisions have to be made for the reproduction, both physical and social, of society. Sexual intercourse (or at least artificial insemination), the upbringing and education of children, and the selection of people to fill various social positions have to be secured and regulated—to mention only the minimum of social institutions required simply because men are mortal.[4] In addition, most utopian constructions have to cope in some way with the division of labor. These regulated processes are, however, no more than the metabolism of society; they are part and parcel of the general consensus on values, and they serve to uphold the existing state of affairs. Although some of its parts are moving in predetermined, calculable ways, utopia as a whole remains a *perpetuum immobile*.

Finally, to add a more obvious observation, utopias generally seem to be curiously isolated from all other communities (if other communities are indeed assumed to exist at all). We have already mentioned isolation in time, but usually we also find isolation in space. Citizens of utopia are seldom allowed to travel; and if they are, their reports serve to magnify rather than lessen the differences between utopia and the rest of the world. Utopias are monolithic and homogeneous communities, suspended not only in time but also in space, shut off from the outside world, which might, after all, present a threat to the cherished immobility of the social structure.

[3] Although many writers have toyed with the idea of immortality as conveyed by either divine grace or the progress of medical science. Why utopian writers should be concerned with this idea may be explained, in part, by the observations offered in this essay.

[4] In fact, the subjects of sex, education, role allocation, and division of labor loom large in utopian writing from its Platonic beginnings.

There are other features that most utopias have in common, and that it might be interesting for the sociologist to investigate. Also, the question might be asked, Just how pleasant would it be to live in even the most benevolent of utopias? Karl Popper, in his *Open Society and Its Enemies,* has explored this and other aspects of closed and utopian societies in considerable detail, and there is little to add to his incisive analyses.[5] In any case, our concern is of a rather more specific nature than the investigation of some common structural elements of utopia. We now propose to ask the seemingly pointless, and even naïve, question of whether we actually encounter all or any of these elements in *real* societies.

One advantage of the naïveté of this question is that it is easily answered. A society without history? There are, of course, "new societies" like the United States in the seventeenth and eighteenth centuries; there are "primitive societies" in a period of transition from pre-literate to literate culture. But in either case it would be not only misleading but downright false to say that there are no antecedents, no historical roots, no developmental patterns linking these societies with the past. A society with universal consensus? One without conflict? We know that without the assistance of a secret police it has never been possible to produce such a state, and that even the threat of police persecution can at best stifle dissent and conflict for limited periods of time. A society isolated in space and devoid of processes tending to upset it or change its design? Anthropologists have occasionally asserted the existence of such societies, but it has never taken very long to disprove their assertions. In fact, there is no need to discuss these questions very seriously. It is obvious that such societies do not exist—just as it is obvious that every known society changes its values and institutions continuously. Change may be rapid or gradual, violent or regulated, comprehensive or piecemeal, but it is never entirely absent where human beings create organizations to live together.

[5] Other authors, of course, have dealt extensively with utopia and its way of life. From a sociologist's point of view, the most rewarding books are Lewis Mumford, *The Story of Utopias* (85); Karl Mannheim, *Ideology and Utopia* (82); and Martin Buber, *Paths in Utopia* (77).

These are commonplaces about which even sociologists will hardly disagree. In any case, utopia means Nowhere, and the very construction of a utopian society implies that it has no equivalent in reality. The writer building his world in Nowhere has the advantage of being able to ignore the commonplaces of the real world. He can populate the moon, telephone to Mars, let flowers speak and horses fly, he can even make history come to a standstill—so long as he does not confound his imagination with reality, in which case he is doomed to the fate of Plato in Syracuse, Owen in Harmony, Lenin in Russia.

Obvious as these observations may be, they lead directly to a question that explains our interest in the social structure of utopia and that appears to merit detailed examination. That question is this: If the immobility of utopia, its isolation in time and space, the absence of conflict and disruptive processes, are a product of poetic imagination divorced from the commonplaces of reality—how is it that so much of recent sociological theory has been based on exactly these assumptions, and has, in fact, consistently operated with a utopian model of society?[6] What are the causes and what the consequences of the fact that every one of the elements we found to be characteristic of the social structure of utopia reappears in the attempt to systematize our knowledge of society and formulate sociological propositions of a general nature?

It would evidently be both misleading and unfair to impute to any sociologist the explicit intention of viewing society as unmoving and eternally stable. In fact, the commonplace that wherever there is social life there is change can be found at the outset of most sociological treatises. In this essay, however, I am contending (1) that recent theoretical approaches, by analyzing social structure in terms of the elements characteristic of immobile societies, have in fact assumed the utopian image of society; (2) that this assumption,

[6] In this essay I am concerned mainly with recent sociological theory. I have the impression, however, that much of the analysis offered here also applies to earlier works in social theory, and that in fact the utopian model of society is one of two models which reappear throughout the history of Western philosophy. Expansion of the argument to a more general historical analysis of social thought might be both instructive and rewarding.

particularly if associated with the claim to being the most general, or even the only possible, model, has been detrimental to sociological research; and (3) that it has to be replaced by a more useful and realistic approach to the analysis of social structure and social process.

II

Much of the theoretical discussion in contemporary sociology reminds me of a Platonic dialogue. The two modes share an atmosphere of unreality, lack of controversy, and irrelevance. To be sure, I am not suggesting that there is or has been a Socrates in our profession. But, as with Plato's dialogues, somebody selects for essentially arbitrary reasons a topic, or more often a general area of inquiry, and at the same time states his position. Then there is some initial disagreement. Gradually disagreement gives way to an applauding, but disengaged and unconvincing, murmur of "Indeed," or "You don't say." Then the topic is forgotten—it has nothing to do with anything in particular anyway—and we move on to another one, starting the game all over again (or else we turn away in disgust from the enterprise of theory altogether). In this process, Plato at least managed to convey to us a moral and metaphysical view of the world; we, the scientists, have not even been able to do that.

I am reminded of Plato in yet a more specific sense. There is a curious similarity between the *Republic*—at least from the second book onward[7]—and a certain line of sociological reasoning that is rather prominent these days and is by no means associated with only one or two names. In the *Republic,* Socrates and his partners set out to explore the meaning of δικαιοσύνη, "justice." In modern sociological theory we have set out to explore the meaning of "equilibrium" or, as it is sometimes called, "homeostasis." Socrates soon

[7] The first book of the *Republic* has always struck me as a remarkable exception to the general pattern of Plato's Socratic dialogues. (It is, of course, well established that this book was written considerably earlier than the rest of the *Republic.*) For an argument in support of the main protagonist of this dialogue, Thrasymachus, see the following essay, "In Praise of Thrasymachus."

finds out that justice really means τὸ ἑαυτοῦ πράττειν, that everybody does what it is proper for him to do. We have discovered that equilibrium means that everybody plays his role. To illustrate this point, Socrates and his friends go about the business of constructing a theoretical—and presumably ideal—πόλις. We have constructed the "social system." In the end, both Plato and we are left with a perfect society, one that has a structure, is functioning, is in equilibrium, and is therefore just. However, what are we going to do with it? With his blueprint for an ideal society in mind, Plato went to the assistance of his friend Dion in Syracuse and tried to put his ideas into practice. He failed miserably. Plato was wise; he admitted defeat. Without abandoning his idea of the best of all possible worlds, he decided that perhaps, so far as real human beings and real circumstances were concerned, democracy with all its shortcomings was a more effective way to proceed.[8] We have not yet been quite as wise. Although what we still tend to call "theory" has failed as miserably in tackling real problems as Plato's blueprint, we have so far not admitted defeat.

The social system, like utopia, has not grown out of familiar reality. Instead of abstracting a limited number of variables and postulating their relevance for the explanation of a particular problem, it represents a huge and allegedly all-embracing superstructure of concepts that do not describe, propositions that do not explain, and models from which nothing follows. At least they do not describe or explain (or underlie explanations of) the real world with which we are concerned. For much of our theorizing about social systems the same objection holds that Milton Friedman raised against Oscar Lange's "Economic System":

> [He] largely dispenses with the initial step of theory—a full and comprehensive set of observed and related facts to be generalized—and in the main reaches conclusions no observed facts can contradict. His emphasis is on the formal structure of the

---

8 I am aware that this account telescopes the known facts considerably and over-stresses Plato's intention of realizing the ideal state in Syracuse. The education of Dion's son was obviously a very indirect way of doing so. However, there is enough truth even in the overstatement offered here to make it a useful argument.

theory, the logical interrelations of the parts. He considers it largely unnecessary to test the validity of his theoretical structure except for conformity to the canons of formal logic. His categories are selected primarily to facilitate logical analysis, not empirical application or test. For the most part, the crucial question, "What observed facts would contradict the generalization suggested and what operations could be followed to observe such critical facts?" is never asked; and the theory is so set up that it could seldom be answered if it were asked. The theory provides formal models of imaginary worlds, not generalizations about the real world. (79: 283.)[9]

Consensus on values is one of the prime features of the social system. Some of its advocates make a slight concession to reality and speak of "relative consensus," thereby indicating their contempt for both the canons of scientific theory (in whose models there is no place for "relatives" or "almosts") and the observable facts of reality (which show little evidence of any more than highly formal, and tautological, consensus). That societies are held together by some kind of value consensus seems to me either a definition of societies or a statement clearly contradicted by empirical evidence—unless one is concerned not so much with real societies and their problems as with social systems, in which anything might be true including the integration of all socially held values into a religious doctrine. I have yet to see a problem that requires the assumption of a unified value system for clarification, or a testable prediction that follows from this assumption.

It is hard to see how a social system based on ("almost") universal consensus can allow for structurally generated conflicts. Presumably conflict always implies some kind of dissent or disagreement

[9] The following sentences of Friedman's critique are also pertinent (pp. 283ff): "Lange starts with a number of abstract functions whose relevance—though not their form or content—is suggested by casual observation of the world.... He then largely leaves the real world and, in effect, seeks to enumerate all possible economic systems to which these functions could give rise.... Having completed his enumeration, or gone as far as he can or thinks desirable, Lange then seeks to relate his theoretical structure to the real world by judging to which of his alternative possibilities the real world corresponds. Is it any wonder that 'very special conditions' will have to be satisfied to explain the real world? ... There are an infinite number of theoretical systems; there are only a few real worlds."

about values. In Christian theology original sin was required to explain the transition from paradise to history. Private property was no less a *deus ex machina* in Marx's attempt to account for the transition from an early society, in which "man felt as much at home as a fish in the water," to a world of alienation and class struggles.[10] These explanations may not be very satisfactory; they at least permit recognition of the hard and perhaps unpleasant facts of real life. Modern sociological theory of the structural-functional variety has failed to do even that (unless one wants to regard the curiously out-of-place chapter on change in Talcott Parsons's *Social System* as the original sin of this approach). By no feat of the imagination, not even by the residual category of "dysfunction," can the integrated and equilibrated social system be made to produce serious and patterned conflicts in its structure.

What the social system can produce, however, is that well-known disturber of the peace of utopia, the "deviant." Even he requires some considerable argument and the introduction of a chance, or at least an undetermined, variable—in this case, individual psychology. Although the system is perfect and in a state of equilibrium, individuals cannot always live up to this perfection. "Deviance is a motivated tendency for an actor to behave in contravention of one or more institutionalized normative patterns." (Parsons 53: 250.) Motivated by what, though? Deviance occurs either if an individual happens to be pathological, or if *"from whatever source* [this, of course, being unspecified], a disturbance is introduced into the system." (53: 252; my italics.) In other words, it occurs for sociologically—and that means structurally—unknown and unknowable reasons. It is the bacillus that attacks the system from the dark depths of the individual psyche or the nebulous reaches of the outside world. Fortunately, the system has at its disposal certain mechanisms for dealing with the deviant and for "re-equilibrating" itself, i.e., the mechanisms of social control.

The striking preoccupation of sociological theory with the re-

---

10 Marx tackled this problem in the *Economic and Philosophical Manuscripts of 1844*. This entire work offers an outstanding illustration of the philosophical and analytical problems faced in any attempt to relate utopia and reality.

lated problems of reproduction, socialization, and role allocation—or, in institutional terms, with the family, the educational system, and the division of labor—bears out our comparison of this type of theory with utopian societies. Plato carefully avoided Justinian's static definition of justice as *suum cuique*; in his definition the emphasis is on πράττειν, on the active and, to apply a much abused term, dynamic aspect. Similarly, the structural-functionalist insists that his equilibrium is not static but moving. But what does he mean by a moving equilibrium? He means, in the last analysis, that the system is a structure not of the building type but of the organism type. Homeostasis is maintained by the regular occurrence of certain patterned processes which, far from disturbing the tranquillity of the village pond, in fact *are* the village pond. Heraclitus's saying, "We enter the same river, and it is not the same," does not hold here. The system is the same however often we look at it. Children are born and socialized and allocated until they die; new children are born, and the same happens all over again. What a peaceful, what an idyllic, world the system is! Of course, it is not static in the sense of being dead; things happen all the time; but happily they are under control, and they all help to maintain that precious equilibrium of the whole. Things not only happen, they function, and so long as they do, all is well.

One of the more unfortunate connotations of the word "system" is its closedness. Although some structural-functionalists have tried, there is no getting away from the fact that a system—even if only "for purposes of analysis"—is essentially something self-sufficient, internally consistent, and closed to the outside. A leg cannot be called a system; a body can. Actually, advocates of the system have little reason to be unhappy with this term; abandoning it would rob their analysis of much of its neatness, and above all would leave no function for the "whatever sources"—the villainous outsiders they can now introduce to "account" for unwanted realities. I do not want to carry my polemicizing too far, but I cannot help feeling that it is only a step from thinking about societies in terms of equilibrated systems to asserting that every disturber of the equilibrium, every deviant, is a "spy" or an "imperialist agent." By implication, the system theory of society comes dangerously close to the conspiracy theory of history—which is not only the end of all sociology but also rather silly.[11] There is nothing logically wrong with the term "system." It begins to give birth to undesirable consequences only when it is applied to total societies and is made the ultimate frame of reference of analysis. It is certainly true that sociology deals with society. But it is equally true that physics deals with nature, and yet physicists would hardly see an advance in calling nature a system and trying to analyze it as such. In fact, any such analysis would probably—and justly—be discarded as metaphysics.

To repeat, the social system as conceived by some recent sociological theorists appears to have the same features that characterize utopian societies. This being so, we are forced to conclude that structural-functional theory also deals with societies from which historical change is absent, and that it is, in this sense, utopian. To be sure, it is utopian not because some of the assumptions of this theory are "unrealistic"—this would be true for the assumptions of almost any scientific theory—but because it is exclusively concerned with spelling out the conditions of the functioning of a utopian social system. Structural-functional theory does not introduce unrealistic assumptions for the purpose of explaining real problems; it introduces many kinds of assumptions, concepts, and models for the sole purpose of describing a social system that has never existed and is not likely ever to come into being.

In thus comparing the social system with utopia, I feel I have done an injustice to the majority of utopian writers that needs to be corrected. With few exceptions, the purpose behind utopias has been the criticism, even the indictment, of existing societies. The story of utopias is the story of an intensely moral and polemical branch of human thinking; and although from a realistic and political point of view utopian writers may have chosen doubtful means to express their values, they have certainly succeeded in con-

---

11 It could, for instance, be argued that only totalitarian states display one unified value system, and that only in the case of totalitarian systems do we have to assume some outside influence ("from whatever source") to account for change—an argument that clearly reduces the extreme structural-functional position to absurdity.

veying to their times a strong concern with the practical and ethical shortcomings of existing institutions and beliefs. This can hardly be said of modern sociological theory. The complacent acceptance, if not justification, of the status quo which by intention or default pervades the structural-functional school of social thought is unheard of in utopian literature. Even as utopias go, the social system has little to contribute to a tradition of penetrating and often radical criticism. I do not want to suggest that sociology should be primarily concerned with uncovering and indicting the evils of society; but I do want to assert that those sociologists who felt impelled to embark on a utopian venture were rather ill-advised in retaining the technical imperfections, while at the same time abandoning the moral impulses, of their numerous forerunners.

III

It is easy to be polemical, hard to be constructive, and—at least for me—impossible to be as impressively and happily catholic as those at whom my critical comments are directed. However, I do not propose to evade the just demand that I specify whose work I mean when I refer to the utopian nature of sociological theory, that I explain why I think that an approach of this kind is useless and even detrimental to our discipline, and that I describe what better ways there are in my opinion to deal with our problems.

The name that comes to mind immediately when one speaks about sociological theory these days is Talcott Parsons. Already, in many discussions and for many people, Parsons appears to be more of a symbol than a reality. Let me therefore state quite explicitly that my criticism applies neither to Parsons's total work nor to his work only. I am not concerned with Parsons's excellent and important philosophical analysis of *The Structure of Social Action,* nor am I concerned with his numerous perceptive contributions to the understanding of empirical phenomena. I do think, however, that much of his theoretical work in the last ten years represents an outstanding illustration of what I mean by the utopian bent in sociological theory. The double emphasis on the articulation of purely formal conceptual frameworks and on the social system as the beginning and end of sociological analysis involves all the vices, and in his case none of the virtues, of a utopian approach. To be sure, Parsons is by no means alone in this approach; at one time or another, many prominent American sociologists and some British anthropologists have engaged in the same kind of reasoning.

Two main remedies have been proposed in recent years against the malady of utopianism, but in my opinion both have been based on a wrong diagnosis. By correcting this diagnostic error, we may hope to get at the root of the trouble and at the same time find a way out of utopia.

For some time now it has been quite popular in our profession to support T. H. Marshall's demand for "sociological stepping-stones in the middle distance" or Robert K. Merton's plea for "theories of the middle range." I cannot say that I am very happy with these formulations. True, both Marshall and Merton explain at some length what they mean by their formulas. In particular, they advocate something they call a "convergence" of theory and research. But "convergence" is a very mechanical notion of a process that defies the laws of mechanics. Above all, this conception implies that sociological theory and sociological research are two separate activities that can be divided or joined. I do not believe that this is so. In fact, I think that so long as we hold this belief, our theory will be logical and philosophical, and our research will at best be sociographic, with sociology disappearing in the void between these two. The admonitions of Marshall and Merton may actually have led to a commendable rediscovery of empirical problems for investigation, but it seems clear that this has been a by-product rather than the intended consequence of their statements.[12]

There is no theory that can be divorced from empirical research; but of course the reverse is equally true. I have no sympathy with formulations in which the just demand that sociological analysis be

---

12 Most of the works of Marshall and Merton do display the kind of concern with problems that I am here advocating. My objection to their formulations is therefore directed not against these works, but against their explicit assumption that nothing is wrong with recent theory but its generality, and that by simply reducing the level of generality we can solve all problems.

inspired by empirical problems is confused with the unjust demand that it be based on, or even exclusively concerned with, something called "empirical research." As a matter of fact, the advocates of "empirical research" and the defenders of abstract theory have been strikingly similar in one, to my mind crucial, respect (which explains, by the way, why they have been able to coexist with comparatively little friction and controversy): they have both largely dispensed with that prime impulse of all science and scholarship, the concern with getting to the bottom of specific, concrete, and— if this word must be used—empirical problems. Many sociologists have lost the simple impulse of curiosity, the desire to solve riddles of experience, the concern with problems. This, rather than anything else, explains both the success and the danger of the utopian fallacy in sociological thinking and the related fallacy of empirical research.

It is perhaps fairly obvious that a book like *The Social System* displays but a minimal concern with riddles of experience. But I do not want to be misunderstood. My plea for a reinstatement of empirical problems in the central place that is due to them is by no means merely a plea for greater recognition of "facts," "data," or "empirical evidence." I think that from the point of view of concern with problems, there is very little to choose between *The Social System* and the ever-increasing number of undoubtedly well-documented Ph.D. theses on such subjects as "The Social Structure of a Hospital," "The Role of the Professional Football Player," and "Family Relations in a New York Suburb." "Areas of investigation," "fields of inquiry," "subjects," and "topics," chosen because nobody has studied them before or for some other random reason, are not problems. What I mean is that at the outset of every scientific investigation there has to be a fact or set of facts that is puzzling the investigator: children of businessmen prefer professional to business occupations; workers in the automobile industry of Detroit go on strike; there is a higher incidence of suicides among upwardly mobile persons than among others; Socialist parties in predominantly Catholic countries of Europe seem unable to get more than 30 per cent of the popular vote; Hungarians revolt against the

Communist regime. There is no need to enumerate more such facts; what matters is that every one of them invites the question "Why?" and it is this question, after all, which has always inspired that noble human activity in which we are engaged—science.

There is little point in restating methodological platitudes. Let me confine myself, therefore, to saying that a scientific discipline that is problem-conscious at every stage of its development is very unlikely ever to find itself in the prison of utopian thought or to separate theory and research. Problems require explanation; explanations require assumptions or models and hypotheses derived from such models; hypotheses, which are always, by implication, predictions as well as explanatory propositions, require testing by further facts; testing often generates new problems.[13] If anyone wants to distinguish theory from research in this process, he is welcome to do so; my own feeling is that this distinction confuses, rather than clarifies, our thinking.

The loss of problem-consciousness in modern sociology explains many of the drawbacks of the present state of our discipline, and in particular the utopian character of sociological theory; moreover, it is in itself a problem worthy of investigation. How is it possible that sociologists, of all people, should have lost touch with actual social problems and questions, of which there are so many in the world? At this point, I think, the ideological interpretation of sociological development that has recently been advanced by a number of authors is pertinent.[14] By turning away from the critical facts of experience, sociologists have both followed and strengthened the trend toward conservatism that is so powerful in the intellectual world today. What is more, their conservatism is not of the militant kind found in the so-called Left Wing of conservative

---

[13] It is, however, essential to this approach—to add one not so trivial methodological point—that we realize the proper function of empirical testing. As Popper has demonstrated in many of his works since 1935 (the year of publication of *Logik der Forschung*), there can be no verification in science; empirical tests serve to falsify accepted theories, and every refutation of a theory is a triumph of scientific research. Testing that is designed to confirm hypotheses neither advances our knowledge nor generates new problems.

[14] I am thinking in particular of the still outstanding articles by S. M. Lipset and Reinhard Bendix (81), and of the early parts of Lewis A. Coser's *The Functions of Social Conflict* (78).

parties in England, France, Germany, and the United States; it is, rather, a conservatism by implication, the conservatism of complacency. I am sure that Parsons and many of those who have joined him in utopia would deny that they are conservatives, and so far as their explicit political convictions go there is no reason to doubt their sincerity. At the same time their way of looking at society, or rather of not looking at society when they should, has promoted a sense of disengagement, of not wanting to worry about things, and has in fact led them to elevate this very attitude of abstinence to the status of a "scientific theory" according to which there is no need to worry. By thus leaving the job of worrying to the powers that be, sociologists have implicitly recognized the legitimacy of these powers; their disengagement has turned out to be an engagement—however involuntary—on the side of the status quo. What a dramatic misunderstanding of Max Weber's attempt to separate the vocation of politics from that of science!

Let me repeat that I am not advocating a sociological science that is politically radical in the content of its theories. In any case, there would be little sense in doing so, since logically speaking there can be no such science. What I am advocating is a sociological science that is inspired by the moral fiber of its forefathers; and I am convinced that if we regain the problem-consciousness which has been lost in the last decades, we cannot fail to recover the critical involvement in the realities of our social world that we need if we are to do our job well. For I hope I have made it quite clear that problem-consciousness is not merely a means of avoiding ideological biases, but is above all an indispensable condition of progress in any discipline of human inquiry. The path out of utopia begins at the point where puzzling social facts are recognized as puzzling and the problems they pose are tackled.

There is yet another reason why I think the utopian character of recent sociological theory has been detrimental to our discipline. It is quite conceivable that to help explain specific problems we shall at some stage want to employ models of a highly general kind or even formulate general laws. Stripped of its more formal and decorative elements, the social system could be, and sometimes has been, regarded as such a model. For instance, we may want to investigate the problem of why achievement in the educational system ranks so high among people's concerns in our society. The social system can be thought of as suggesting that in advanced industrial societies the educational system is the main, and tends to be the only, mechanism of role allocation. In this case, the social system proves to be a useful model. It seems to me, however, that even in this limited sense the social system is a highly problematic, or at least a very one-sided, model, and that here, too, a new departure is needed.

IV

It is perhaps inevitable that the models underlying scientific explanations acquire a life of their own, divorced from the specific purpose for which they have originally been constructed. The *homo oeconomicus* of modern economics, invented in the first place as a useful, even if clearly unrealistic, assumption from which testable hypotheses could be derived, has today become the cardinal figure in a much discussed philosophy of human nature that is far beyond the economist's range of concern. The indeterminacy principle in modern physics, which again is nothing but a useful assumption without claim to any reality other than operational, has been taken as a final refutation of all determinist philosophies of nature. Analogous statements could be made about the equilibrium model of society—although, as I have tried to show, it would unfortunately be wrong to say that the original purpose of this model was to explain specific empirical problems. We face the double task of having to specify the conditions under which this model proves analytically useful and having to cope with the philosophical implications of the model itself.[15] It may seem a digression for a sociologist to

---

[15] The approach here characterized by the catchword "social system" has two aspects, which are not necessarily related and which I am here treating separately. One is its concentration on formal "conceptual frameworks" of no relevance to particular empirical problems, as discussed in the previous section. The other is the application of an equilibrium model of society to the analysis of real societies, and is dealt with in the present section. The emphasis of advocates of the social system on one or the other of these aspects has been shifting, and to an extent it is possible to accept the one without the other. Both aspects, however, betray the impress of utopianism, and it therefore seems appropriate to deal with both of them in an essay that promises to show a way out of utopia.

occupy himself with the latter problem; however, in my opinion it is both dangerous and irresponsible to ignore the implications of one's assumptions, even if these are philosophical rather than scientific in a technical sense. The models with which we work, apart from being useful tools, determine to no small extent our general views, our selection of problems, and the emphasis in our explanations; and I believe that in this respect, too, the utopian social system has played an unfortunate role in our discipline.

There may be some problems that can be approached by assuming an equilibrated, functioning social system based on consensus, absence of conflict, and isolation in time and space. I think there are such problems, although their number is probably much smaller than many contemporary sociologists wish us to believe. The equilibrium model of society also has a long tradition in social thinking, including, of course, not only all utopian thinking but also such works as Rousseau's *Contrat social* and Hegel's *Philosophy of Law*. But neither in the explanation of sociological problems nor in the history of social philosophy is it the only model, and I would strongly contest any implicit or explicit claim that it can be so regarded. Parsons's statement in *The Social System* that this "work constitutes a step toward the development of a generalized theoretical system"[16] is erroneous in every respect I can think of, and in particular insofar as it implies that all sociological problems can be best understood in terms of the equilibrium model of society.

It may be my personal bias that I can think of many more problems to which the social system does not apply than problems to which it does, but I would certainly insist that, even on the highly abstract and largely philosophical level on which Parsons moves, at least one other model of society is required. The model I have in mind has as long a tradition as the equilibrium model, and, I think,

[16] Characteristically, this statement is made in the chapter "The Processes of Change of Social System" (53: 486). In many ways I have here taken this chapter of *The Social System* as a clue to the problems of structural-functionalism—an approach that could easily be justified by a page-by-page interpretation of the amazingly weak argument offered by Parsons in support of his claim (*a*) that the stabilized system is the central point of reference of sociological analysis, and (*b*) that any theory of change is impossible in the present state of our knowledge.

a better one. In spite of this fact, no modern sociologist has as yet formulated its basic tenets in such a way as to render it useful for the explanation of critical social facts. Only in the last year or two has there been some indication that this alternative model, which I shall call the "conflict model of society," is gaining ground in sociological analysis.

The extent to which the social system model has influenced even our thinking about social change and has marred our vision in this important area of problems is truly remarkable. Two facts in particular illustrate this influence. In talking about change, most sociologists today accept the entirely spurious distinction between "change within" and "change of" societies, which makes sense only if we recognize the system as our ultimate and only reference point. At the same time, many sociologists seem convinced that in order to explain processes of change they have to discover certain special circumstances that set these processes in motion; the implication here is that social change is an abnormal, or at least an unusual, state, one that has to be accounted for in terms of deviations from a "normal," equilibrated system.

I think that in both these respects we shall have to revise our assumptions radically. A Galilean reformulation is required; we must realize that all units of social organization are continuously changing unless some force intervenes to arrest this change. It is our task to identify the factors interfering with the normal process of change rather than to look for variables involved in bringing about change. Moreover, change is ubiquitous not only in time but also in space; that is to say, every part of every society is constantly changing, and it is impossible to distinguish between "change within" and "change of," between "microscopic" and "macroscopic" change. Historians discovered a long time ago that in describing the historical process it is insufficient to confine one's attention to such major affairs of state as wars, revolutions, and government actions. Their experience should help us to understand that what happens in Mrs. Smith's house, in a trade union local, or in the parish of a church is just as significant for the social process of history, and in fact *is* just as much the social process of history, as what happens in the White House or the Kremlin.

The great creative force that leads to change in the model I am trying to describe, and that is equally ubiquitous, is social conflict. The notion that wherever there is social life there is conflict may be unpleasant and disturbing. Nevertheless, it is indispensable to our understanding of social problems. As with change, we have grown accustomed to looking for special causes or circumstances whenever we encounter conflict; but again a complete about-face is necessary in our thinking. Not the presence but the absence of conflict is surprising and abnormal, and we have good reason to be suspicious if we find a society or social organization that displays no evidence of conflict. To be sure, we do not have to assume that conflict is always violent and uncontrolled. There is probably a continuum from civil war to parliamentary debate, from strikes and lockouts to collective bargaining. Our problems and their explanations will undoubtedly teach us a great deal about the range of variation in forms of conflict. In formulating such explanations, however, we must never lose sight of the underlying assumption that conflict can be temporarily suppressed, regulated, channeled, and controlled, but that neither a philosopher-king nor a modern dictator can abolish it once and for all.

There is a third notion that goes with change and conflict to make up the armamentarium of the conflict model of society: the notion of constraint. From the point of view of this model, societies and social organizations are held together not by consensus but by constraint, not by universal agreement but by the coercion of some by others. It may be useful for some purposes to speak of the "value system" of a society, but in the conflict model such characteristic values are ruling rather than common, enforced rather than accepted, at any given point of time. And as conflict generates change, so constraint may be thought of as generating conflict. We assume that conflict is ubiquitous, since constraint is ubiquitous wherever human beings set up social organizations. In a highly formal sense, it is always the basis of constraint that is at issue in social conflict.

I have sketched the conflict model of society—as I see it—only very briefly, but I hope it is evident that there is a fundamental difference between the equilibrium and conflict models. Utopia is—to use the language of the economist—a world of certainty. It is par-

adise found; utopians know all the answers. But we live in a world
of uncertainty. We do not know what an ideal society looks like—
and if we think we do, we are fortunately unable to realize our
conception. Because there is no certainty (which, by definition, is
shared by everybody in that condition), there has to be constraint
to assure some livable minimum of coherence. Because we do not
know all the answers, there has to be continuous conflict over values
and policies. Because of uncertainty, there is always change and development. Quite apart from its merits as a tool of scientific analysis, the conflict model is essentially non-utopian; it is the model of
an open society.

I do not intend to make the mistake of many structural-functional theorists and advance for the conflict model a claim to comprehensive and exclusive applicability. As far as I can see, we need
both models for the explanation of sociological problems. Indeed,
it may well be that society, in a philosophical sense, has two faces of
equal reality: one of stability, harmony, and consensus, and one of
change, conflict, and constraint.[17] Strictly speaking, it does not matter whether we select for investigation problems that can be understood only in terms of the equilibrium model or problems for
which the conflict model is required. There is no intrinsic criterion for preferring one to the other. My own feeling is, however,
that in the face of recent developments in our discipline and the
critical considerations offered earlier in this essay, we may be well
advised to concentrate in the future not only on concrete problems
but on such problems as involve explanations in terms of constraint, conflict, and change. This second face of society may be
esthetically rather less pleasing than the first, but if all that sociology had to offer were an easy escape to utopian tranquillity, it
would hardly be worth our efforts.

---

[17] I should not be prepared to claim that these two are the only possible models of
sociological analysis. Without any doubt, we need a considerable number of models
on many levels for the explanation of specific problems, and more often than not the
two models outlined here are too general to be of immediate relevance. In philosophical terms, however, it is hard to imagine other models of society that are not of
either the equilibrium or the conflict type.

5

In Praise of Thrasymachus

Tradition has been rather less than fair to Thrasymachus of Chalcedon, who, even if he has no other claim to fame, deserves to be remembered for the remarkable achievement of holding his own in an encounter with that champion dialectician, Socrates. Despite the impressions of some of the bystanders and perhaps of Socrates himself, Thrasymachus emerged unconvinced by Socrates' arguments, and with his heavy irony intact, from the vicious debate about justice that distinguishes the first book of the *Republic* from so many of Plato's other dialogues. "Well," he said in response to his opponent's final thrust, "this is a feast day, and you may take all this as your share of the entertainment." (86: 39.)

Our reasons for recalling the rude visitor from Chalcedon are by no means merely rhetorical. Indeed, the first book of the *Republic* deserves much more attention from those who have lightly dismissed it as an early and playful prologue to the serious discussions of the nine remaining books. It was in this initial dialogue, or perhaps more appropriately debate, that two incompatible views of society were stated for the first time in the history of social and political thought. The conflict between these two views has since proved to be the single most persistent conflict in the ranks of those who seek to understand the workings of human society, and among today's scholars it rages still. This conflict has assumed many forms since the admittedly rather crude statement of the two views in the first book of the *Republic,* and we shall here be considering some of these forms right down to contemporary sociological and political theory; but its basic terms were set in that apparently accidental encounter between Thrasymachus and Socrates.

What is more, it seems to me that despite his rather formidable temper and abusive language, Thrasymachus had the better arguments on his side. We have to assist him a little, to be sure, to make his case fully convincing; we shall have to interpolate or even extrapolate his arguments rather than simply interpret them; but with the ideas of Thrasymachus as a starting point, we can develop an image of society that helps us to understand both some basic problems of political theory and the patterns of the good society in our time. This is what I shall try to do here.

Let us return for a moment to the home of Cephalus and Polemarchus in Piraeus, the port of Athens. Socrates, on his way home from the festivities in honor of Bendis, is almost literally dragged into the house, where he is greeted with varying degrees of delight and soon finds himself engaged in his favorite sport, talking. After a polite exchange with the aging master of the house about wisdom and old age, he engages Polemarchus, the son of Cephalus, in one of those supposedly educational circular debates in which the dialogues of Plato abound. The subject is justice, and the conclusion is an open question: "Now what, after all that, might justice be?"

Thrasymachus, understandably impatient, forgets his manners ("gathering himself up like a wild beast," says Socrates, "he sprang at us as if he would tear us in pieces") and begins: "What is the matter with you two, Socrates? Why do you go on in this imbecile way, politely deferring to each other's nonsense? . . . I want a clear and precise statement; I won't put up with that sort of verbiage." (86: 15–16.)

After some further interchanges, Thrasymachus proceeds to make himself quite clear in a few stark statements interrupted by Socratic doubts:

> "Listen then," Thrasymachus began. "What I say is that 'just' or 'right' means nothing but what is to the interest of the stronger party. Well, where is your praise? You don't mean to give it me."
>
> "I will, as soon as I understand," I said. "I don't see yet what

you mean by right being the interest of the stronger party. For instance, Polydamas, the athlete, is stronger than we are, and it is to his interest to eat beef for the sake of his muscles; but surely you don't mean that the same diet would be good for weaker men and therefore be right for us?"

"You are trying to be funny, Socrates. It's a low trick to take my words in the sense you think will be most damaging."

"No, no," I protested; "but you must explain."

"Don't you know, then, that a state may be ruled by a despot, or a democracy, or an aristocracy?"

"Of course."

"And that the ruling element is always the strongest?"

"Yes."

"Well then, in every case the laws are made by the ruling party in its own interest; a democracy makes democratic laws, a despot autocratic ones, and so on. By making these laws they define as 'right' for their subjects whatever is for their own interest, and they call anyone who breaks them a 'wrongdoer' and punish him accordingly. That is what I mean: in all states alike 'right' has the same meaning, namely what is for the interest of the party established in power, and that is the strongest. So the sound conclusion is that what is 'right' is the same everywhere: the interest of the stronger party." (86: 18.)

The scene is set, and Socrates is quick to respond. He tries to entangle Thrasymachus in contradictions, making him admit that the powerful may be in error about what is useful to them. Thrasymachus parries rather well by pointing out the difference between positions of power ("the rulers insofar as they are acting as rulers") and their incumbents.

Soon Socrates approaches the central issue of the controversy. He argues that all human activity must be directed toward some goal, and that the value of any such activity must therefore be found in its goal, not in the activity itself. "And so with government of any kind: no ruler, insofar as he is acting as ruler, will study or enjoin what is for his own interest. All that he says and does will be said and done with a view to what is good and proper for the subject for whom he practices his art." (86: 24.)

In response to this apparent reversal of his own original statement, Thrasymachus bursts into a long argument to the effect that
whatever those in power do is bound to be harmful to their subjects. And now that he has lost his temper, Thrasymachus adds
somewhat inconsistently that for this reason injustice pays and a belief in justice is naïve.

This remark provides Socrates with an easy opening for a whole
shower of counterarguments, in the course of which, contrary to his
rhetorical principles, he states a case of his own. He clearly has no
other choice, since no amount of Socratic irony can force his adversary to state the Socratic case. It had been agreed, Socrates claims
(of course he is wrong), "that any kind of authority, in the state or
in private life, must, in its character of authority, consider solely
what is best for those under its care." (86: 27.)

Repeatedly Socrates insists on the essentially harmonious relationship between rulers and ruled. Indeed, he uses an argument
against Thrasymachus that his opponent, had he not by this time
been blind with fury, might well have turned into one for his own
case: namely that if Thrasymachus's notion of justice were correct,
people would be divided, hate one another, and engage in conflict.
And wherever this sort of justice occurs—"in a state or a family or
an army or anywhere else"—the effect is "to make united action impossible because of factions and quarrels, and moreover to set whatever it resides in at enmity with itself as well as with any opponent
and with all who are just." (86: 35.)

"Enjoy your triumph," is all that Thrasymachus can reply. "You
need not fear my contradicting you. I have no wish to give offense
to the company." (86: 36.) The answer is in accord with his theory,
if one assumes that those present were the stronger, but the arsenal
of Thrasymachus was still full. It would be fun to try out the weapons it contained in defense of the proud and angry Sophist from
Chalcedon.

II

But here we must stop for a moment. Though we shall continue
the dialogue with Socrates and his latter-day followers and make at

least some of the points that Thrasymachus failed to make, this is the place to state a little more directly, and a little less historically, what this debate is about.

Socrates and Thrasymachus were concerned with what they called justice, or with that substantival adjective so characteristic of Greek and German philosophical language, "the just," τὸ δίκαιον. What Plato and his characters described with this one complex word defines an area of reflection that is almost equally relevant to three different sets of problems: those central to the theory of society, to social and political analysis, and to political theory. A word about each of these sets of problems may help to clarify the issue.

Georg Simmel's question "How is society possible?" is rarely asked today, although it has lost none of its urgency and is at least implicitly dealt with by every theorist of modern social science. It is easy to assert or assume that man is a social animal, but how social groups persist, and what holds them together, are questions that remain to be answered. Perhaps some die-hard positivists would claim that no answer is needed, since any answer is unlikely to be immediately testable by experience; but they would be wrong on at least two counts. First, there are other avenues to knowledge besides the objective experience of our senses, and there is no reason whatever to block off any of these to the inquiring mind. And second, how one answers Simmel's question is likely to have both direct and indirect effects on how one attacks specific problems of social analysis.

This is why the same type of argument may be equally relevant to the theory of society and to theories about particular social events. No rigorous scientific theory is relevant to all events. But the events I have in mind here are of strategic importance;[1] they are events involving the political processes of total societies. How can we understand the exercise of power? How can we identify the limits of power? How can we rationalize clashes of interest and

[1] One must not be misled by the impressive-sounding word "strategic." Any statement of this kind is based on value judgments; my own should be obvious from this essay.

conflicts of groups? How can we explain those sweeping social changes that we call revolutions, as well as the lesser, almost imperceptible ones that occur in our lives every day? Here observation is indeed the test of knowledge, but here, too, it is useful to reflect on what Plato called justice.

In terms of language and the meaning of words alone, the relevance of Plato's ideas on justice seems strongest and most evident in political theory. What does the good society look like? What institutions can bring about the good society under given conditions of social development? For a variety of reasons, sociologists in particular—but more recently, in the wake of the behavioral vogue, political scientists as well—have come to feel rather hesitant about raising these questions. The questions are not scientific in the rigorous sense required by Max Weber, that dynamic man who was all but destroyed by the conflict between value and fact; and those more concerned about the status of their disciplines than the extent of their knowledge have accordingly seen fit to banish them from social science. Their exclusion has robbed social science of much of its interest, and has probably contributed to the general deterioration of political debate as well. In any case I hope to be able to show how the notion of a good society may be reintroduced into scientific discussion to the mutual advantage of social analysis and political philosophy.

These, then, are the three kinds of contemporary questions evoked by the Piraeus dialogue about justice. But the leap from the excited debate in the home of Cephalus to the all but unrecognizable discussions in the scholarly journals of our own time is rather a long one. As we try to restate the cases made by Thrasymachus and Socrates, we may do well to begin by putting them into a language halfway between that of Greek philosophy and that of modern social science.

III

Thrasymachus was the first to state his case. In all human societies, there are positions that enable their bearers to exercise power. These positions are endowed with sovereignty—the men who hold them lay down the law for their subjects. Obedience is enforced, for the most important single aspect of power is the control of sanctions. (Sanctions do not always have to be applied: mere anticipation of their effect may suffice to guarantee compliance with the law.) It follows from this notion of power and sanctions that there is always resistance to the exercise of power, and that both the effectiveness and the legitimacy of power—if there is any difference between these two concepts—are precarious. Normally those in power manage to stay in power. Theirs is the stronger group, and society is held together by the exercise of their strength, that is, by constraint.

Now for Socrates' position. It is true, he says, that power is exercised in human societies, but it is exercised on behalf of societies rather than against them. Positions of power are created to give active expression to a general will that represents the consensus of the society's members. What appears to be obedience is in many ways but an expression of this consensus. The exercise of power is dependent on the support of those who are apparently subject to it. Subjection never involves a renunciation of sovereignty; rather, sovereignty remains with the total body politic, with all the citizens of a society. Any differences and divisions in a society are due to outside interference with a basically legitimate system; such divisive influences are in any case destructive of society. Normally, society is held together by the agreement of all citizens on certain fundamental tenets, to which they then adhere voluntarily as a way of protecting their own interests.

This language, of course, is no longer that of Thrasymachus and Socrates, but that of a much later pair of political thinkers, Thomas Hobbes and Jean-Jacques Rousseau. Though separated by more than a century, Hobbes and Rousseau are properly discussed together, as the brilliant article on Hobbes in the *Encyclopédie* was the first to point out.[2] It was they who wrote the next act in our drama.

---

[2] "The philosophy of M. Rousseau of Geneva is almost exactly the reverse of Hobbes's" (92: 589). The two philosophers are seen as opposites not only in approach but in their social theories: "If one believes Hobbes, laws and the formation of society have improved man; if one believes M. Rousseau, they have corrupted him."

In the extended debate over the social contract (yet another translation of Plato's "justice") two conflicting notions were repeatedly advanced.[3] One was the notion of the social contract of association (*pacte d'association*), according to which society was originally formed by a free agreement to join in a common enterprise involving no abdication of any participant's rights. An odd contract this, or so one might think, but then there are other weaknesses of the Socratic—or Rousseauist—position. The other notion, that of the contract of government (*pacte de gouvernement*), postulated an original agreement setting up an agency responsible for holding society together, an agency to which every party to the agreement must be to some extent subject. This agency is, of course, government, and in this form the social contract becomes a real contract with all the attendant problems.

The consequences of this conflict between notions of the social contract were many, although there is little agreement even today on exactly what they were. Hobbes has been called the father of authoritarianism; he has even been used by German sociologists to clothe Nazi rule in an ancient ideology; but the same Hobbes has also been regarded as a forefather of modern liberal theory. Rousseau was long considered the great theorist of democracy; only recently have some political historians discovered that this notion of democracy is distinctly ambiguous, and that perhaps Rousseau bears as much responsibility for totalitarian democracy as for its liberal counterpart.

In the social contract debate, the ancient dispute about the basis of justice was resumed on a more sophisticated level, but with inconclusive results. Its nineteenth-century version, the many-sided conflict between a Socratic *Gemeinschaft* and a Thrasymachean *Gesellschaft*, was equally inconclusive. To find definitive answers, we shall have to take the final step to the present-day version of this debate.

When we do, the first discovery we make is a telling reversal of order. Today, it is the party of Socrates that has stated its case first,

<hr />

[3] For a historical account of the social contract debate that is informed by a sense of its sociological relevance, see the study by J. W. Gough (93).

and the party of Thrasymachus that has so far confined itself to putting its opposition on record in the most general terms. The surnames of Socrates in our time are many; indeed one can hardly speak of a "party" here, so varied are the approaches of Socratic theorists today. This group includes economists like Kenneth Arrow and Anthony Downs, political scientists like Karl Deutsch and David Easton, sociologists like Talcott Parsons and Neil Smelser, and many others whose analysis rests on an equilibrium model of social life.[4]

Equilibrium theories differ greatly in the degree to which their basic concepts are reified. Not all of them, for example, assume explicitly that there is a general consensus on values among the members of a society. In one way or another, however, they all regard the exercise of power as an exchange in which all citizens participate, and which in theory makes it possible to think of society as a system held in equilibrium so far as its constituent parts are concerned. Disturbances of the system are either ruled out as beyond the boundaries of this type of analysis (i.e., regarded as unfortunate intrusions of the complicated world of uncertainty) or classified as unexplained accidents. Although such disturbances may produce stress or failure of communication within the system, they are generated outside it. The system is regarded as persisting through time by virtue of the equilibrium created either by its internal cycles of power and support, or by the flow of communications, or by the interchange between subsystems as mediated by the currency of power.

What resistance there has been to this approach has been much less subtle than the various versions of the equilibrium theory it-

---

4 The list of names is incomplete, which is only to be expected; it is also somewhat unfair, and can perhaps stand qualification. "Equilibrium theorist" is scarcely an adequate description of any of these men, especially the economists: Downs, for example, makes it quite clear that the conditions of certainty are merely an assumption for one part (the simpler one) of his *Economic Theory of Democracy,* and Arrow's analyses merely share the general assumptions of economic theory. Also, of course, the classification does not imply any judgment of quality; all the authors mentioned are of the first order. My point is simply that in the work of all these men, the assumption, or discovery, of equilibrium counts for more than the sense of structural change of uncertain direction.

self. In this respect, at least, the school of Thrasymachus has re-mained true to its founder. There have been noisy and ambitious proclamations of a new sociology or a true science of politics, but these have so far resulted in little more than some rather old-fashioned protestations to the effect that power is important, con-flict and change omnipresent, and the political process incalculable. There has not yet been any considered statement of how else one might look at society, or explain the political process, or argue for the good society, without abandoning the indubitable technical ad-vances of modern social science.[5] Not infrequently, laudable senti-ments have taken the place of necessary arguments. This is as true, it seems to me, of C. Wright Mills and his numerous followers to-day as it is of Raymond Aron. (The pairing of these two names may perhaps suggest the profound ambiguity in any Thrasymachean position!)

There is no intrinsic objection to an analysis of society in which power figures as an agent of constraint. To be sure, we see in mod-ern economics a remarkable contrast between the technical refine-ment of equilibrium theories and the nineteenth-century crudeness of theories of development; and our concern here is with a similar contrast between an emphasis on continuity and an emphasis on change. But refinement is not necessarily a sign of truth; and it might be suggested that if Thrasymachean theories seem crude, it is only because the imagination that has gone into formulating them has so far not been accompanied by a corresponding preci-sion of craftsmanship.

In a Thrasymachean theory, power is a central notion. It is seen as unequally divided, and therefore as a lasting source of friction; legitimacy amounts at best to a precarious preponderance of power over the resistance it engenders. Of all states, equilibrium is the least likely, a freakish accident rather than the rule; and there is

[5] Once again, distinctions are necessary in the interests of fairness. The statement above is truer of C. Wright Mills than of Wilbert E. Moore; truer of Irving L. Horo-witz than of Dennis Wrong; and only after considerable qualification would it apply to Raymond Aron. As for the "leftist" opposition to orthodox social science, *The New Sociology* (94), edited by Horowitz, affords a clear view of the opportunities and limits of a modern Thrasymachus.

little to be gained by making it a basic assumption. The dialectic of power and resistance determines the rate and direction of change.

IV

At the point we have now reached, general statements are no longer very helpful. Let me turn, therefore, to the three sets of questions I spoke of earlier, and apply our two approaches to them in some detail.

How is society possible? This is, of course, what Talcott Parsons called the Hobbesian problem of order, even though he proposed a very Rousseauist solution to it. According to Parsons, society is possible by virtue of some assumed general agreement on a set of values that define the boundaries and coordinates of the social order and of individual identity in social groups. Societies vary—and change—in their degree of internal differentiation, but at any given time social roles and institutions are integrated by the functional contribution of every one of them to the maintenance of the whole as a going concern. The concern is a going one in the sense that it can adapt to changing environmental conditions, to internal processes of differentiation and functional reallocation, and perhaps even to stresses caused by internal factors (of mysterious origin). Its adaptations are made possible in part by the processes of interchange variously described as feedback processes, as input-output relations, or as manifestations of the flow of power in a system of support and initiative.

By pointing to concrete historical experiences such as revolutions, or to the constraints involved in the actual exercise of power, it is relatively easy to make Parsons's modern equilibrium approach appear hopelessly abstract and formal—even absurd. But the approach was not primarily intended to be descriptive, and as an explanation of the continuity of society it is less easily dismissed.

There is, however, another approach, closer to the experience of the historian and the politician, to problems that do not yield to the equilibrium approach. Continuity is without doubt one of the fundamental puzzles of social life; but continuity may be regarded as a result not of equilibrium but of constraint, if not force. Whereas in the equilibrium approach the notion of power has but a marginal place—"Power," says Deutsch in summarizing Parsons, "is thus neither the center nor the essence of politics" (89: 124), to say nothing of society—it is a fundamental category of the constraint approach to social analysis. Societies are moral entities, i.e., definable by normative structures; to this extent the two approaches agree. But according to the constraint approach norms are established and maintained only by power, and their substance may well be explained in terms of the interests of the powerful.

If one states the case this way, a third concept is necessary: sanctions. Norms differ from values—"mere" values—in being associated with sanctions and thus having a binding force. But the translation of values into norms, the application of sanctions, and the maintenance of stability all refer back to power as a constraining force rather than a currency of exchange or an expression of social integration. Political power, then, to summarize this view in John Locke's words, is seen as "a right of making laws with penalties of death and, consequently, all less penalties" (95: 4).

The ramifications of these different approaches to the Hobbesian problem of order are numerous and fascinating. In the sociology of law, for example, the equilibrium approach is likely to be associated with the old—and demonstrably unsatisfactory, if not wrong —theory that laws grow "organically" out of people's values and habits, whereas the constraint approach would lead to a more adequate, if apparently more Machiavellian, view of the genesis of laws. To the equilibrium theorist, conflict must forever remain a *diabolus ex machina,* the product of an abstract enemy without or an inexplicable dysfunction within, whereas to the constraint theorist it comes of necessity from the resistance provoked by the exercise of power. Social stratification in the equilibrium approach expresses an objective consensus on the "functional importance" of social positions; in the constraint approach it comes from the selective application of sanctions and thus expresses the relationship between social positions and the ruling values.[6]

[6] Two of these three subjects are dealt with more extensively in this volume: social stratification in the essay "On the Origin of Inequality among Men," conflict in "Out

If we pursued these ramifications of our two approaches to the Hobbesian problem of order, we might be able to establish that even such seemingly unscientific, if not irrelevant, attitudes toward society—general orientations, as Merton would call them, or para-theories—have implications for a more empirical type of analysis. But there is one question to which we would still have no answer: Which of the two competing approaches is correct? Perhaps this question cannot be answered in any ultimate sense; perhaps it will forever remain a matter of argument and persuasion. Though I believe that despite this reservation there are good reasons for praising Thrasymachus at this point, we have so far arrived at rather less than a satisfactory conclusion to our discussion, one that leaves the empirically oriented scholar with an unhappy suspicion of its irrelevance to his concerns.

V

Let us move on, therefore, to the second kind of question raised by the ancient problem of justice, namely the analysis of the political process, or of more specific events involving total societies. How do Socratic and Thrasymachean views of justice fare if we apply them to specific problems whose theoretical solutions we are in a position to test empirically?

Clearly, there is no answering this question in the abstract. I have therefore selected a problem that to my mind critically tests any total social analysis purporting to explain the political process: the rise and success of National Socialism in Germany. Here we encounter a dramatic sequence of political events with obvious social undercurrents and ramifications. If our theories of the political process are worth anything at all, they should enable us to explain why what happened had to happen. Since ample documentation of the events that took place in Germany both before and after 1933 is available today, it would seem possible to test almost any theory put forward.

---

of Utopia" (not to mention my *Class and Class Conflict*). The third, the genesis of norms, is a crucial problem in the theory of social change that has so far not received sufficient attention from sociologists.

The difficulty of accounting for the rise and persistence of Nazism by traditional social theories makes this problem even better for our purposes. A Marxian theory of class conflict does little to explain why the working class was as hopelessly divided as the entrepreneurial class. Some of the historians who have described the events of the 1920's and 1930's in Germany in great detail have pronounced them inevitable, i.e., have claimed that by some mysterious transformation the chronological sequence of events is a causal sequence as well; but they have scarcely succeeded in convincing even their colleagues. Inveterate metaphysicians continue to speak, following Tacitus, of some strange infection in the German soul that pervades Germany's body politic and causes occasional outbreaks of fever; but they pay little heed to the extraordinary changeability of social structures and indeed of human nature, which exceeds even the imagination of social scientists. Champions of comparative research have brought out certain features of German society that may well have a bearing on the rise of National Socialism, but that unfortunately were also present in countries whose political history took a very different course from Germany's for reasons that usually go unexplained. There are other explanations, but to this day none that can be called fully satisfactory, so that the attempt to apply our competing orientations to this problem is more than a pedagogical exercise.[7]

In his *Framework for Political Analysis,* David Easton mentions National Socialism twice; and though he would obviously have much more to say on the subject if he dealt with it systematically, these two remarks so clearly reveal the deficiencies of the equilibrium approach that I should like to take them as a point of departure for my argument against it. First, Easton observes that despite various profound changes "a political system has managed to persist in the United States over the years." This is a rather cautious remark, but it is followed by a surprisingly incautious one: "Similarly in Germany, although the Imperial order fell to the Weimar

Republic which in turn yielded to the Nazi regime to be succeeded by a third order after World War II, some form of political system persisted. Change does not seem to be incompatible with continuity." (91: 84.) This may well be true—but what a miserable, indeed almost inhuman, way to describe the most dramatic changes in the composition and substance of Germany's political order!

Even in its own context, Easton's formulation is rather extreme; but it serves to show that an equilibrium approach cannot come to terms with certain substantive problems of change. Equilibrium theorists are interested above all in the continuity of the system, and in this respect the Nazis did them the special favor of establishing their rule within the existing order, which was then changed —adapted perhaps?—in a series of steps, in other words gradually, after 1933. What analysis of change there is in studies based on the equilibrium model never penetrates to such substantive questions as whether a regime is liberal or totalitarian, or whether the determining elements of a society are military, economic, or narrowly political. The equilibrium theorist may claim, of course, that he never wanted to tackle this type of question in the first place, and there is some justice to this claim. But the fact remains that even if he wanted to, he could not do so with the theoretical resources at his disposal, and that a good deal can be said for wanting to look at the substance of change. Equilibrium theories lend themselves to explaining continuity alone, and even this only with respect to the most formal aspects of the political system.

It is only to be expected, then, that when equilibrium theorists come to explaining the changes they like to describe as adaptations, they generally have recourse to random factors, which they often introduce very crudely. Later in the same book Easton says, "Although the German political system shifted [*shifted*!] from the Weimar Republic to a totalitarian regime and in this way adapted to the stresses attendant upon defeat in World War I and its ensuing economic inflation, a considerable range of alternatives was possible." (91: 89.) We learn that Germany's political regime "shifted," and that it did so by a process of "adaptation," which was a response to "stresses." But where did the "stresses" come from? Here

Easton seriously offers us the half-baked explanation of the Nazis' seizure of power that has been offered so often in the past, notably by the Nazis themselves. The stresses came from defeat in World War I, that is, from the Treaty of Versailles. Did the treaty make a National Socialist response inevitable? And if so, by what strange law of human nature or society? The inflation, of course, was not "ensuing" in any sense, but by impoverishing the self-employed middle classes it was bound to have some effect on Germany's politics; yet it would seem that the German political system adapted very well to this stress, since the five years following the inflation were the only stable years of the Weimar Republic!

Finally, and most important, how does Easton set about identifying his "stresses"? Does their identification follow in any way from his general approach? Seemingly not; in fact, the "stresses" are introduced at random. To be sure, Easton has done rather badly even for an equilibrium theorist; Parsons, for example, did much better in "Democracy and Social Structure in Pre-Nazi Germany." But the methodological basis is the same in both cases, and its weakness shows that the equilibrium theory is ill-adapted to identifying the rate, depth, and direction of social change in pre-Nazi and Nazi Germany.

However, we must now ask how Thrasymachus would acquit himself if he were faced with the problem of explaining National Socialism. Would he really do much better? Probably not well enough to satisfy our rigorous methodological standards; still, some of the broad advantages of his approach are readily demonstrated. To begin with, a constraint approach leads us to recognize the Nazi seizure of power as an important problem for analysis. Second, it enables us to focus on the internal processes in German society that may account for the events of 1933. Third, a developed Thrasymachean approach would systematically guide us to some of the factors that determine the rate, depth, and direction of change. Where we would fail, or at least temporarily fall short of our expectations, would be in the technical refinement of identifying empirically some of the conditions that we can describe in general theoretical terms.

Any given political situation—such as that of January 29, 1933, in Germany—may be described in terms of the antagonism between power and resistance. As long as power is exercised within certain boundaries set by social structures, and is therefore stronger than the resistance inevitably offered to it—or, in less abstract terms, so long as the ruling groups are effectively superior to the ruled—we can analyze the course a society takes in terms of the interests, goals, and social personalities of those in power. From 1929 on, the interplay of power and resistance in Germany found the powerful increasingly weak, and their opponents correspondingly strong. In the end, it became virtually impossible to exercise power effectively, and completely impossible to control those in opposition. As the status of those in power became more and more precarious, their opponents prepared to take over and translate their interests into norms.

So far, this description seems no less formal than the equilibrium theorist's. But then, a description is merely the beginning of analysis, and the crucial step is the next one. Both power and resistance are structured socially. Those in power pursue certain interests by virtue of their position; and by these interests certain groups in society are tied to them. Similarly, opposition is based on interests, and social groups with these interests adhere to the opposition cause. As the history of the Weimar Republic took its course, there were fewer and fewer groups whose interests could best be satisfied within the existing constitutional order, and, conversely, more and more groups who impatiently demanded a new political system. In the end, even those in positions of power began to doubt their seemingly vested interest in the status quo, and at least three in many respects incompatible groups—the National Socialists, the Communists, and the traditionalist German Nationalists—united for a short time, a very short time, to dislodge those in power and replace them with a new set of leaders.

The next step in our analysis would take us to the conditions under which such alliances, doubts, and ambitions come into being. Note, however, that the direction of the changes of the early 1930's can already be inferred to a considerable extent from the analysis to this point. Given the broad range of the opposition and the weakness of those in power in the final stages of the Weimar Republic, it was predictable that even sweeping changes would meet with little effective resistance for a while. It was clear, moreover, from the interests of those who tried to destroy the Weimar Republic that the new regime would not be democratic; and equally clear from the relative strengths of the interest groups involved that it would not be Communist either.

In this brief outline, we have passed over literally dozens of questions to which this approach gives rise. For example, who were the elites and what were their politics? At what point and why did middle-class groups reject the existing order and go over to resistance? To what extent can an analysis of this sort predict which points in the National Socialist program would be realized and which dropped? How are we to explain the temporary union between traditionalists and totalitarian modernists?

As we go on asking these questions, two things at least become obvious. One is that we are still a long way from a satisfactory explanation of the Nazis' rise to power; the other is that in any such explanation we shall have to supplant formal theories with historical description and apt interpretation. It follows that the framework of a Thrasymachean analysis of change is also quite unfinished, and to this extent praising Thrasymachus is praising a mere program after all. But there is more to be said: namely, that by taking the approach I am urging here, we can escape the melancholy emptiness of formal analysis. To be sure, an equilibrium theorist can pride himself on being at least scientific, even if he does not have much to tell us about his subject; but a constraint theorist can afford to remain much closer to the richness and color of events.

There is no conflict, no basic methodological incompatibility, between the study of history and a Thrasymachean approach to the study of society, much as the epistemological goals of historiography and sociology may differ. The historian's insistence on the uniqueness of events (as opposed to the search for empty generalities) and his preference for interpretative analysis may be unsatisfactory in strict theoretical terms, but they are essential, both as a stimulus and as a component, to the approach I am advocating here. In this sense, our approach may combine the vitality of an account of real events with the excitement of theoretical explanation.[8]

There are events more obviously suited to this approach than the National Socialist seizure of power in Germany. Traditional revolutions, for example (the French, the Russian, perhaps the Cuban and the Hungarian), defy all but the most vacuous analysis in equilibrium terms; for when we say that in all cases internal stresses became so severe as to disrupt temporarily the very continuity of the system, we are saying almost nothing. In the theory of revolution, which has been one of the more distinguished branches of social analysis since Tocqueville and Marx, power has never figured as a mere medium of exchange or an almost randomly chosen point in a feedback process. Of course revolutions are exceptional events— but are they more exceptional than the perfect equilibrium of stagnation? And if not, might we not find a better clue to the more ordinary types of change in the special case of revolutions than in the special case of stagnation?

VI

Though I have made my own opinion clear, I realize that so far I have offered no dramatic proof for the superiority of the Thrasymachean approach over the Socratic. Given the present technical refinement of social science, it may well be impossible today to offer such proof with respect to the area we have just discussed, that of social analysis. But when it comes to our third and final area of discussion, political theory, the picture is considerably clearer; indeed, it is with regard to the problem of constructing the good society that our two approaches have their most dramatically contrary implications. And at all times, or so it seems to me, the arguments

---

8 It is desirable to discriminate here between the two very different forms taken by analysis of change. One is structural, based on the analysis of roles and role interests, and is thus largely formal. The other is historical, a matter of actual groups and their actual goals, and is accordingly substantive. Although the two may be related, they are by no means identical. For example, whereas the work of C. Wright Mills might be put in the historical class, my *Class and Class Conflict* (7) is closer to the structural.

have overwhelmingly favored a Hobbesian solution to the Hobbesian problem of order.

One may imagine a delightful country in which power is exercised on behalf of the whole of society and with its support. Political decisions are essentially the expression of a common or general will. Power is not a zero-sum concept, but a currency of which every citizen has his share. A universal system of participation, an undisturbed flow of communications, characterizes the political process and its inherent "justice."

But, as so often, it is worth taking a second look at this pleasing picture. What happens, for example, if somebody does not agree with the alleged general will? This should not happen, of course, but what if it does? If the theory of the general will is made a dogma, the deviant will have to be persecuted, and if necessary exiled; if he is not, the theory is refuted. What happens if someone gets an idea about how to do things better and gathers support for it? And above all, what if those in power forget about the feedback processes and begin to hoard the cherished currency of power?

The answer is the same in every case. Either the general will is upheld by the use of force (it is for urging the use of force in this circumstance that Rousseau is sometimes called the father of totalitarian democracy), or force is not used and the general will is discredited. In terms of political theory, the assumption of certainty implicit in all equilibrium theories, or at least in their ideal-type extremes, turns out to be a deadly weapon against individual freedom in a living, changing society.

By contrast, the society envisioned by Hobbes, or Thrasymachus, is not very appealing at first sight. Its virtues become clear only when we consider that institutions exist to protect men from the badness of their fellowmen rather than as monuments of consensus.[9] The underlying assumption of all constraint theories of politics is that man lives in a world of uncertainty. Since nobody is capable of giving only right answers, we have to protect ourselves from the tyranny of wrong answers, and that includes the tyranny

9 This somewhat cynical definition of institutions I owe to my former colleague, the Tübingen political scientist Theodor Eschenburg.

of a stagnant status quo. Institutions have to be set up in such a way as to accommodate change, conflict, and the interplay of power and resistance. There is no foolproof recipe for creating such institutions, and someday we may well conclude that parliaments, elections, and the other traditional democratic political machinery are only one of many arrangements of roughly equal effectiveness. In any case, such institutions should allow for conflict; they should be designed to control power rather than to camouflage it behind an ideology of consensus, and they should permit change even in the unwieldy structure of a complex modern society.

These conflicting principles of political theory—totalitarianism and liberalism—are what Karl Popper and others would call the pragmatic implications of the two views I have discussed in this essay.[10] Human beings need not be consistent to survive, and it may well be fortunate that they are often very inconsistent indeed. One may hold a view but be horrified by its implications; and I suspect that few of the equilibrium theorists, certainly none of those I mentioned, deserve to be identified with totalitarian political theory. But the fact that inconsistency is psychologically viable does not lessen the logical force, and above all the moral force, of consistency. A liberal theory of politics is plausible in part because it shares certain assumptions with scientific analysis and para-theory. One is the assumption of uncertainty. Another is the relation between power, conflict, and change. In view of the apparent persistence of change, this assumption seems likely to play a part in any effort to formulate a general explanatory theory.

The pragmatic implications of our two approaches for the shape of the good society may thus be turned around, so that the theoretical and para-theoretical approaches appear as implications of a pragmatic, normative notion of justice. It is this relationship that seems to me to tip the scales finally in favor of Thrasymachus. I make this statement without qualification; that is to say, I no longer take the tolerant view that the two approaches discussed are essen-

---

[10] For further discussion of the notion of "pragmatic implication" (as well as this particular pragmatic implication), see the essay "Uncertainty, Science, and Democracy" below.

tially equivalent ways of understanding a given problem or of understanding two different sets of problems.[11]

It can be argued, I think—and I have at least tried to argue—that the constraint approach is superior to the equilibrium approach. There is no problem that can be described in equilibrium terms that cannot be described at least as well in constraint terms, and there are many problems that Thrasymachus can tackle but Socrates cannot. The constraint approach, being more general, more plausible, and generally more informative about the problems of social and political life, should for these reasons replace the approach now so surprisingly in vogue in social science.

Socrates became the first functionalist when he described justice as the state in which everybody does what he is supposed to do, τὸ ἑαυτοῦ πράττειν. This is clearly a miserable state, a world without rebels or retreatists, without change, without liberty. If this is justice, one can understand Thrasymachus's ill-tempered preference for injustice. But fortunately neither Socrates nor his latter-day followers have had the power to enforce their notion of what justice is and what it is not. They, too, live in a world of conflict, and even for them (as they may yet come to see) competitive diversity is a condition of living in the real world and of rationally explaining what happens in it. Justice, then, would appear to be not an unchanging state of affairs, whether real or imagined, but the permanently changing outcome of the dialectic of power and resistance.

---

[11] I tentatively espoused the more tolerant view in "Out of Utopia" (see above) as well as in *Class and Class Conflict*. Another repudiation of it appears in "On the Origin of Inequality among Men" (see below).

6

On the Origin of Inequality among Men

Even in the affluent society, it remains a stubborn and remarkable fact that men are unequally placed. There are children who are ashamed of their parents because they think that a university degree has made them "better." There are people who decorate their houses with antennas without having the television sets to go with them, in order to convince their neighbors that they can afford television. There are firms that build their offices with movable walls because the status of their employees is measured in square feet and an office has to be enlarged when its occupant is promoted. There are clerical workers whose ambition it is to achieve a position in which they not only can afford, but are socially permitted to own, a two-tone car. Of course, such differences are no longer directly sustained by the force of legal sanction, which upholds the system of privilege in a caste or estate society. Nevertheless, our society— quite apart from the cruder gradations of property and income, prestige and power—is characterized by a multitude of differences of rank so subtle and yet so penetrating that one cannot but be skeptical of the claim one sometimes hears that a leveling process has caused all inequalities to disappear. It is no longer usual to investigate the anxiety, suffering, and hardship that inequalities cause among men—yet there are suicides because of poor examination results, divorces based on "social" incompatibility, crimes occasioned by a feeling of social inequality. Throughout our society, social inequality is still turning men against men.

These remarks are not meant as a plea for equality. On the contrary, I shall later agree with Kant, who called "inequality among men" a "rich source of much that is evil, but also of everything that is good." (104: 325.) Yet the extreme effects of inequality may give a general idea of the problem that concerns me. Diderot has our sympathy when he states in his article "Société" in the *Encyclo-pédie*:

> There is no more inequality between the different stations in life than there is among the different characters in a comedy: the end of the play finds all the players once again in the same posi-tion, and the brief period for which their play lasted did not and could not convince any two of them that one was really above or below the other. (92: 208.)

But the life of men in society is not merely a comedy, and the hope that all will be equal in death is a feeble consolation for most. The question remains: Why is there inequality among men? Where do its causes lie? Can it be reduced, or even abolished altogether? Or do we have to accept it as a necessary element in the structure of human society?

I shall try to show that historically these were the first questions asked by sociology. By surveying the various attempts to answer them a whole history of sociological thought might be written, and I shall at least give some indication of how this may be so. So far, however, as the problem of inequality itself is concerned, this his-tory has achieved little more than to give it a different name: what was called in the eighteenth century the origin of inequality and in the nineteenth the formation of classes, we describe today as the theory of social stratification—all this even though the original problem has not changed and no satisfactory solution to it has been found. In this essay I shall attempt a new explanation of the old problem, one that in my opinion will take us a few steps beyond the present state of our thinking.

II

The younger a branch of scholarship is, the more concerned are its historians to pursue its origins back at least as far as Greek an-tiquity. Historians of sociology are no exception to this rule. But if one regards the problem of inequality as a key to the history of sociology, it can be clearly shown not only that Plato and Aristotle were definitely not sociologists, but also why they were not. It is always awkward to ascribe to an academic discipline a precise date of birth, but this discussion may help us to date the beginnings of sociology with reasonable plausibility.

In 1792, a gentleman by the name of Meiners, described as a "Royal British Councillor and *rite* teacher of worldly wisdom in Göttingen," wrote some reflections on "the causes of the inequality of estates among the most prominent European peoples." His results were not especially original:

> In all times inequality of natures has unfailingly produced inequality of rights. . . . If the negligent, the lazy, the untrained, and the ignorant were to enjoy equal rights with those who display the corresponding virtues, this would be as unnatural and unjust as if the child had rights equal to those of the adult, the weak and cowardly woman rights equal to those of the strong and courageous man, the villain the same security and respect as the meritorious citizen. (108: 41.)

Meiners's reflections are a version, highly characteristic of his time, of an ideology that to the present day, and with only minor refinements, is invoked by all societies that are worried about their survival to reassure themselves of the justice of their injustices. By repeating in a simplified form the errors of Aristotle, such societies assert a preestablished harmony of things natural and social, and above all a congruence of natural differences between men and social differences between their positions. It was Aristotle, after all, who said:

> It is thus clear that there are *by nature* free men and slaves, and that servitude is agreeable and just for the latter. . . . Equally, the relation of the male to the female is *by nature* such that one is superior and the other inferior, one dominates and the other is dominated. . . . With the barbarians, of course, the female and the dominated have the same rank. This is because they do not possess a naturally dominating element. . . . This is why the poets

say, "It is just that Greeks rule over barbarians," because the bar-barian and the slave are *by nature* the same. (97: 1254b, 1252a.)

Now this is just the attitude that makes impossible a sociological treatment of the problem, i.e., an explanation of inequality in terms of specifically social factors expressed in propositions capable of be-ing empirically tested.

So far, I have talked about social inequality as if it were clear what is meant by this notion. Obviously, this is a somewhat opti-mistic assumption. The lathe operator and the pipe fitter, the gen-eral and the sergeant, the artistically gifted child and the mechani-cally gifted child, the talented and the untalented, are all pairs of unequals. Yet these inequalities are evidently themselves rather un-equal, and have to be distinguished from one another in at least two respects. First, we must distinguish between inequalities of na-tural capability and those of social position; second, we must dis-tinguish between inequalities that do not involve any evaluative rank order and those that do. If we combine these two approaches, four types of inequality emerge, all of which we shall have to dis-cuss. In relation to the individual there are (1) *natural differences of kind* in features, character, and interests, and (2) *natural differ-ences of rank* in intelligence, talent, and strength (leaving open the question of whether such differences do in fact exist). Correspond-ingly, in relation to society (and in the language of contemporary sociology) there are (3) *social differentiation* of positions essentially equal in rank, and (4) *social stratification* based on reputation and wealth and expressed in a rank order of social status.[1]

Our interest here is primarily in inequalities of the stratification type. On the question of what these are, or, more technically speak-ing, how they can be measured, no consensus has so far been reached, nor has a suggestion been offered that would make a con-

---

[1] The distinction between natural and social inequalities can be found in Rousseau; indeed, it constitutes the core of his argument. "I perceive two kinds of inequality among men: one I call natural or physical . . . ; the other might be called moral or political." (111: 39.) The distinction between social stratification and social differenti-ation, by contrast, has only recently been made unambiguously, for example by Mel-vin M. Tumin (119) and Walter Buckley (98). Yet this distinction is no less important than the other, as the attempt to explain social stratification in terms of social differ-entiation shows.

sensus possible. I am accordingly making an arbitrary decision here
when I distinguish the distributive area of stratification—the ex-
plicandum of our theoretical discussion—from nondistributive inequalities such as those of power.[2] According to this distinction,
wealth and prestige belong to the area of stratification, even if they
are assembled to a considerable extent by one person; property and
charisma, by contrast, are nondistributive. How wealth and prestige relate to each other, and especially whether they are mutually
convertible and can therefore be reduced to one concept, one single
"currency" of social stratification, is an important technical question that I cannot go into here.[3]

III

Aristotle was concerned as we are here to examine the origin of
the fourth type of inequality, social stratification. However, by trying to explain social stratification—as so many authors of antiq-
uity, the Christian middle ages, and modern times did after him—
in terms of assumed natural differences of rank between men, he
missed precisely that type of analysis which we should today describe as sociology. In consequence, his analysis subjects a potentially sociological problem to assumptions that transcend the realm
of social fact and defy the test of historical experience. That this
attitude helped to delay the birth of sociology by more than twenty
centuries is perhaps no great loss, considering the political consequences of so unhistorical an explanation. I believe that Rousseau
was right, for all his polemical tone, when he argued that it did not
make sense

to investigate whether there might not be an essential connection
between the two inequalities [the natural and the social]. For it

[2] For what has here been called "distributive" and "nondistributive" one could
also use the terms "intransitive" and "transitive" (in the grammatical sense). Transitive or nondistributive inequalities are the creators of the more passive intransitive
or distributive ones.
[3] A possible currency of this kind might be the (structured) "chances of participation"—or, in Weber's terms, "life chances"—that we acquire by virtue of our positions.

would mean that we must ask whether rulers are necessarily worth more than the ruled, and whether strength of body and mind, wisdom, and virtue are always found in the same individuals, and found, moreover, in direct relation to their power or wealth; a question that slaves who think they are being overheard by their masters may find it useful to discuss, but that has no meaning for reasonable and free men in search of the truth. (111: 39.)[4]

This is Rousseau's argument in his prize essay of 1754 on "The Origin of Inequality among Men and Whether It Is Legitimated by Natural Law." Unlike his earlier essay of 1750 on "The Moral Consequences of Progress in the Arts and Sciences," this essay was not awarded the prize of the Dijon Academy. I do not know why the judges preferred the essay of "a certain Abbé Talbert" (as one editor of Rousseau's work describes him); but conceivably they began to feel uneasy about the radical implications of their own question. For the new meaning given by Rousseau and his contemporaries to the question of the origin of inequality involved a revolution in politics as well as intellectual history.

The pivotal point of the Aristotelian argument—if I may use this formula as an abbreviation for all treatments of the problem before the eighteenth century—was the assumption that men are by nature unequal in rank, and that there is therefore a natural rank order among men. This presupposition collapsed in the face of the assumption of natural law that the natural rank of all men is equal. Politically, this meant that together with all other hierarchies, the hierarchies of society also lost their claim to unquestioning respect. If men are equal by nature, then social inequalities cannot be established by nature or God; and if they are

---

[4] Clearly Aristotle and numerous thinkers between his time and the revolutionary period had important sociological insights; one need only mention the way Aristotle relates social strata to political constitutions in the *Politics*. Nor would it be correct to charge Aristotle with having naïvely asserted the congruence of natural and social inequalities. But Aristotle (to say nothing of Plato) and all others down to the eighteenth century lacked what one might call pervasive "sociological thinking," i.e., an unwavering sense of the autonomously social (and thus historical) level of reality. Such thinking required a radical break with the undisputed constants of earlier epochs, a break that first became general in the age of the great revolutions. For this reason one may well derive the birth of sociology from the spirit of revolution.

not so established, then they are subject to change, and the privileged of today may be the outcasts of tomorrow; it may then even be possible to abolish all inequalities. A straight road leads from such reflections to the Declaration of the Rights of Man and Citizen of 1789: "Men are born and remain free and equal in rights. Social differences, therefore, can only be based on general utility."

In terms of intellectual history, the same process meant that the question of the origin of inequality was now phrased in a new and different, i.e. sociological, manner. If men are by nature equal in rank, where do social inequalities come from? If all men are born free and equal in rights, how can we explain that some are rich and others poor, some respected and others ignored, some powerful and others in servitude? Once the question was posed in these terms, only a sociological answer was possible.[5] With good reason, then, Werner Sombart and others have seen the beginnings of sociology in the works of those authors who first tried to give a sociological answer to this question—notably the French *philosophes,* the Scottish moral philosophers and political economists, and the thinkers of the German Enlightenment in the second half of the eighteenth century.[6]

IV

The first sociological explanation of the origin of inequality proved disappointing, though for a century it reappeared in a suc-

---

[5] Historically, therefore, one necessary condition of the sociological mode of inquiry into the origin of inequality was the assumption of the natural equality (equality of rank) of all men. But here as so often what was historically necessary is logically superfluous: once the question of the origin of inequality is posed in a sociological way (i.e., without recourse to natural inequalities), its answer has nothing to do with whether or not men are by nature equal or unequal. Thus the difficult philosophical question of the natural rank of men can be set aside here as irrelevant to the truth or falsity of sociological explanations of social stratification. We rule out only explanations based on the assumed congruence, or tendency to congruence, of the natural and social rank orders.

[6] Few historians of sociology have taken up Sombart's reference to the Scottish moral philosophers and their attack on natural law (116); apart from a recently published dissertation (103), only William C. Lehmann has elaborated on it (105, 106). Parallel developments on the Continent are described even more rarely. One can write the history of sociology in many ways, of course; but it seems to me that the origin of inequality would be far from the worst central theme.

cession of new forms. It consisted in a figure of thought, which may be demonstrated by further reference to Rousseau's prize essay.

As we have seen, Rousseau begins by assuming the natural equality of men. In the style of his time, he then projects this assumption into history and constructs a pre-social original state in which there was complete equality of all, where no one was superior to anyone else in either rank or status. Inequality, he argues, came about as a result of leaving the state of nature; it is a kind of original sin, which he links with the emergence of private property. How private property itself came into existence, Rousseau does not explain; instead, he confines himself to a statement as obscure as it is concrete: "The first man who fenced in an area and said, 'This is mine,' and who found people simple enough to believe him, was the real founder of civil society." (111: 66.)

Not all of Rousseau's contemporaries, even those who shared most of his assumptions, accepted the one-sidedness of his explanation or his evaluation of the process he described. Adam Ferguson's *History of Civil Society* (1767) and John Millar's *Origin of the Distinction of Ranks* (1771) come quite close to Rousseau in assuming a natural state of equality and ascribing to property the crucial part (Millar) or at least an important part (Ferguson) in destroying this natural state. But both of them regard the fact that men have learned "to strive for riches and admire distinctions," and thus to differentiate according to income and prestige, not as a curse but as a step toward the civilization of "civil society." (See 102: II, 2, 3.)

Even further removed from Rousseau the romantic utopian are Schiller's Jena lectures of 1789, "On the First Human Society"; the title is a clear, if implicit, reference to Kant's essay on the "Probable Beginning of Human History," which in turn referred explicitly to Rousseau's essay (see 112: 322, 325). Schiller praises the "abolition of equality of status" as the step that enabled man to leave the "tranquil nausea of his paradise" (112: 600–601). But the assumption of an original state of equality, and the explanation of the origin of inequality in terms of private property, remained unchallenged from Rousseau to Lorenz von Stein and Karl Marx.[7]

---

[7] Obviously these men's arguments were not as simple as this account may suggest. The most unambiguous emphasis on property as a cause of inequality is found in

For many writers between 1750 and 1850, and for their public, the explanation of inequality in terms of private property remained politically attractive. A society without private property is at least conceivable; and if the idea of equality is associated with this notion, the abolition of private property may become the supreme goal of political action. Indeed, it can be argued that two great revolutions have been abetted to no small extent by the association of inequality with private property, one by Rousseau's dream of reestablishing the original, natural equality of man, the other by Marx's dream of a communist society. Attractive as this explanation may be to some people, however, and though it represents an undeniable methodological advance over the Aristotelian argument, it does not stand the test of historical experience.

To be sure, private property was never completely abolished in the Soviet Union. Nevertheless, the disappointment of the Webbs and other Socialist visitors in the 1930's, caused by the evident inequalities of income and rank in the Soviet Union, may be taken as an experimental refutation of the thesis of Rousseau and Millar, Ferguson and Schiller, Stein and Marx. In the Soviet Union, in Yugoslavia, in Israel, and wherever else private property has been reduced to virtual insignificance, we still find social stratification. Even if such stratification is prevented for a short period from manifesting itself in differences of possessions and income (as in the *kibbutzim* of Israel), the undefinable yet effective force of prestige continues to create a noticeable rank order. If social inequality were

---

Rousseau, Millar, Stein, and Marx. Millar displays a nice historical concreteness on this point: "The invention of taming and pasturing cattle gives rise to a more remarkable and permanent distinction of ranks. Some persons, by being more industrious or more fortunate than others, are led in a short time to acquire more numerous herds and flocks." (109: 204.) Property here has a very definite sociological sense which becomes even clearer in Stein (118: 275): "Class formation is that process by which the distribution of property leads to a distribution of spiritual rights, goods, and functions among the individual members of society, such that the attributes of persistence and fixity are transferred from property to social position and function." This means that property both causes inequality and stabilizes it socially; as Ferguson aptly puts it, "Possessions descend, and the luster of family grows brighter with age." (102: 166.)

The other authors mentioned here do not give property quite the same prominence; in varying degrees they invoke the division of labor, the motive of conquest, and natural differences in rank between men. Rousseau and Marx are unrivaled in their radical insistence on property as the sole cause of social inequality.

really based on private property, the abolition of private property would have to result in the elimination of inequality. Experience in propertyless and quasi-propertyless societies does not confirm this proposition. We may therefore regard it as disproved.[8]

V

Stein and Marx are only marginal members of the group of writers who, by explaining the origin of stratification in terms of property, contributed to the emergence of sociology. Both Stein and Marx (and, to a lesser extent, Ferguson and several political economists of the late eighteenth century) mention a second factor in addition to property, one that came to dominate the discussion of the formation of classes, as our problem was now called, throughout the second half of the nineteenth century and the beginning of the twentieth. This factor was the division of labor.

As early as the 1870's Engels, in his *Anti-Dühring,* had developed a theory of class formation on the basis of the division of labor. The subsequent discussion, however, is associated preeminently with the name of Gustav Schmoller. It began with the famous controversy between Schmoller and Treitschke over Schmoller's essay on "The Social Question and the Prussian State"—a controversy that is of interest to us here because it raised once again the question of whether a sociological science was possible. Against Schmoller, Treitschke argued (one would be tempted to say a century too late, if this were not characteristic of the whole of German history) for a congruence of natural and social rank orders. Schmoller (with arguments often no less curious) tried to explain the formation of classes by the division of labor.

Schmoller's essays on "The Facts of the Division of Labor" and

8 The scientific significance of Communism can hardly be overestimated in this context, though it provides yet another example of the human cost of historical experiments. For almost two centuries, property dominated social and political thought: as a source of everything good or evil, as a principle to be retained or abolished. Today we know (though we do not yet have the most rigorous sort of proof) that the abolition of property merely replaces the old classes with new ones, so that from Locke to Lenin the social and political significance of property has been vastly overestimated.

"The Nature of the Division of Labor and the Formation of Classes," published in 1889 and 1890, prompted Karl Bücher's polemical Leipzig inaugural lecture of 1892 on "The Division of Labor and the Formation of Social Classes," which was later extended and modified in his book *The Emergence of Economy*. This in turn was attacked not only by Schmoller, but by Emile Durkheim in his *Division of Labor in Society*. Durkheim also discussed at some length Georg Simmel's "On Social Differentiation," which had appeared in 1890 in Schmoller's *Staatswissenschaftliche Forschungen*. Schmoller greeted Durkheim gladly in a review "as one striving to the same end, although he has not convinced us altogether," and continued to pursue the subject and his thesis. After Schmoller's death in 1917, however, both the subject and his view of it found few friends—only Pontus Fahlbeck and (with reservations) Franz Oppenheimer and Joseph Schumpeter come to mind—before they were forgotten, at which point, of course, the dispute remained unresolved.

Many of the issues that came up in the course of this prolonged debate cannot be discussed here, either because they lead us too far from our subject or because they are merely historical curiosities. Notable among the other issues was Simmel's and Durkheim's discussion of the relation between the division of labor and social integration.[9] Among the historical curiosities is Schmoller's theory of the genetics of special abilities acquired by the progressive division of labor. Bücher rightly attacked this theory repeatedly and

[9] For Simmel and Durkheim, and to some extent for Bücher and even Schmoller, the division of labor was the main concern, and class formation merely one of its aspects. There would certainly be a point in reexamining the origin of inequality of the differentiation type as well as inequality of the stratification type. The main question is whether the division of labor is based on the natural differences among men (between man and woman, adult and child, etc.), or whether it might be explained by purely social factors (such as technical development). As with stratification, one of the problems of the division of labor is whether it is a universal phenomenon, or a historically developed and therefore at least potentially ephemeral one (as Marx as well as Schmoller and Bücher believed). The consequences of the division of labor, too, require a reexamination that goes beyond Durkheim's at many points. I mention these problems to show that in confining ourselves to explanations of class formation by the division of labor, we are considering only a small segment of the sociological debate of the turn of the century.

violently, without succeeding in forcing out of Schmoller more than
very minor concessions. Yet Schmoller's position, especially in his
early papers of 1889 and 1890, contains elements of a theory of class
formation that has to be taken quite seriously, if only because in a
new (but not very different) form it seems to play a certain role in
contemporary sociology.

According to Schmoller's theory, class formation (that is, inequality of rank) is based on the fact that occupations are differentiated.
However one may wish to explain the division of labor itself—
Schmoller explains it in terms of the exchange principle, Bücher
in terms of property (and neither regards it as universal)—differentiation precedes the stratification of social positions. "The emergence of social classes always depends in the first instance on an
advance in the division of labor within a people or a nation."
(114: 74.) Or even more clearly: "The difference in social rank and
property, in prestige and income, is merely a secondary consequence
of social differentiation." (See 114: 29.)

Schmoller later modified his position without disavowing the
principles on which it rested (see 23: 428ff). It must be admitted,
however, that the crucial arguments against his views were not made
in the literature of the time. To state them, we must remember the
distinction between social differentiation and social stratification
introduced above.

Since we tend, particularly in modern society, to associate social
rank with occupational position, one might be led to suspect that
differences of rank are in fact based on the differentiation of occupations. On the contrary, it must be emphasized that the notion of
differentiation does not in itself imply any distinctions of rank or
value among the differentiated elements. From the point of view
of the division of labor (the "functional organization" of industrial
sociology), there is no difference in rank between the director, the
typist, the foreman, the pipe fitter, and the unskilled laborer of an
enterprise: these are all partial activities equally indispensable for
the attainment of the goal in question. If in fact we do associate a
rank order (or "scalar organization") with these activities, we do
so as an additional act of evaluation, one that is neither caused nor

explained by the division of labor; indeed, the same activities may be evaluated quite differently in different societies. What we have, then, is a rank order (i.e., a social stratification) of activities that in functional terms are merely differentiated in kind.[10]

Schmoller seems to have sensed this gap in his argument when, in later editions, he suddenly inserted a "psychological fact" between the division of labor and the formation of classes: "the need for human thought and feeling to bring all related phenomena of any kind into a sequence, and estimate and order them according to their value." (23: 428–29.) However factual this fact may be, that Schmoller felt compelled to introduce it serves as further evidence that social differentiation and social stratification cannot explain each other without some intermediate agency.

VI

This conclusion played an important part in the third major historical phase of sociological theorizing about the origin of inequality: the American discussion of the theory of social stratification. Since Talcott Parsons first published his "Analytical Approach to the Theory of Social Stratification" in 1940, there has been an unceasing debate over the so-called "functional" theory of social stratification. Almost all major American sociologists have taken part in this debate, which—unknown though it still is on the Continent—represents one of the more significant contributions of American sociology toward our understanding of social structures.

The chief immediate effect of Parsons's essay of 1940 was to acquaint American sociologists with the idea of a theory of social stratification. The largely conceptual paper published by Parsons's disciple Kingsley Davis in 1942 was also mainly preparatory in character. The discussion proper did not begin until 1945, when Davis and Wilbert E. Moore published "Some Principles of Stratification."

---

[10] One difficult question remains unresolved here: whether there are two different kinds of coordination of partial activities—one "functional," which merely follows "inherent necessities" and completes the division of labor, and one "scalar," which produces a rank order founded on other requirements.

Both Rousseau and his successors and Schmoller and his adherents had regarded inequality as a historical phenomenon. For both, since there had once been a period of equality, the elimination of inequality was conceivable. Davis and Moore, by contrast, saw inequality as a functional necessity in all human societies—i.e., as indispensable for the maintenance of any social structure whatever —and hence as impossible to eliminate.

Their argument, at least in its weaknesses, is not altogether dissimilar to Schmoller's. It runs as follows. There are in every society different social positions. These positions—e.g. occupations—are not equally pleasant, nor are they equally important or difficult. In order to guarantee the complete and frictionless allocation of all positions, certain rewards have to be associated with them—namely, the very rewards that constitute the criteria of social stratification. In all societies, the importance of different positions to the society and the market value of the required qualifications determine the unequal distribution of income, prestige, and power. Inequality is necessary because without it the differentiated (occupational) positions of societies cannot be adequately filled.

Several other writers, among them Marion J. Levy and Bernard Barber, have adopted this theory more or less without modification. But it has been subjected to severe criticism, and despite several thoughtful replies by the original authors, some of the criticisms seem to be gaining ground. The most persistent critic, Melvin M. Tumin, has presented two main arguments against Davis and Moore (in two essays published in 1953 and 1955). The first is that the notion of the "functional importance" of positions is extremely imprecise, and that it probably implies the very differentiation of value that it allegedly explains. The second is that two of the assumptions made by Davis and Moore—that of a harmonious congruence between stratification and the distribution of talent, and that of differential motivation by unequal incentives—are theoretically problematical and empirically uncertain.

This second argument was bolstered in 1955 by Richard Schwartz, whose analysis of two Israeli communities showed that it is in fact possible to fill positions adequately without an unequal distribution of social rewards (115). Buckley charged Davis and Moore in 1958 with confusing differentiation and stratification; unfortunately, however, his legitimate objection to the evaluative undertones of the notion of "functional importance" led in the end to an unpromising terminological dispute. Since then, criticism of the functional theory of stratification has taken two forms. Some critics have followed Dennis Wrong, who in 1959 took up Tumin's suggestion that Davis and Moore had underestimated the "dysfunctions" of social stratification, i.e., the disruptive consequences of social inequality (122); the conservative character of the functional theory has been emphasized even more clearly by Gerhard Lenski (107). Other critics have raised methodological objections, questioning the value of a discussion of sociological universals that ignores variations observed in the workings of real societies.[11]

But the significance of the American debate on stratification is only partly to be found in its subject matter. In this respect, its main conclusion would seem to be that social inequality has many functions and dysfunctions (that is, many consequences for the structure of societies), but that there can be no satisfactory functional explanation of the origin of inequality. This is because every such explanation is bound either to have recourse to dubious assumptions about human nature or to commit the *petitio principii* error of explanation in terms of the object to be explained. Yet this discussion, like its historical predecessors, has at several points produced valuable propositions, some of them mere remarks made in passing. With the help of these propositions, let us now attempt to formulate a theory of social stratification that is theoretically satisfactory and, above all, empirically fruitful.[12]

[11] The origin of inequality has been only one of several subjects of dispute in the American debate on stratification. Davis and Moore, for example, after their first few pages, turn to the empirical problems of the effect and variability of stratification. Their critics do much the same thing. But the dispute was ignited by the "functional explanation of inequality": its substantive justification, its scientific fruitfulness, and its political significance. The dispute, which still continues, may be seen as a commentary on the subterranean conflicts in American sociology.

[12] The concentration of my historical account of discussions of inequality on three epochs and positions—property in the eighteenth century, division of labor in the nineteenth, and function in the twentieth—rests on my conviction that these are the

166 ESSAYS IN THE THEORY OF SOCIETY

VII

The very first contribution to the American debate on stratification, the essay by Parsons, contained an idea which, although untenable in Parsons's form, may still advance our understanding of the problem. Parsons tries to derive the necessity of a differentiated rank order from the existence of the concept of evaluation and its significance for social systems. The effort to formulate an ontological proof of stratification is more surprising than convincing—as Parsons himself seems to have felt, for in the revised version of his essay, published in 1953, he relates the existence of a concept of evaluation to the mere probability, not the necessity, of inequality.[13] In fact, Parsons's thesis contains little more than the suggestion, formulated much more simply by Barber, that men tend to evaluate themselves and the things of their world differently (26: 2). This suggestion in turn refers back to Schmoller's "psychological assumption" of a human tendency to produce evaluative rank orders, but it also refers—and here the relation between evaluation and stratification begins to be sociologically relevant—to Durkheim's famous proposition that "every society is a moral community." Durkheim rightly remarks that "the state of nature of the eighteenth-century philosophers is, if not immoral, at least amoral" (100: 394). The idea of the social contract is nothing but the idea

most important stages in the discussion of the subject. But historically this account involves some questionable simplifications. As early as 1922, Fahlbeck (101: 13–15) distinguished four explanations of inequality: (1) "differences in estate are exclusively the work of war and conquest in large things, force and perfidy in little ones"; (2) "in property and its differential distribution" can be found "the real reason for all social differences"; (3) "the origin and raison d'être of classes" can be traced to "the connections with the general economic factors of nature, capital, and labor"; and (4) "classes are a fruit of the division of labor." (Fahlbeck favors the last.) To these we should have to add at least the natural-differences explanation and the functional explanation. All six notions found support, at times side by side in the same works, and all six would have to be taken into account in a reasonably complete historical account of the problem. It is another question whether such an account would advance our knowledge.

13 Parsons 1940 (110: 843): "If both human individuals as units and moral evaluation are essential to social systems, it follows that these individuals *will be* evaluated as units." And 1953 (96: 387): "Given the process of evaluation, *the probability is* that it will serve to differentiate entities in a rank order of some kind." (My emphases.) In both cases, as so often at those points of Parsons's work where classification is less important than conceptual imagination and rigor of statement, his argument is remarkably weak.

of the institution of compulsory social norms backed by sanctions. It is at this point that the possibility arises of connecting the concept of human society with the problem of the origin of inequality —a possibility that is occasionally hinted at in the literature but that has so far gone unrealized.[14]

Human society always means that people's behavior is being removed from the randomness of chance and regulated by established and inescapable expectations. The compulsory character of these expectations or norms[15] is based on the operation of sanctions, i.e., of rewards or punishments for conformist or deviant behavior. If every society is in this sense a moral community, it follows that there must always be at least that inequality of rank which results from the necessity of sanctioning behavior according to whether it does or does not conform to established norms. Under whatever aspect given historical societies may introduce additional distinctions between their members, whatever symbols they may declare to be outward signs of inequality, and whatever may be the precise content of their social norms, the hard core of social inequality can always be found in the fact that men as the incumbents of social roles are subject, according to how their roles relate to the dominant expectational principles of society, to sanctions designed to enforce these principles.[16]

[14] An attempt in this direction has recently been made by Lenski, but his approach and the one offered here differ significantly in their para-theoretical and methodological presuppositions.

[15] Since expectations, as constituent parts of roles, are always related to concrete social positions, whereas norms are general in their formulation and their claim to validity, the "or" in the phrase "expectations or norms" may at first seem misleading. Actually, this is just a compressed way of expressing the idea that role expectations are nothing but concretized social norms ("institutions").

[16] A similar idea may be found at one point in the American discussion of stratification—as distinguished, perhaps, from Othmar Spann's biology-based argument (117: 293), "The law of stratification of society is the ordering of value strata," which might seem superficially similar—in a passing remark by Tumin (119: 392). "What does seem to be unavoidable," Tumin says, "is that differential prestige shall be given to those in any society who conform to the normative order as against those who deviate from that order in a way judged immoral and detrimental. On the assumption that the continuity of a society depends on the continuity and stability of its normative order, some such distinction between conformists and deviants seems inescapable." It seems to me that the assumption of a "continuity and stability of the normative order" is quite superfluous; it shows how closely Tumin remains tied to the functional approach.

Let me try to illustrate what I mean by some examples which, however difficult they may seem, are equally relevant. If the ladies of a neighborhood are expected to exchange secrets and scandals with their neighbors, this norm will lead at the very least to a distinction between those held in high regard (who really enjoy gossip, and offer tea and cakes as well), those with average prestige, and the outsiders (who, for whatever reasons, take no part in the gossiping). If, in a factory, high individual output is expected from the workers and rewarded by piecework rates, there will be some who take home a relatively high paycheck and others who take home a relatively low one. If the citizens (or better, perhaps, subjects) of a state are expected to defend its official ideology as frequently and convincingly as possible, this will lead to a distinction between those who get ahead (becoming, say, civil servants or party secretaries); the mere followers, who lead a quiet but somewhat anxious existence; and those who pay with their liberty or even their lives for their deviant behavior.

One might think that individual, not social, inequalities are in fact established by the distinction between those who for essentially personal reasons (as we must initially assume, and have assumed in the examples) are either unprepared for or incapable of conformism and those who punctiliously fulfill every norm. For example, social stratification is always a rank order in terms of prestige and not esteem, i.e., a rank order of positions (worker, woman, resident of a certain area, etc.), which can be thought of independently of their individual incumbents. By contrast, attitudes toward norms as governed by sanctions seem to be attitudes of individuals. There might therefore seem to be a link missing between the sanctioning of individual behavior and the inequality of social positions. This missing link is, however, contained in the notion of social norm as we have used it so far.

It appears plausible to assume that the number of values capable of regulating human behavior is unlimited. Our imagination permits the construction of an infinite number of customs and laws. Norms, i.e., socially established values, are therefore always a selection from the universe of possible established values. At this point, however, we should remember that the selection of norms always involves discrimination, not only against persons holding sociologically random moral convictions, but also against social positions that may debar their incumbents from conformity with established values.

Thus if gossip among neighbors becomes a norm, the professional woman necessarily becomes an outsider who cannot compete in prestige with ordinary housewives. If piecework rates are in force in a factory, the older worker is at a disadvantage by comparison with the younger ones, the woman by comparison with men. If it becomes the duty of the citizen to defend the ideology of the state, those who went to school before the establishment of this state cannot compete with those born into it. Professional woman, old man, young man, and child of a given state are all social positions, which may be thought of independently of their individual human incumbents. Since every society discriminates in this sense against certain positions (and thereby all their incumbents, actual and potential), and since, moreover, every society uses sanctions to make such discrimination effective, social norms and sanctions are the basis not only of ephemeral individual rankings but also of lasting structures of social positions.

The origin of inequality is thus to be found in the existence in all human societies of norms of behavior to which sanctions are attached. What we normally call the law, i.e., the system of laws and penalties, does not in ordinary usage comprise the whole range of the sociological notions of norm and sanction. If, however, we take the law in its broadest sense as the epitome of all norms and sanctions, including those not codified, we may say that the law is both a necessary and a sufficient condition of social inequality. There is inequality because there is law; if there is law, there must also be inequality among men.

This is, of course, equally true in societies where equality before the law is recognized as a constitutional principle. If I may be allowed a somewhat flippant formulation, which is nevertheless seriously meant, my proposed explanation of inequality means in the case of our own society that all men are equal *before* the law but they are no longer equal *after* it: i.e., after they have, as we put it, "come in contact with" the law. So long as norms do not exist, and insofar as they do not effectively act on people ("before the law"), there is no social stratification; once there are norms that impose inescapable requirements on people's behavior and once their actual behavior is measured in terms of these norms ("after the law"), a rank order of social status is bound to emerge.

Important though it is to emphasize that by norms and sanctions we also mean laws and penalties in the sense of positive law, the introduction of the legal system as an illustrative *pars pro toto* can itself be very misleading. Ordinarily, it is only the idea of punishment that we associate with legal norms as the guarantee of their compulsory character.[17] The force of legal sanctions produces the distinction between the lawbreaker and those who succeed in never coming into conflict with any legal rule. Conformism in this sense is at best rewarded with the absence of penalties. Certainly, this crude division between "conformists" and "deviants" constitutes an element of social inequality, and it should be possible in principle to use legal norms to demonstrate the relation between legal sanctions and social stratification. But an argument along these lines would limit both concepts—sanction and stratification—to a rather feeble residual meaning.

It is by no means necessary (although customary in ordinary language) to conceive of sanctions solely as penalties. For the present argument, at least, it is important to recognize positive sanctions (rewards) as both equal in kind and similar in function to negative sanctions (punishments). Only if we regard reward and punishment, incentive and threat, as related instruments for maintaining social norms do we begin to see that applying social norms to human behavior in the form of sanctions necessarily creates a system of inequality of rank, and that social stratification is therefore an

---

[17] Possibly this is a vulgar interpretation of the law, in the sense that legal norms (which are after all only a special case of social norms) probably have their validity guaranteed by positive as well as negative sanctions. It may be suspected, however, that negative sanctions are preponderant to the extent to which norms are compulsory—and since most legal norms (almost by definition) are compulsory to a particularly great extent, behavior conforming to legal norms is generally not rewarded.

immediate result of the control of social behavior by positive and negative sanctions. Apart from their immediate task of enforcing the normative patterns of social behavior, sanctions always create, almost as a by-product, a rank order of distributive status, whether this is measured in terms of prestige, or wealth, or both.

The presuppositions of this explanation are obvious. Using eighteenth-century concepts, one might describe them in terms of the social contract (*pacte d'association*) and the contract of government (*pacte de gouvernement*). The explanation sketched here presupposes (1) that every society is a moral community, and therefore recognizes norms that regulate the conduct of its members; (2) that these norms require sanctions to enforce them by rewarding conformity and penalizing deviance.

It may perhaps be argued that by relating social stratification to these presuppositions we have not solved our problem but relegated its solution to a different level. Indeed, it might seem necessary from both a philosophical and a sociological point of view to ask some further questions. Where do the norms that regulate social behavior come from? Under what conditions do these norms change in historical societies? Why must their compulsory character be enforced by sanctions? Is this in fact the case in all historical societies? I think, however, that whatever the answers to these questions may be, it has been helpful to reduce social stratification to the existence of social norms backed by sanctions, since this explanation shows the derivative nature of the problem of inequality. In addition, the derivation suggested here has the advantage of leading back to presuppositions (the existence of norms and the necessity of sanctions) that may be regarded as axiomatic, at least in the context of sociological theory, and therefore do not require further analysis for the time being.

To sum up, the origin of social inequality lies neither in human nature nor in a historically dubious conception of private property. It lies rather in certain features of all human societies, which are (or can be seen as) necessary to them. Although the differentiation of social positions—the division of labor, or more generally the multiplicity of roles—may be one such universal feature of all societies, it lacks the element of evaluation necessary to explain distinctions of rank. Evaluative differentiation, the ordering of social positions and their incumbent scales of prestige or income, is effected only by the sanctioning of social behavior in terms of normative expectations. Because there are norms and because sanctions are necessary to enforce conformity of human conduct, there has to be inequality of rank among men.

VIII

Social stratification is a very real element of our everyday lives, much more so than this highly abstract and indeed seemingly inconsequential discussion would suggest. It is necessary, then, to make clear the empirical relevance of these reflections, or at least to indicate what follows from this kind of analysis for our knowledge of society. Such a clarification is all the more necessary since the preceding discussion is informed, however remotely, by a view of sociology as an empirical science, a science in which observation can decide the truth or falsity of statements. What, then, do our considerations imply for sociological analysis?

First, let us consider its conceptual implications. Social stratification, as I have used the term, is above all a system of distributive status, i.e., a system of differential distribution of desired and scarce things. Honor and wealth, or, as we say today, prestige and income, may be the most general means of effecting such a differentiation of rank, but there is no reason to assume that it could not be effected by entirely different criteria.[18] As far as legitimate power is concerned, however, it has only one aspect that can be seen as affecting social stratification, namely patronage, or the distribution of power as a reward for certain deeds or virtues. Thus to explain differences of rank in terms of the necessity of sanctions is not to explain the power structure of societies;[19] it is rather to explain stratification in

[18] Honor and wealth (or prestige and income) are general in the sense that they epitomize the ideal and the material differences in rank among men.

[19] Thus the theory advanced here does not explain the origin of power and of inequalities in the distribution of power. That the origin of power also requires explanation, at least in a para-theoretical context, is evident from the discussion of the

terms of the social structure of power and authority (using these terms to express Weber's distinction between *Macht* and *Herrschaft*). If the explanation of inequality offered here is correct, power and power structures logically precede the structures of social stratification.[20]

It is hard to imagine a society whose system of norms and sanctions functions without an authority structure to sustain it. Time and again, anthropologists have told us of "tribes without rulers," and sociologists of societies that regulate themselves without power or authority. But in opposition to such fantasies, I incline with Weber to describe "every order that is not based on the personal, free agreement of all involved" (i.e., every order that does not rest on the voluntary consensus of all its members) as "imposed," i.e., based on authority and subordination (121: xiii, 27). Since a *volonté de tous* seems possible only in flights of fancy, we have to assume that a third fundamental category of sociological analysis belongs alongside the two concepts of norm and sanction: that of institutionalized power. Society *means* that norms regulate human conduct; this regulation is guaranteed by the incentive or threat of sanctions; the possibility of imposing sanctions is the abstract core of all power.

---

universality of historicity of power (see below). What an explanation of inequalities of power might look like is hard to say; Heinrich Popitz suggests that the social corollaries of the succession of generations are responsible for such inequalities.

20 This conclusion implies a substantial revision of my previously published views. For a long time I was convinced that there was a strict logical equivalence between the analysis of social classes and constraint theory, and between the analysis of social stratification and integration theory. The considerations developed in the present essay changed my mind. I have now come to believe that stratification is merely a consequence of the structure of power, integration a special case of constraint, and thus the structural-functional approach a subset of a broader approach. The assumption that constraint theory and integration theory are two approaches of equal rank, i.e., two different perspectives on the same material, is not so much false as superfluous; we get the same result by assuming that stratification follows from power, integration from constraint, stability from change. Since the latter assumption is the simpler one, it is to be preferred.

This conclusion may also be seen as opposing the "synthesis" of "conservative" and "radical" theories of stratification proposed by Lenski (108). It seems to me that this synthesis is in fact merely a superficial compromise, which is superseded at important points by Lenski himself: "The distribution of rewards in a society is a function of the distribution of power, not of system needs." (108: 63.)

I am inclined to believe that all other categories of sociological analysis may be derived from the unequal but closely related trinity of norm, sanction, and power.[21] At any rate, this is true of social stratification, which therefore belongs on a lower level of generality than power. To reveal the explosiveness of this analysis we need only turn it into an empirical proposition: the system of inequality that we call social stratification is only a secondary consequence of the social structure of power.

The establishment of norms in a society means that conformity is rewarded and deviance punished. The sanctioning of conformity and deviance in this sense means that the ruling groups of society have thrown their power behind the maintenance of norms. In the last analysis, established norms are nothing but ruling norms, i.e., norms defended by the sanctioning agencies of society and those who control them. This means that the person who will be most favorably placed in society is the person who best succeeds in adapting himself to the ruling norms; conversely, it means that the established or ruling values of a society may be studied in their purest form by looking at its upper class. Anyone whose place in the coordinate system of social positions and roles makes him unable to conform punctiliously to his society's expectations must not be surprised if the higher grades of prestige and income remain closed to him and go to others who find it easier to conform. In this sense, every society honors the conformity that sustains it, i.e., sustains its ruling groups; but by the same token every society also produces within itself the resistance that brings it down.

Naturally, the basic equating of conformist or deviant behavior with high or low status is deflected and complicated in historical

21 This is a large claim, which would justify at least an essay of its own. For our present purposes only two remarks need be added. First, the three categories are obviously disparate. Sanction is primarily a kind of intermediate concept (between norm and power), although as such it is quite decisive. Norm has to be understood as anterior to power, just as the social contract is anterior to the contract of government (this may help as a standard of orientation). Second, we must ask whether the "elementary category" of social role can also be derived from the trinity norm-sanction-power. I tend to think it can, at least insofar as roles are complexes of norms concretized into expectations. Beyond that, however, the question is open.

societies by many secondary factors. (In general, it must be emphasized that the explanation of inequality proposed here has no immediate extension to the history of inequality or the philosophy behind it.) Among other things, the ascriptive character of the criteria determining social status in a given epoch (such as nobility or property) may bring about a kind of stratification lag: that is, status structures may lag behind changes in norms and power relations, so that the upper class of a bygone epoch may retain its status position for a while under new conditions. Yet normally we do not have to wait long for such processes as the *"déclassement* of the nobility" or the "loss of function of property" which have occurred in several contemporary societies.

There are good reasons to think that our own society is tending toward a period of "meritocracy" as predicted by Michael Young, i.e., rule by the possessors of diplomas and other tickets of admission to the upper reaches of society issued by the educational system. If this is so, the hypothesis of stratification lag would suggest that in due course the members of the traditional upper strata (the nobility, the inheritors of wealth and property) will have to bestir themselves to obtain diplomas and academic titles in order to keep their position; for the ruling groups of every society have a tendency to try to adapt the existing system of social inequality to the established norms and values, i.e., their own. Nevertheless, despite this basic tendency we can never expect historical societies to exhibit full congruence between the scales of stratification and the structures of power.[22]

IX

The image of society that follows from this exceedingly general and abstract analysis is in two respects non-utopian and thereby

[22] The variability of historical patterns of stratification is so great that any abstract and general analysis of the kind offered here is bound to mislead. The criteria, forms, and symbols of stratification vary, as does their meaning for human behavior, and in every historical epoch we find manifold superimpositions. The question of what form stratification took in the earliest known societies is entirely open. This is but one of the many limitations of the present analysis.

anti-utopian as well.[23] On the one hand, it has none of the explicit or concealed romanticism of a revolutionary utopia à la Rousseau or Marx. If it is true that inequalities among men follow from the very concept of societies as moral communities, then there cannot be, in the world of our experience, a society of absolute equals. Of course, equality before the law, equal suffrage, equal chances of education, and other concrete equalities are not only possible but in many countries real. But the idea of a society in which all distinctions of rank between men are abolished transcends what is sociologically possible and has a place only in the sphere of poetic imagination. Wherever political programs promise societies without class or strata, a harmonious community of comrades who are all equals in rank, the reduction of all inequalities to functional differences, and the like, we have reason to be suspicious, if only because political promises are often merely a thin veil for the threat of terror and constraint. Wherever ruling groups or their ideologists try to tell us that in their society all men are equal, we can rely on George Orwell's suspicion that "some are more equal than others."

The approach put forward here is in yet another sense a path out of utopia. If we survey the explanations of inequality in recent American sociology—and this holds for Parsons and Barber as it does for Davis and Moore—we find that they betray a view of society from which there is no road leading to an understanding of the historical quality of social structures. In a less obvious sense this is also true, I think, of Rousseau and Marx; but it is more easily demonstrable by reference to recent sociological theory.[24] The American functionalists tell us that we ought to look at societies as entities functioning without friction, and that inequality among men

[23] The following para-theoretical discussion is *inter alia* a criticism of Lenski's oversimple dichotomy between "conservative" and "radical" theories of stratification. Our approach is "radical" in assuming the dominant force of power structures, but "conservative" in its suspicion that the unequal distribution of power and status cannot be abolished. Other combinations are conceivable.

[24] The assumption that history follows a predetermined and recognizable plan is static, at least in the sense in which the development of an organism into an entelechy lacks the historical dimension of openness into the future. For this reason, and because of the static-utopian notion of an ultimate state necessarily connected with such a conception, a lack of historicity might also be imputed to Rousseau and Marx.

(since it happens to exist) abets this functioning. This point of view, however useful in other ways, may then lead to conclusions like the following by Barber: "Men have a sense of justice fulfilled and of virtue rewarded when they feel that they are fairly ranked as superior and inferior by the value standards of their own moral community." (98: 7.) Even Barber's subsequent treatment of the "dysfunctions" of stratification cannot wipe out the impression that the society he is thinking of does not need history anymore because everything has been settled in the best possible way already: everybody, wherever he stands, is content with his place in society, and a common value system unites all men in a big, happy family.

It seems to me that whereas an instrument of this kind may enable us to understand Plato's Republic, it does not describe any real society in history. Possibly social inequality has some importance for the integration of societies. But another consequence of its operation seems rather more interesting. If the analysis proposed here proves useful, inequality is closely related to the social constraint that grows out of sanctions and structures of power. This would mean that the system of stratification, like sanctions and structures of institutionalized power, always tends to its own abolition. The assumption that those who are less favorably placed in society will strive to impose a system of norms that promises them a better rank is certainly more plausible and fruitful than the assumption that the poor in reputation and wealth will love their society for its justice.

Since the "value system" of a society is universal only in the sense that it applies to everyone (it is in fact merely dominant), and since, therefore, the system of social stratification is only a measure of conformity in the behavior of social groups, inequality becomes the dynamic impulse that serves to keep social structures alive. Inequality always implies the gain of one group at the expense of others; thus every system of social stratification generates protest against its principles and bears the seeds of its own suppression. Since human society without inequality is not realistically possible and the complete abolition of inequality is therefore ruled out, the intrinsic explosiveness of every system of social stratification confirms the general view that there cannot be an ideal, perfectly just, and therefore non-historical human society.

This is the place to recall once again Kant's critical rejoinder to Rousseau, that inequality is a "rich source of much that is evil, but also of everything that is good." There is certainly reason to regret that children are ashamed of their parents, that people are anxious and poor, that they suffer and are made unhappy, and many other consequences of inequality. There are also many good reasons to strive against the historical and therefore, in an ultimate sense, arbitrary forces that erect insuperable barriers of caste or estate between men. The very existence of social inequality, however, is an impetus toward liberty because it guarantees a society's ongoing, dynamic, historical quality. The idea of a perfectly egalitarian society is not only unrealistic; it is terrible. Utopia is not the home of freedom, the forever imperfect scheme for an uncertain future; it is the home of total terror or absolute boredom.[25]

---

[25] These last paragraphs contain in highly abridged form—and in part imply—two arguments. One is that the attempt to realize a utopia, i.e., a society beyond concrete realization, must lead to totalitarianism, because only by terror can the appearance of paradise gained (of the classless society, the people's community) be created. The other is that within certain limits defined by the equality of citizenship, inequalities of social status, considered as a medium of human development, are a condition of a free society.

7

Liberty and Equality
Reflections of a Sociologist on a Classical Theme of Politics

> A proposal to solve all problems and answer all questions would
> be such a piece of boastful impertinence, such an extravagant
> conceit, that its author would immediately forfeit all claim to
> our trust.
>
> *Kant*

At one point in *Reason and Faith in Modern Society,* Eduard Heimann raises the old problem of the compatibility of liberty and
equality in the political community. "Everything," he asserts, "in
the institutions of democracy hinges on the reconciliation of liberty
and equality." Heimann contrasts this position of his with the record of what he calls "rationalist development," which, he says, has
torn "the two halves of democracy" asunder and placed them "at
opposite extremes of its fateful dialectics." He sees both varieties of
"social rationalism"—namely, liberalism or individualism, and
Marxism or Communism—as having failed, the first by developing
liberty at the expense of equality, the second by enforcing equality
at the expense of liberty. Thus, both have departed from that
"vision of democracy" which Heimann tries to derive from man's
prerational memory or "religious inheritance," where in his view
the supposedly opposite values of liberty and equality are reconciled (124: 233). For Heimann, the alternatives of liberal freedom
without equality and total equality without freedom serve as a
backdrop for his own essentially Christian conception of a society
that is both liberal and egalitarian.

Between the two poles of liberalism and Marxism as characterized by Heimann, however, there exists a considerable body of political theory which is neither unequivocally "liberalist" nor unequivocally Marxist, and which endeavors to reconcile liberty and
equality within the framework of what might be called a "rational

autonomy." Harold Laski, for example—a socialist, but no Marxist; a liberal, but no liberalist—believes that equality "properly understood" is quite compatible with the freedom of men in society, and indeed that it is necessary to such freedom. In his *Grammar of Politics* Laski develops a syllogistic argument. "Liberty," he says, "means absence of restraint." And "equality . . . means first of all the absence of special privilege." (127: 147, 153.) Since, however, "special privilege" amounts to a "restraint" on those who do not enjoy it, inequality and liberty are incompatible; indeed (Laski does not say this explicitly, but it follows from his argument), equality is a component of liberty. Liberty and equality are thus "reconciled" in a rational conception of the good society.

Laski goes on to deplore the views of earlier thinkers who in his opinion mistakenly regarded liberty and equality as "antithetic things," notably Tocqueville and Lord Acton (127: 152). But Tocqueville, at least, can by no means be placed unambiguously among Laski's opponents. To be sure, Tocqueville emphasizes the possibility of tension between liberty and equality, but he stresses at the same time the chances of reconciling them. "There is in fact a manly and lawful passion for equality that incites men to wish all to be powerful and honored. This passion tends to raise the humble to the rank of the great; but there exists also in the human heart a depraved taste for equality which impels the weak to attempt to lower the powerful to their own level and reduces men to preferring equality in slavery to inequality with freedom." (135: 39–40.) Unlike Laski and Heimann, then, Tocqueville sees no necessary relation between liberty and equality; whether they are reconciled or not depends on a *tertium,* which Tocqueville seeks somewhat vaguely in the "historical circumstances" of a people, their "origin," their "intelligence," and especially their "morals." But that liberty and equality can be reconciled Tocqueville documents impressively by the example of American society in his time.

One could go on with the game of tracing the question of liberty and equality back into history. For example, Tocqueville's description of the United States as both "democratic" (egalitarian) and free was an indirect criticism of the France of the French Revolu tion—i.e., of a doctrine that regarded liberty and equality as not only compatible, but necessarily associated. Going on with the game would lead not to a *reductio ad absurdum,* but to a *reductio ad Aristotelem*; for it is with Aristotle that we find the relationship between liberty and equality first posed as a problem, and also first asserted as a contradiction. But we are not concerned here with the history of the problem. Rather, I have cited these conflicting ideas and viewpoints by way of background for a more fundamental question: How can the true relationship between liberty and equality be determined? Although Heimann and Laski, Tocqueville and the revolutionaries of 1789, would agree that liberty and equality are compatible, on other matters their notions of the good society differ greatly. Unless we are content with declaring arbitrarily that one is right and the other wrong, we must start with some less exciting but perhaps more promising questions. How can one demonstrate differences of viewpoint in apparently identical statements? How are we to understand these differences? How can we decide whether liberty and equality are compatible or incompatible values?

The statements "Liberty and equality are compatible" and "Liberty and equality are incompatible" are in themselves remarkably imprecise. They bear a certain resemblance to statements like "$x \times y = z$, where z is an even number" and "$x \times y = z$, where z is an odd number." Obviously these statements in themselves are neither true nor untrue. If x, or y, or both are even numbers, the first equation is correct; if both x and y are odd numbers, the second one is correct. But for us both x and y are unknowns. All we can say is that either equation *may* be correct. Similarly, whether liberty and equality are or are not compatible depends on what one means by liberty and equality. Yet this commonplace assertion is important. It may be taken as a challenge to begin with the most naïve possible definitions of our terms, definitions shorn so far as possible of their customary content and connotations, while at the same time remaining within the exacting framework of arguable statements and testable assumptions.

It would certainly be possible to proceed differently. Today conceptual nominalism is so widely accepted that we are inclined to grant every author his own "definitions," thereby so alienating thought from its objects that any statement, however inconsequential by any outside standards, is adjudged valid if it complies with its author's standards of validity. To apply this observation to the authors quoted above, one cannot say that they discuss the compatibility of liberty and equality purely as such, i.e., as unknowns. I have already quoted Laski's definitions. Heimann's concern is with the liberty and equality of men "as God's children"; he has examined the consequences of this notion for the economic and social order in several of his works. For Tocqueville, equality is equality of opportunity (*égalité des conditions*), an idea whose fame owes much to his work and to which we shall return; liberty is the opposite of slavery, of subjection to others. Any of these men's views might be isolated and examined for its logical consistency. But instead I intend to break through the circle of what is often wrongly praised as "immanent criticism," and to question not the compatibility of liberty and equality "according to Heimann," "according to Laski," or "according to Tocqueville," but their compatibility as such.

Does this intention make sense? Does it not presuppose a conceptual realism in which liberty and equality figure as fixed, unchangeable quantities that may be identified as such? I think not. There is at least one way to avoid both the pitfalls of metaphysics and the relativism of arbitrary definitions. To return to the metaphor of an equation with several unknowns: if we do not know x and y but nevertheless want to say something about z's likelihood of being odd or even, we can dissolve x into its possible values $x_1, x_2, \ldots, x_n$ and $y_1, y_2, \ldots, y_n$ and see which of the possible x and y combinations make z even and which odd. In the following pages I shall try to apply this procedure to the problem of the compatibility of liberty and equality. Thus we must ask which of the possible meanings of liberty is compatible or incompatible with which of the possible meanings of equality. Since this is obviously too bold an enterprise—who could claim to know all the possible meanings of liberty and equality?—we shall, more precisely, try to contrast some of the important meanings of the two concepts in order to prepare the way for a more definite understanding of the problem.

II

That liberty always means the absence of restraint and force seems clear from the very etymology of the word "freedom." At least one root of the word, and of its German equivalent, *Freiheit*, leads us back (as the etymological dictionary tells us) to the Gothic word *freihals* and the Old and Middle High German word *frihals:* whereas slaves had to wear a ring around their throat (*Hals*), their masters had a "free throat"; they were thus "free men" (cf. 126). In the course of history, the ring around the throat of the slave may have turned from an instrument of force into a symbol of status; in any case it represents a restriction to which the free-throated, i.e. the free, are not subjected. Thus freedom in at least one of its meanings implies an absence of restrictions on human behavior, a freedom from constraint of any kind.

Although the example of the slave's throat ring may help to explain this meaning of liberty, its very concreteness makes it misleading. For we must go on to ask which particular restrictions and constraints must be absent for men to be free. It may be obvious that slavery and serfdom, the physical dependence of one man on another, are conditions of unfreedom, but what about men's dependence on food, clothing, shelter, and physical safety? The arbitrary operations of a secret police are easily recognized as a sign of unfreedom, but what about the unrecognized and thus possibly arbitrary operation of divine forces through the instrumentality of man? Is an ascetic life a necessary element of freedom understood as the absence of constraint, and in particular is free will such an element? In philosophical and theological contexts it is undeniably important to decide these questions; but fortunately they do not concern the freedom of men in society. From the point of view taken here, there are certain constraints from which no one is free, and which may therefore be regarded simply as "data" or constants: man's possibly unfree will, his bodily nature and its consequences,

and indeed the fact that man is a social being and as such necessarily exposed to alien controls and sanctions. On the other hand,
there are certain constraints that are more strictly of human making and do not hold in the same manner for all times: slavery and
serfdom, economic dependence, political terrorism, censorship, the
suppression of parties and unions, and many others. With respect
to society, then, freedom from constraint can only mean freedom
from such restrictions as do not stem from human nature itself with
universally binding force.

Clearly this definition, too, is far from adequate. What is to be
attributed to human nature and what to social structure is a question that has been answered very differently at different times by
different men. We shall return to it later, in our discussion of the
natural equality of rank.

In recent times in particular, many writers have emphasized that
it is not sufficient to define human freedom as a "freedom from"
this or that, i.e., as a "merely negative" value; rather, it should be
understood primarily as "freedom to," as a "positive" value. And
indeed, in the history of political theory, there is scarcely a single
negative definition of liberty that is not accompanied by certain
positive notions. Moreover, these positive notions are characterized
by a remarkable degree of at least formal agreement, notably on the
importance of the self-fulfillment of man in society, i.e., of liberty
as freedom for human development. Marx's view of "personal liberty" as a state in which "every individual has the means to develop
[all] his endowments in all directions" (129: 64) would be as acceptable to Aristotle as to modern Christian thinkers, to Thomas Aquinas as to the Neoliberals, to Kant as to Hegel. At least in the formal
sense, the Christian Socialist Heimann ("For we have learned that
man has been created in the image of his creator, i.e. creative, able
to add to God's creation. Creativity is the highest revelation of liberty; man is free because he is creative" [124: 215]) and the rational
socialist Laski ("By liberty I mean the eager maintenance of that
atmosphere in which men have the opportunity to be their best
selves" [127: 142]) meet in defining liberty as self-fulfillment. All
this is hardly surprising, for the so-called positive definition of liberty is nothing more than the other side of its "negative" definition

as the absence of constraint. What can the "absence of constraint" mean if not the freedom to behave in accordance with one's inner nature, and by so doing to fulfill oneself? Freedom from society-imposed constraints and freedom for self-fulfillment are simply two ways of expressing the same idea. The effort to contrast them rests on a misunderstanding.

The assertion that most political thinkers agree in their "positive" concept of liberty may sound like a crude simplification, even if we limit ourselves to the statements and authors quoted. It is in fact a simplification, but it seems to me a permissible one. Our formal analysis makes it clear that there is a view of human nature behind every view of liberty. Aristotle's *vita contemplativa,* Kant's "guiding thread of reason" as the "natural endowment" of man, Marx's "objectivization," Laski's "best self," and Heimann's "creativity" are obviously not the same thing. The meaning of self-fulfillment has been defined in many different ways by different people at different times. But we may ignore these differences so long as we merely want to consider liberty in its possible relations to equality. For a discussion of this kind it is sufficient to understand self-fulfillment, whatever its particular character, as the reverse side of the absence of arbitrary constraint.

Our equating of the "negative" and "positive" definitions of liberty holds only on the condition that liberty is understood simply as a chance, an opportunity, for self-fulfillment. The absence of arbitrary constraints makes self-fulfillment possible; it says nothing about man's capacity for making use of the chance offered him. According to this concept, which I shall call the *problematic* concept of liberty, liberty prevails in a society that frees man from all restrictions not attributable to his nature; liberty is thus the possibility of self-fulfillment in definable conditions. Most of the writers quoted (and most of those not quoted) incline toward this concept of liberty. Nevertheless, there is a second concept, clearly distinct from the first, which I shall call the *assertoric* concept of liberty. According to this second concept, liberty exists only where men in fact take advantage of the opportunity for self-fulfillment, where self-fulfillment is demonstrably an aspect of their behavior.

The difference between problematic and assertoric liberty may be illustrated by the problem of leisure in modern society. Marx considered shorter working hours essential to "the true realm of freedom" (45: 874). The necessity of working for the wherewithal to satisfy material needs is undoubtedly a constraint that is susceptible, if not to abolition, at least to mitigation; and it is therefore an arbitrary constraint, at least to the extent that mitigation is possible. Leisure and liberty are thus terms that certainly belong together. Indeed, according to the problematic concept, liberty and leisure coincide, since both are defined as the absence of constraint and the chance for self-fulfillment. According to the assertoric concept, by contrast, leisure means not the fact of liberty but its mere possibility; liberty itself exists only if leisure time is actually used for the purpose of self-fulfillment. In the assertoric sense liberty is not a setting, but a mode of human existence; it exists only in specific realities of behavior. Whereas liberty in the problematic sense exists wherever and whenever, in Laski's words, "men have the opportunity to be their best selves," liberty in the assertoric sense exists only where and when men really use this opportunity. "Man is free because he is creative," Heimann says. If we rephrased this statement to accord with the assertoric sense (and possibly with what Heimann meant), it would read "man is free *when* he is creative." It follows from the assertoric concept that we cannot say of anyone at every minute of his existence that he is free; it follows above all that we cannot say that any society is free. There is such a thing as a "free society" only in the problematic sense of liberty; in the assertoric sense, society can at best make liberty possible.

The distinction between these two concepts of liberty is of more than philosophical interest. It involves the far more significant distinction between two views of politics: one that sees politics exclusively as an instrument of institutional change, and another that sees the range of social organization accessible to politics as extending beyond institutions. It follows from the problematic concept of liberty that the only task of politics is to abolish all constraints on liberty; that men will then actively seek self-fulfillment is either assumed as a matter of course or excluded from consideration as irrelevant to public policy. From this point of view, the reduction of working hours is a proper concern of politics, but beyond that the individual is left to his own resources. According to the assertoric concept of liberty, by contrast, the concerns of politics extend to the matter of how the chance for self-fulfillment is used. The reduction of working hours thus becomes a necessary, but not a sufficient, goal of liberal politics. In this way, the seemingly minor distinction between two concepts of liberty reveals a political choice of considerable consequence.[1]

Are there other concepts of liberty besides the problematic and the assertoric? The question is legitimate, but must go unanswered here. It would be difficult to answer it in the abstract; but historically it seems to me that almost all concepts of liberty may be subsumed under these two—to repeat, formal—categories. We must now ask whether each of these concepts is compatible with any of the possible concepts of equality, and if so in what way. In the following discussion we shall again confine ourselves (in a manner that is necessarily arbitrary, but in effect remains subject to the conventions of scientific discourse) to a selected few of the various conceivable ideas of equality.

III

When we think of equality, we think first of human nature, with its uniformities and differences. It is certainly no accident that immediately after asserting the equality of men as children of God, Heimann emphasizes that "men are not naturally equal" (124: 233); that Laski couples his demand for equality with the qualification that the "native endowments of men" are "by no means equal" (127: 154); and that even Marx, in discussing equality, adds the commonplace that "men would not be different if they were not unequal" (129: 20). Behind the problem of the compatibility of liberty and equality lies the question: Are men equal or unequal by nature? Does equality—whatever it may be—correspond to hu-

---

[1] The choice is in fact between liberal and totalitarian democracy, or two fundamentally different concepts of rationality; on this subject see the following essay, "Market and Plan."

man nature or not? Now we certainly cannot hope even to begin
to answer this important and far-reaching question here. But it may
help to phrase the question in a more precise way than is usual, and
to relate it more precisely to the problem of liberty and equality.

In the beginning of Book II of the *Politics,* Aristotle develops an
argument which, *mutatis mutandis,* may help us here. He proposes
to "investigate which is the best political community of all, so that
people can live so far as possible according to their wishes." For this
purpose, he decides to "begin with what is the natural beginning
in an investigation of this kind. Either all citizens have everything
in common, or they have nothing in common, or they have some
things in common" (97: 1261a). Just so, let us begin by asking
whether all men are naturally equal in everything, in nothing, or
in some things. Insofar as this question touches on basic questions
of philosophy and natural law, we shall again take a more modest
course. Our concern here will be to examine the compatibility
of liberty and equality under conditions of the total inequality, the
total equality, and the partial equality of men.

Let us begin by assuming that men are by nature entirely unequal in every respect. "Human nature" then becomes a meaningless fiction; there are as many human natures as there are human
beings. Any apparent identities that we perceive are superficial,
since anything deeper would contradict our assumption of total
inequality. Aristotle has shown that human society is impossible
under such conditions: people must have something in common,
something that brings them together—if only the Hobbesian in-
stinct of self-preservation, on which the social contract is founded.
Liberty may conceivably be possible under conditions of total inequality; indeed, total inequality may offer the chance of total liberty, a liberty unimpeded by "data." But any question of the compatibility of liberty and equality necessarily disappears where equality does not exist.

The opposite assumption, a complete identity of human nature
in all respects, is not so easily dealt with, even from our limited
point of view. In terms of our mathematical metaphor, $y = \infty$,
and thus z becomes a value to which the categories "even" and
"odd" either can be arbitrarily assigned or no longer apply. Here,

too, the problem of compatibility would have no meaning. Complete equality implies that all human beings have by nature the same abilities and needs, the same desires and habits, the same character and views of life, the same rank and the same rights. Any apparent differences that we perceive are accidental, the work of men and of history, not of human nature.

Aristotle argues—somewhat superficially, it seems to me—that "The state consists . . . not only of many people, but also of such as are different in kind. When all are equal, there can be no state." (97: 1261a.) Must the inequality of men in the state be inequality in kind? Is it not conceivable (as Marx, Hegel, and others indeed thought) that before the state came into being there was a community of equals, out of which the state arose as a result of inequalities that had developed in the course of history? In this event, one might regard the demand for liberty as a demand for the abolition of the unnatural inequalities generated by history, and to this extent see liberty and equality as brothers. But this argument does not stand up on closer examination. If liberty is defined in terms of the reestablishment of a natural state of complete equality, it must abolish itself by its realization: for where all men exist in total "natural" equality, all behavior is either a mere "datum," a given beyond human control and thus beyond the reach of liberty, or else nature's mechanism for effecting man's predetermined self-fulfillment, in which case it is beyond the reach of constraint and once again inaccessible to human control. A state of total natural equality would not only put an end to liberty and the tension of its relationship to equality, but reduce all history to a nauseating procession of necessary events. Human self-fulfillment would no longer exist even as an idea.

Thus the relationship between liberty and equality is worth discussing only if we assume that men are by nature partly equal and partly unequal. The harmonious or discordant counterplay of liberty and equality, indeed these very concepts and values, become meaningful only if natural as well as social inequalities substitute history for the terrible perfection of constant equality and thus expose man's freedom, his efforts toward self-fulfillment, to the threats of the world. Our question should therefore be: In what respects are all men equal, and in what respects unequal? Once again we are concerned only with the comparatively narrow problem of the compatibility of liberty and equality.

The extreme cases of total equality and total inequality suggest a plausible (if rather brief and dogmatic) answer to our question. Men are equal by nature (or so we might assume) with respect to the data of their existence, the constants at the basis of all social life. They are equal in their bodily nature, which ties them to the "realm of necessity" and forces them to work for their living; they are equal in their instinctive nature, which imposes certain restrictions on their rational development; they are equal, moreover, in the possible dependence of their will on transcendent forces. Furthermore, men are equal by nature with respect to rank, and in particular in their access to the possibility of liberty in terms of the absence of arbitrary restrictions on self-fulfillment. It is this equality that we refer to when we say that all men are equal "as men," "in their dignity as men," or "as God's children." Men are unequal, by contrast, with respect to the mode of their existence, i.e. in their endowments and abilities, their needs and means of expression, and in what they do with what they have.

Though a rapid formulation like this may provoke objections, I think it is defensible. One point only seems to me to require proof: the equality of rank. Whereas the equality of the data of human existence and the inequality of its modes may both be regarded as nearly self-evident, the natural equality of rank has time and again been questioned. Distinctions between lower and higher races (in a sense, between "primitive" and "developed" peoples), between natural aristocracies and masses born to serve, between a "stronger" and a "weaker" sex, all reject the natural equality of rank. All three of these alleged rank orders of nature were first asserted by Aristotle:

> It is thus clear that there are *by nature* free men and slaves, and that servitude is agreeable and just for the latter. Equally, the relation of the male to the female is *by nature* such that one is superior and the other inferior, one dominates and the other is dominated. . . . With the barbarians, of course, the female and the dominated have the same rank. This is because they do not

possess a naturally dominating element. . . . This is why the poets say, "It is just that Greeks rule over barbarians," because the barbarian and the slave are *by nature* the same. (97: 1254b, 1252a.)

If Aristotle is right (and especially if the same may be said of his rather less human successors in this line of thought), our delimitation of equality and inequality in human nature disappears, and with it the possibility of liberty in the traditional sense.

But is Aristotle right? He sees the natural inequality of rank primarily in terms of ruling and serving; indeed, he derives the three theses quoted from the universality of power. The core of his argument is: "Ruling and serving are not only necessary, but wholesome. Many things are separated from birth onward, the ones to serve, the others to rule." (97: 1254a.) Ruling and serving are necessary, then, but necessary for what? Presumably for the functioning of society, since without power order is not conceivable. Thus ruling and serving are indeed universal, but nevertheless social, conditions. To this insight, Aristotle adds the observation (for an observation it is) that men are divided "from birth onward" into rulers and ruled. But how is this statement to be understood? Either it means that in a given society a person's social origin determines his chances of power (which was certainly the case in Aristotle's world), or it means that society has declared certain unequally distributed talents to be qualifications for power (which is the case in any society, although the talents in question keep changing). But in no case does the division of men into rulers and ruled imply that the social relations of power are reproduced in human nature in the sense that some are destined to rule and others to serve. Aristotle's mistake is to present as a constant of human existence a demonstrably arbitrary, i.e. society-imposed, inequality; in short, from the universal inequality of social roles he wrongly infers a natural inequality of rank.[2] Confusion on this point has persisted for centuries, and has had many a terrible consequence to the present day.

And liberty? Is liberty compatible with human nature if, as we

---

[2] The mistake is excusable, seeing that it occurs to the present day, notably in the work of "structural anthropologists" who interpret social universals—assumed social universals, to be precise—as elements of human nature. This, if anything, is an example of reification in the social sciences.

have assumed, human nature is a peculiar blend of equality and inequality? Put this way, the question certainly must be answered in the affirmative. We have seen that if men were by nature either wholly equal or wholly unequal, liberty would be meaningless and its relationship to equality nonexistent. The tension between liberty and equality, the very problem of their compatibility, exist only if we assume that men are equal in some respects and unequal in others.

Beyond this general compatibility, however, the relationship between the equality of human nature and the possibility of individual self-fulfillment cannot be expressed in a simple formula. The natural equality of rank implies that man, every man, has the capacity for self-fulfillment in the absence of arbitrary constraints. Thus it implies a claim of man, every man, on the society he lives in. Here the combination of liberty and equality proposed by Heimann and others applies: if all men are by nature equal in rank, all men by nature have an equal claim to the chance of liberty, the opportunity for self-fulfillment. The natural equality of rank is accordingly the precondition of the possibility of liberty for all, without regard to social rank and status.

Our other natural equality, however, the equality of the data of human existence, is by no means as plainly compatible with the chance of liberty. Indeed, this equality represents the inherent limitations on man's liberty, just as the inequality of the modes of existence represents his hope of liberty. It may be said that we are unequal by nature with respect to the things that make us free, and unfree with respect to the things in which we are equal. As a constant threat to human liberty, the data of our existence enter into our social life as well: as Marx observes, for example, the world of work remains forever "a realm of necessity" (45: 874). Self-fulfillment in the modes of our existence begins only after the constants of our life have been established. With respect to human nature, therefore, we have the chance of liberty only insofar as we are unequal; for insofar as we are equal, our actions are governed by a common law outside ourselves. The interplay of necessary equality and possible liberty serves as both boundary and stimulus to the creative and moral existence.

As a constant of human existence, the natural equality of men is beyond the reach of social forces. The interplay of liberty and equality in human nature is equally anterior to social development; its forms are determined by society, but in itself it is pre-social. One cannot make human nature more or less equal the way one can make social conditions more or less egalitarian. Our discussion to this point is therefore merely preliminary to an investigation of the compatibility of social equality and liberty. Whereas in this section our considerations have been largely philosophical, only sociological analysis can help us relate the other possible meanings of equality to the problematic and assertoric concepts of liberty.

IV

Equality of human rights in society corresponds to the natural equality of rank of all men, a point made explicitly in theories of natural law. This equality of citizenship status, which is the basis of all social equality, is associated with the French Revolution. By creating a state of equal rights for all citizens, the Revolution signaled the advent of a new historical epoch, an epoch in which Stoic, Christian, natural-law ideas of the equal rank of all men became the basis of social organization. For the first time, inequalities among men were not thought of in terms of natural and social rights and privileges; and differences in social status were confined to increasingly trivial sublegal social differentiations. From that time on, all men have been held not only to be "created equal," but also to be sent equal into the unequal world of society; from that time on, social differences were not to be allowed to affect the chance of liberty promised to all.

When people refer to the equality of men in a democracy, they are thinking primarily of equal citizenship. Tocqueville's "equality of opportunity," Laski's equality as the "absence of special privilege," the equality of the French revolutionaries, and Heimann's equality of the children of God all boil down to the idea that society guarantees everyone an equal opportunity for self-fulfillment. The notion of social inequality has two possible interpretations with radically different historical backgrounds and political consequences.

In the first, to quote T. H. Marshall, unequal status is a matter of "legal rights and fixed customs which have the essentially obligatory character of the law. In its extreme form a system of this kind divides society into a plurality of different, inherited kinds—patricians, plebeians, villains [villeins], slaves, and so forth." In the second, differences of status are "not fixed and defined by the laws and customs of society (in the medieval sense of this term), but they emerge from the interplay of a multitude of factors in connection with the institutions of property and of education and of the structure of the economy" (128: 30–31). What the revolutionary principle of equal citizenship rights did was destroy the "total inequality" of a status fixed in law and custom and reduce all differences of social position to what they are in essence: ranks relating to man's existence as a social being, which are necessary in terms of social structure but arbitrary in terms of human nature.

The historical leveling-out of human rights has accompanied the emergence and definition of the social role of the citizen. The leveling-out process has two essential elements: the first a matter of content, the creating of a general set of expectations relating to inviolable opportunities and unexceedable limits; the second a matter of form, the transforming of these expectations into obligations guaranteed by law. Thus the role of citizen provides a man with certain rights that make possible his own self-fulfillment and certain obligations that make possible everybody else's. In Laski's useful formulation, "It means that no man shall be so placed in society that he can overreach his neighbor to the extent which constitutes a denial of the latter's citizenship." (127: 153.)

Even in the developed societies of today, full equality of citizenship status is not yet an accomplished fact. The first step in the process was the equality of all citizens before the law; next came the equalization of political rights, and in particular the practice of universal, equal, and secret suffrage; most recently we have seen the equalization of social opportunities with respect to education, income, and social security benefits. We do not know what further rights and obligations may become associated with the citizen's role; nor do we know whether the two-hundred-year-old trend toward broader citizenship rights will continue or give way to counter-trends. Here as elsewhere, a historical necessity exists only in the dangerous naïveté of utopian fantasy.

Whatever the future may hold, however, the equalization of basic social rights has made available the chance of liberty on a scale unknown to all earlier patterns of society. Equal citizenship is not only compatible with the chance of liberty; it is a condition of the possibility of liberty for all men. By it, and by it alone, the opportunity for self-fulfillment becomes a legal claim open to everyone instead of a privilege for the few. Without this kind of equality, the liberty of all is inconceivable. It must be emphasized, however, that equality of citizenship status can create problematic liberty only. Equal citizenship constitutes by its nature a basis of social differentiation; it is significant precisely because it makes inequality possible. Because all men are equal as citizens they may be unequal in the mode of their existence; without equality of rights and obligations, the multiplicity of forms and styles of life is impossible. But if the rights and obligations of the citizen's role are extended beyond what is necessary for creating the basis of social existence, if they are applied to regulating the mode of human self-development as well, they change from a necessary condition of liberty into its destroyer. Thus only the possibility of assertoric liberty can be created by equal citizenship. In a society of equal citizens, it remains up to the individual to achieve liberty in the fullest sense. His success is made possible, but is not guaranteed, by equality of citizenship.

V

In the pure world of ideas, equal citizenship seems clearly compatible with the possibility of liberty. But here as elsewhere reality does not reproduce the purity of ideas. To demonstrate this, let us examine further the statement that citizenship creates problematic but not assertoric liberty, that it makes participation in the social process possible but does not bring it about. The right to vote is a condition of the possibility of liberty, but the legal obligation to vote is at least potentially a restriction of liberty—a restriction, moreover, that cannot sensibly be conceived of as essential to the status of citizen, since the nonvoter's decision can by no means be said to constitute a denial of his neighbor's citizenship. The contrast between the right to vote and the obligation to vote is rather clear; more often, however, the line between permitting and compelling the individual to participate in society is unclear, and in some cases shifting. The distinction between equality of citizenship status and equality of social status in particular—in theory decisive, and especially so in terms of the compatibility of liberty and equality—is in practice difficult to make. Should a legally guaranteed minimum wage be associated with equality of citizenship, or with equality of social status? Should old age and disability insurance be regarded as a citizenship right, or as an infringement on individual liberty? What about prohibitive taxes on high incomes, antitrust legislation, the nationalization of major industries? Are these unwarranted restrictions on the opportunity for self-fulfillment, or conditions of the freedom of all? In the recent history of developed countries, many equalities of social status have been transformed into legal rights, and thus into role expectations of citizenship. This process is important in our context, since, as we shall see, equality of social status and equality of citizenship status differ significantly in their relationship to liberty.

Unlike equality of citizenship, equality of social status implies a leveling of the modes of social participation. It refers not to the basis of social existence, but to its forms. Men are equal as citizens if they have the same opportunity to earn a certain income or achieve a certain level of education; men are equal in social status if in fact they do earn a certain sum or achieve a certain educational status. The four factors conventionally invoked in describing social status are income or property, social prestige, authority, and level of education or training.[3] Since equality with respect to these factors is clearly conceivable, at least in a utopian flight of fancy, we have

---

[3] It hardly need be added that this is a pre-theoretical understanding of status. Possibly the notion of chances of participation in the social process is more useful than any combination of the four "factors." See the preceding essay, "On the Origin of Inequality among Men."

here still another concept of equality, whose compatibility with the chance of liberty has to be examined.

The relationship between liberty and equality of social status is a favorite subject of modern political economy, one that divides liberals and socialists, proponents of a "social market economy" and proponents of "economic democracy." There is therefore a considerable body of literature on the subject, and for this very reason I shall be careful to proceed "naïvely" here as before, i.e., to consider the problem without apparent regard to earlier attempts to solve it. It may be argued that such a procedure makes possible theoretical solutions only; but this corresponds exactly to my intention.

We shall approach the complex relationship between social equality and individual liberty by examining as limiting cases the lower and upper limits of the status hierarchy. Is there a social rank below which nobody may fall without losing the chance of liberty? Conversely, are there social positions so far above the general level that they endanger the chances of liberty of those in lesser positions? How compatible are liberty and equality at the base and the peak of the social pyramid? In answering these questions, we shall confine ourselves to examples from advanced industrial societies.

In terms of the four factors of social stratification, the lowest social rank would consist of people who have enjoyed no training or education whatsoever, who are subordinated to others in all their social relations and thus completely without authority, whose prestige is the lowest possible, and who have no property and too low an income to satisfy their elementary needs. It is obvious that for such people equal citizenship, and thus the opportunity for self-fulfillment, is of doubtful value—to put it mildly. Absolute exclusion from the rewards and life chances of society makes equal citizenship meaningless by curtailing the equal chance of liberty that equal citizenship theoretically guarantees. A minimum level of social status (one that is equal for all) is thus a condition of the possibility of liberty. In other words, a minimum of social status—in the sense of the abolition of society-imposed restrictions on the chances of liberty—is a necessary ingredient of equal citizenship.

How can this minimum be determined? The case of extreme deprivation is obviously so rare in the developed societies of the present day that we can ignore it so far as theory is concerned. If one takes as a standard the "poverty line" of physiological subsistence as developed by B. S. Rowntree and others (see 133, 134), a minimum equality of social status is hardly in question today. It might reasonably be argued, however, that the minimum of authority, education, prestige, and especially income necessary to the chance of liberty should be determined not in physiological terms but in cultural terms. Under certain social conditions, for example, this minimum might reasonably include not only food and shelter, but an automobile, a higher education, and a house of one's own.

We need not decide this question here. For us a more important question is whether this minimum should be set as high or as low as possible. Specifically, what would happen to the chance of liberty if the minimum social status guaranteed every citizen were so low that many citizens remained (and felt) relatively deprived? And conversely, what would be the fate of liberty if, for example, every citizen were guaranteed a minimum income that not only took care of his needs but permitted him many a "luxury" as well? The answer to the first question may be inferred from our earlier discussion. If the minimum is too low, some people's chances of liberty will be threatened; if our concern is to extend the chance of liberty to all, we must accordingly avoid too low a minimum. In answering the second question, we must anticipate the discussion that follows. In a word, if the minimum status guaranteed all citizens is put as high as possible, this does not constitute a threat to the chance of liberty, so long as there remains above this minimum space enough for many different levels and kinds of education, authority, prestige, and income. Anyone who places a high value on liberty should do his best to see that the minimum social status of all citizens is set high rather than low, but at the same time to make sure that the space between the floor and the ceiling of the status hierarchy does not become too narrow.

The theoretical peak of the modern society's status pyramid, the status conferred on men at the highest levels of property and income, authority, prestige, and education, poses problems of a different kind. In the first place, it is clear that success on one or more of these scales is at least potentially a sign of self-fulfillment. Even if we assume that most such qualifications have nothing to do with self-fulfillment but instead are the result of social origin, inheritance, or even "connections," the mere possibility that self-fulfillment may be involved means that any limitation on what may be achieved or acquired amounts to a restriction on the chance of liberty. For example, a law forbidding private monopolies might restrict a dynamic entrepreneur's opportunity for self-fulfillment, irrespective of whether such a law is essential to equal citizenship in Laski's sense, i.e., designed to ensure that no man's place in society shall so overreach his neighbor's as to constitute a denial of the latter's citizenship. In short, even if it should be in the interest of the liberty of all to fix an upper limit on achievable social status, to do so would limit the liberty of some. On the other hand, it may well be that the effective equality of all is undermined not only by the low social status that prevents some citizens from exercising their rights, but also by the overpowering status that enables a few citizens to curtail the rights of others. To appraise the real weight of this question, we must examine the four factors of social stratification individually.

The potential danger of extreme success is less plausible with respect to education. A protracted and thorough education of the few curtails the liberty of the many only where it is offered at the expense of a reasonable level of general education, i.e., where the right to education implied by citizenship is in effect denied. Here, higher education might in fact create monopolies of knowledge affecting the relative rights of neighbors and the power structure of society.[4]

At first sight, the peaks of social prestige seem scarcely more threatening to the liberty of the many. The high prestige of the doctor, the judge, and (in Germany) the university professor is more

---

[4] There is also, of course, the problem suggested by Michael Young in his *Rise of the Meritocracy*, i.e., the monopoly of power by those who have achieved the highest educational status.

amusing than threatening. There is a point, however, at which the prestige of a position becomes the charisma of a person—at which, in other words, a prestigious man rises above all normal measures of esteem and translates his prestige into power. Such a charismatic leader may use his personal power to suspend existing norms and to restrict the liberty of his constituents. Indeed, for this reason, measures to control charisma are one of the main (and tragic) features of modern political institutions: the separation of powers, elective democracy, political party organizations, bureaucracy. Such institutions have not succeeded in eliminating the possibility of charismatic leadership; nor are they likely to, for prestige and charisma are probably the least manipulable attributes of social status. Although a contradiction between the chance of liberty and inequality of social prestige is thus conceivable as a marginal case, it does not lend itself to political control.

Consequently, the traditional economic and political arguments for and against establishing a maximum permissible social status have to do not with prestige or education, but with income and property. Perhaps property and income are not always distinguished with sufficient clarity. Mere income, whatever its level, seems as "harmless" as mere prestige to the rights of others. A man with an income of $100,000 a year, whether earned or unearned, prevents no one from exercising his rights as a citizen. Income turns into a potential threat to liberty only if, in the form of property, it becomes an instrument of power. Like prestige as charisma, income as property can become a means of curtailing other people's opportunity for self-fulfillment. In both cases, then, the impulse to establish a maximum permissible status comes not from the unequal distribution of the ostensible determinants of status, but from their translation into power or authority. Thus according to Laski's definition equal citizenship "means that I must not find that there are persons in the state whose authority is qualitatively different from my own" (127: 153). But the charismatic leader and the powerful property owner—so one might argue—have an authority that is qualitatively different from the "ordinary" citizen's; their means of enforcing subordination and obedience do not stem from the rights that all citizens share as such. It follows that the liberty of all requires a limitation on the "private power" of individuals, and hence a curtailment of freedom at the peak of the status scale. This is the crucial problem in the present-day discussion of political equality.

Power and subordination are universal social relations; they can be abolished only in a utopian world. This being so, the only way of eliminating inequalities in the chance of liberty is by rendering all power rational in Weber's sense: i.e., by making power subject to legitimation by the voluntary assent of those who are subject to it. The rational legitimation of power is thus an implicit but decisive feature of equality of citizenship. Where everyone has access to the chance of power and to a voice in legitimating power (politically, to active and passive suffrage), ruling and serving both lose their arbitrary character and become compatible with the equal chance of liberty for all. It is from this point of view, I think, that the relationship between liberty and equality of social status must be judged. If I am right, all power that is not rationally legitimated must be abolished before there can be equal chances of liberty for all. In economic terms, legitimation by property is not sufficient without a measure of consent on the part of the unpropertied; i.e., group conflicts must be recognized. In political terms, power based strictly on economic power is illegitimate and must be eliminated; i.e., there must be institutional pluralism. Such a restriction on achievable social status (and unquestionably a ceiling on permissible property and power must be considered a restriction) does not imply the abolition or even the nationalization of property. It is merely a limitation on the possibilities of illegitimate power derived from property, particularly public property—i.e., a restriction on the rights that property can confer.

As our analysis has shown, power and authority—not property, income, prestige, or education—are the crucial factors in social status. Any effort to bring about equal chances of liberty for all would therefore have to begin not with income or property, but with the control (and, under certain conditions, the elimination)

of the private power both of individuals and of the state—for the
state may also exercise "private," i.e. illegitimate, power. Necessary as such restrictions may be, however, to protect the liberty of
all, it seems clear that the limits on achievable social status should
be placed too high rather than too low, in an effort to keep the
opportunities for human self-fulfillment as wide open as possible
for as many people as possible. In historical societies there are no
permanent structures; today's solution may be at the root of tomorrow's conflicts. Since in this sense all political measures are
unpredictable in their effects, even more weight should be given to
their general direction than to their immediate content. And from
this point of view, an excessively low ceiling on social status is as
dangerous to the liberty of all as an excessive inequality that turns
into qualitative differences of power and authority.

At the two extremes of the status hierarchy, we have found social
equality (in the sense of the exclusion of extremes) and individual
liberty (in the sense of the opportunity for self-fulfillment) to be
clearly compatible; indeed, we have found equality a condition of
the possibility of liberty. But the equality that our restrictions seek
to guarantee is not equality of social status but equality of citizenship. In the vast domain between the ceiling and the floor of the
status hierarchy, the domain in which equality of citizenship can
be taken for granted, equality of social status is an enemy of liberty.
As a stimulus, a medium, and a reward of personal self-development, social stratification is essential to human freedom. The more
monolithic, the less differentiated, a society is, the more it restricts
its citizens' chances of liberty; the more pluralistic and differentiated a system of social stratification is, the more easily can it do
justice to the citizens' multifarious individual needs and talents.
Once equality of citizenship is assured, inequality of social status is
necessary to the chance of liberty.

VI

So far we have avoided a key question: Is equality of social status
possible? Are there not certain inherent qualities in human society,

perhaps corresponding to the data of human nature, that are universal and not alterable by the intervention of historical forces? How much equality and how much liberty can we hope for without forsaking the structural conditions and hopes of real societies for the arbitrary conditions and hopes of utopia? I can do no more here than consider these questions briefly in the hope of rendering them a bit more precise. But some such excursus seems necessary in order to get at the true meaning of our concepts of equality and liberty.

In discussing equality and inequality of social status, we have implicitly assumed a scale (or several scales) of historically real (or at least historically realizable) social positions. This assumption needs correction at two points. First, it is obvious that for a society characterized by total inequality, the notion of a scale makes little sense. In such a society some people (in the extreme case, one person) monopolize all the attributes of status—property and income, power, prestige, and education—leaving all others no share whatever in these attributes, and hence no possibility even of physical survival. In this event, the idea of stratification simply disappears. Stratification exists only so long as the goods and chances of society are unequally distributed, but still distributed, i.e., not completely monopolized by the few. In reality, even an oligopoly of the attributes of social status is probably possible only as a marginal case. Any excessively unequal distribution of income, prestige, and education creates a threat to stratification itself and thus, at least in principle, to the very people who have greatest access to society's benefits. Thus the notion of stratification itself sets certain limits to the extreme forms of inequality.

It is equally true, if more difficult to demonstrate, that total equality of social status is not realistically possible. Here the emphasis is on the word "realistically." In our imagination there may well exist a society in which no man enjoys more prestige, a higher income, or a better education than any other. However, no such "ideal" society has ever existed; and supposing one were created, it would hardly be able to function. To prove this last statement—i.e., that some minimum of hierarchical differentiation is one of the structural conditions of a functioning society—let us turn to one of the time-honored subjects of sociological discussion: the origin of inequality, of class formation, or of social stratification, as the phenomenon was called in successive centuries.[5] In taking up this discussion, which has to date been inconclusive, we might argue as follows. Insofar as any human society is, in Durkheim's phrase, a "moral community," i.e., has norms whose compulsory character is guaranteed by sanctions, it necessarily generates the rudimentary inequality that results from the application of these norms and sanctions to the behavior of individuals and groups. Every social norm represents a selection from the large reservoir of conceivable values; but any such selection discriminates by gratifying one social group as opposed to others. Thus in any society some groups are better placed than others. This argument tends to confirm the historical observation that whereas over the centuries the forms and symbols of stratification have undergone many changes, these changes have never affected the system of inequality that we call "social stratification."

If we assume the universality of social stratification in this sense, and thus the impossibility of both total equality and total inequality, the chance of liberty seems guaranteed under all conditions; it seems clear, that is, that wherever society exists, social stratification offers the possibility of self-fulfillment. But the situation is not so simple. For one thing, between the realistically impossible extremes of total equality and total inequality there remains a broad range of historical variations, some of them favorable to the chance of liberty, others unfavorable. More important, inequality of social status is always, as we have seen, a potential threat to the chance of liberty for all. Where social inequality stops being a result and becomes a precondition of self-fulfillment, it may lead to qualitative differences of social position and thus undermine the equal citizenship that makes possible the equal chance of liberty.

The same uncertainty characterizes a second and even more basic datum of man's social existence: the universality of power and subordination. In arguing against Aristotle's equating of natu-

---

[5] The argument sketched here is the subject of the preceding essay, "On the Origin of Inequality among Men."

ral and social rank, I emphasized that even though ruling and
serving are universal, they are not natural conditions of man, but
social conditions. Despite occasional tales of distant societies in
which power plays no part, the historical evidence is clear: there
is no known society and no known association within a society in
which some men are not empowered by their social position to issue
commands and have them obeyed. Inequalities of social status are
thus reducible to inequalities of power. But this is merely to give
our question another form: Why are there structures of power in
all human societies? A plausible reply would be that the coordination of socially differentiated positions—in the family and the
business, the church and the state—requires among other things a
structure of authority, of command and subordination; but this
plausible formulation is rather less than a convincing proof. One
might suppose further that the tradition of norms associated with
the sequence of generations presupposes certain authority relations
between age groups; but this supposition, too, can hardly be regarded as proof. Political philosophers have usually taken refuge
in the notion of a social contract, in which the necessity of power is
argued on the basis of certain hypotheses about the nature of man,
among them the idea of a "natural" *bellum omnium contra omnes*
and the idea of a Golden Age. Perhaps we must indeed assume
something like Kant's "unsociable sociability" of man in order to
find a convincing argument for the universality of ruling and
serving.

The unequal distribution of authority does not at first glance
appear compatible with the chance of liberty, since even the rationally legitimated necessity of serving restricts a man's chances of self-
fulfillment. And yet the maintenance of equal citizenship status
for all, like the maintenance of any other social norm, requires
laws and constitutions, and therefore power; only after the social
contract, and as a result of it, can there be equality of citizenship.
It follows that the inequality of power inherent in society does not
in itself determine the individual's chance of liberty, but leaves
open a wide range of more or less liberal patterns and types of
authority.

All the data of human society lead us back to their common basis, the fact of society itself. Man is a social animal. Since by his nature he lives in society, he can fulfill himself only in social terms. Man's social existence is a condition of his possible freedom—and at the same time of his possible unfreedom, for society always means force and constraint. To belong to society is to subject oneself to the rules of the game, to accept norms and controls. Kant's argument rings true: "Man has an inclination to associate because in such a state he feels more human, i.e., better able to develop his natural endowments. But at the same time he has a great tendency to remain apart because his own unsociable desire to have everything his own way leads him to expect resistance everywhere, just as he himself is inclined to resist others." Society is the struggle of liberty with itself. For the free man—i.e., the man who carries within him a claim to liberty—society is simultaneously an attraction and a vexation, an opportunity and a danger, a support and a threat. Kant believed that this "antagonism" was the ultimate motive force of all history, without which "men, like the docile sheep in their pastures . . . , would hardly value their existence" (104: 210–11). But it has to be remembered that the unsociable sociability of man, like all the other givens of his social existence, is merely part of the ambiguous framework within which various historical solutions to our problem of the compatibility of liberty and equality remain possible, and with which any such solution must come to terms.

VII

When the political theorists of the nineteenth century spoke of social equality, they were thinking almost exclusively of equal citizenship and equal social status. Neither Kant nor Hegel, neither Tocqueville nor Marx, neither Lassalle nor the Fabians, conceived of that third form of social equality which in our century has jeopardized liberty in a new and sinister way. John Stuart Mill, who has been widely and unjustly scorned, was a remarkable exception. In his treatise *On Liberty,* the familiar notion of the "tyranny of the majority" leads him to what, if I am not mistaken, was a novel idea at the time: what he calls the "tyranny of society":

Society can exercise its own authority and it does so: and if it gives false orders instead of right ones, or gives orders at all in matters with which it should not be concerned, it is practicing a social tyranny which is more terrible than many forms of political suppression, because although it is usually not based on such extreme sanctions it leaves fewer chances of escape, penetrates deeper into the details of life, and enslaves the soul itself.

More precisely, Mill sees a tendency on the part of society "to enforce its own ideas with other means than legal punishments on those who have different opinions; to disturb the development and formation of that individuality which does not harmonize with its ways, and prevent it if possible; and to force all characters to direct themselves by the model of its own character." (131: 5–6.) It remains to be asked who this personified "society" of Mill's really is; but the tendency Mill described is no less significant for leaving this question unanswered. Equality of social character is indeed one form of social equality, and one, as Mill has impressively shown, that particularly threatens men's chances of liberty.

Man's participation in society involves a strange mixture of dependence and spontaneity. On the one hand, there is the possibility of flinging himself into society, setting or changing its course, fulfilling himself within it, forging his individuality in the social struggle. At the same time, society is always placing restrictions on his liberty and spontaneity. He is subject to the rules of the game, the norms and role expectations of the society around him; he can throw them off only at great cost to himself, if at all. Conformity, the honoring of the social contract by all parties concerned, is a structural condition of any functioning society. For the sake of society, but for his own sake as well, a man must conform to society's predetermined behavior patterns in wide areas of his life, must establish at least some minimum of congruence between the social reality outside him and the individual reality within. Thus conformity as such does not derive from equality of social character. Rather, the relationship between them can best be understood by examining the variability of conformity under different social conditions: by considering to what extent "society" enforces conformity with its norms, to what extent it regulates the behavior of its members, and in what manner it undertakes to determine their behavior.

The degree of social control and the extent of the regulation of social behavior are two important measures of conformity. Not every society imposes severe sanctions on "deviant behavior." In some societies, for example, political radicalism, however unpopular it may be with the majority, is nonetheless tolerated in the sense that no radical need fear occupational, "social," or legal reprisals. In other societies, by contrast, the mere suspicion of radicalism leads to such reprisals. Similarly, not every society tries to regulate every minute in the lives of its citizens. In some societies, for example, what a man does with his free time is entirely his own affair, whereas in others the expectations associated with his profession, age, family, or class position apply to his leisure time as well. "Society," then, can threaten or abet a man's chance of achieving liberty by subjecting him to stronger or weaker measures of social control, or by extending or restricting the regulation of his behavior. These various possibilities, and notably the possible combination of extremely strong control and extremely far-reaching regulation, were probably what Mill had in mind in describing the tyranny of society.

However, there is still another dimension to equality of social character. Even in a society characterized by intense social control and far-reaching regulation of behavior, a man might conceivably have so large a choice of socially acceptable behavior patterns as to be likely to find the combination that corresponds perfectly to his unique needs. Social control and the social regulation of behavior as such do not establish a principle of equality. Equality comes about only when and where socially regulated and controlled behavior becomes *uniform,* i.e., where only a few behavior patterns are permitted, or perhaps only a single pattern, with the result that all individuality of behavior disappears in the gray broth of conformity. Where people not only are exposed to expectations, but are all exposed to the same expectations, we find true equality of social character.

An example may help to illustrate how and to what extent equality of social character represents a realistic possibility. A British journalist who lived in the United States for some time, and whose seven-year-old son went to school there, later reported an amusing if unnerving experience:

> Some weeks before Valentine's Day we got a circular letter from the director of the school with the information that "the day" was approaching and the school would like to help us with the distribution of Valentine cards. But, so the letter added frankly, no cards would be distributed in the school from any particular child to any other particular child, unless every child who brings such cards brings them for every member of the class. In this way no child would receive more cards than any other; there would be no discrimination for the most popular or against the least popular child: every child would receive exactly as many messages of love as any other child. And in order to guarantee this happy, abstract democracy of love, a list was added to the circular letter with the names of all children in the class of our son. (125: 29–30.)

Totalitarianism? No, this is unplanned, spontaneous uniformity, unplanned at least by political agencies. There is conformity also when everyone sends his best friend a Valentine because that is the custom; but only when everyone sends everyone else a Valentine is there uniformity, and thus equality of social character. Equality of social character means that within a given broad social role everyone is expected to behave like everyone else: everyone must hate the Communists today and McCarthy tomorrow; everyone must keep his office door open; every young man must take his girl friend out on Saturday night; every white-collar worker must spend his vacation in Miami Beach; everyone must be interested in football or satellites or the best-seller of the month—unless he is prepared to accept the unbearable position of outsider, in which he risks losing his friends, his job, possibly even his physical freedom. Where equality of social character is coupled with severe measures of social control, every spark of spontaneity threatens the social status quo; in such a society only the mask is acceptable, because only this is equal for all.

It need hardly be emphasized that, of the three kinds of equality we have discussed, equality of social character is not only the hardest to find in fully realized form, but the hardest to bring about. American schoolchildren on Valentine's Day no doubt find ways both to do the expected (to conform) and to express their own personal wishes (not to be uniform)—for example, by bringing Valentines for all their classmates but writing longer messages on some than on others. Probably it can be shown here, too, that the theoretical extremes of equality and inequality are impossible in practice. Clearly, however, several contemporary societies can be seen as exhibiting a tendency toward more uniform social character types. To demonstrate this tendency is David Riesman's concern in the study from which we have borrowed the term "social character." Riesman's "other-directed man," who takes his cues from an internal radar screen that registers the preferences of "society," is nothing but the embodied will to equality of social character (see 132). If we assume that unsociable sociability may take any of a number of historical forms, the egalitarian character of other-directed man describes the extreme case of almost unlimited sociability, in which everything unsociable has been repressed or destroyed. Once equality of social character becomes a social command, the free man is wholly alienated from himself.

Liberty is the opportunity for human self-fulfillment; but where equality of social character prevails, whatever man does serves only the ends of the society around him. Where men try to make their behavior conform entirely to their neighbor's, they subject their existence to the egalitarian tyranny of society. Liberty, the inequality of human nature with respect to the modes of existence, becomes taboo: personal talents, wishes, and interests have to be repressed, not developed, in order to satisfy society's demand. Between the chance of liberty for all men and the equality of social character there is therefore no connecting link. Men are potentially free to the extent that they are unequal in their social character, and unfree to the extent that they are equal. Among all possible concepts of equality, equality of social character contains the clearest and most dangerous threat to the chance of human liberty: "The idea that men are created free and equal is both true and misleading. Men are created different; they lose their social liberty and their individual autonomy if they try to become equal to each other." (132: 373.)

VIII

Inevitably, the more closely we scrutinize a problem, the more complicated it becomes, so that in the end it is more difficult than ever to capture in simple formulas. The gratifying puzzlement of the first moment is soon lost, and is hard to recapture by reflection. We have examined some of the possible concepts of liberty and equality for their compatibility. This examination has yielded only one wholly unambiguous result, namely that the relationship between the two values is too complex to express in such an unqualified statement as "Liberty and equality are compatible" or "Liberty and equality are incompatible." Our equation has multiple solutions. In the circumstances, all we can do in conclusion is ask whether the threads we have spun in the preceding pages can be woven into any kind of pattern. Can any general principle be derived from our discussion? Is there some limit to which the counterplay of liberty and equality converges in all its solutions? Or are there really as many answers to our initial question as there are concepts and combinations of liberty and equality?

It seems to me that a general principle has in fact become apparent: namely, that equality is a condition of the possibility of liberty wherever it relates to the rank of human existence, but that it constitutes a threat to the possibility of liberty wherever it relates to the modes of human existence. Only with respect to the data of human existence does the relationship of equality to liberty remain uncertain, unless one chooses to regard the very existence of such data as a threat to liberty. This "pattern," which represents the main finding of our discussion, thus reproduces for society that multi-layered yet transparent relationship between equality and liberty which we have found to be characteristic of human nature.

In human nature as in society, certain data are beyond the reach of history or spontaneous individual action. The bodily nature of man, like the stratification of society, is a constant, and as such makes both freedom and unfreedom possible. We can indeed go a step further and say that the idea of liberty in society becomes meaningful only if we accept the data of human nature and of society as given; liberty always means liberty within the bounds defined by these data. Man can realize himself only as what he is, i.e., with and through the human nature peculiar to him, with and through the ineluctable conditions of human society. But in order for all men to have the chance of liberty, all men must be equal in natural and social rank. Wherever equality means equality of rank, it is unreservedly compatible with the chance of liberty. With respect to human nature we have to assume that equality of rank accompanies all history as a constant; with respect to society, however, equality of rank is a historical achievement. Citizenship rights alone make the chance of liberty available to those who are least favorably placed in the hierarchies of social differentiation. But if equality of citizenship status is thus necessary to the liberty of all, it is not sufficient. Where it does not exist, the liberty of all is impossible; where it does exist, it merely creates problematic liberty, only the possibility of human self-fulfillment. For liberty in the assertoric sense, the actuality of self-fulfillment, further conditions must be met.

The concept of liberty refers to the modes of human existence. Free men are men who are free to fulfill themselves within the bounds set by the data of their existence, without interference from alien purposes or forces. It follows that insofar as equality aims at rendering the modes of human existence more nearly uniform, it is not compatible with liberty. In this sense we have found liberty incompatible with both equality of social status and equality of social character; the possibility of liberty requires inequality, institutional pluralism, differentiation of strata, and a multiplicity of character patterns. Again, however, only problematic liberty is possible in these terms. Although leveling of status and uniformity of character make liberty in any sense impossible, multiplicity and inequality are not in themselves enough to create assertoric liberty.

Neither positively nor negatively is the actuality of self-fulfillment a function of equality.

Comparing this conclusion with Heimann's notion of liberty and equality as quoted at the beginning of this essay, we find a strange historical dialectic of political ideas (one certainly not intended by Heimann). As we have seen, Heimann feels that liberalism and socialism have both failed, liberalism by emphasizing liberty at the expense of equality, socialism by enforcing equality at the expense of liberty. What is needed, says Heimann, is the reconciliation of liberty and equality in democracy: "Liberty and equality are the two halves of democracy; equal liberty is required for democracy." (124: 233.)

Political movements rarely attain the goals they start out with. Political practice has its own laws, some complex, others simple, which tend to reduce highly differentiated ideological constructions to their core meanings, and often, if unintentionally, to make them appear more unambiguous than they are. With this reservation in mind, we may say that it was the historical function of liberalism to force the tough and vexatious reality of society to yield a place to liberty. One cannot fairly charge the theorists of liberalism with rejecting all forms of equality, since at least one aspect of equal citizenship, the equal right to conclude contracts (which Marx so scorned), derives squarely from liberal theory. But it was nonetheless one of the political effects of liberal thought to create the possibility of liberty at the expense of equality, so that liberal liberty frequently became liberty for the few at the expense of the many. Historically, then, liberalism succeeded, in our terms, insofar as it established the claim of liberty for all, especially against the constraints and restrictions of arbitrary public authority. It "failed" insofar as it destroyed, rather than developed, the social equality necessary for its success.

Socialism, on the other hand, may in historical retrospect be characterized by the reality it gave to equality of citizenship, without which the liberty of all remains an empty declaration. Socialism was not merely egalitarian any more than liberalism was merely liberal; each of the two traditional opponents in the political arena shared a good many of the other's convictions. But the effect of socialism may be seen above all in the protracted process of the equalizing of social position, a process that began with citizenship status and was later extended to social status and social character. Historically, then, socialism succeeded, in our terms, insofar as it gave reality to the social equality of rank, which for the first time in history made the liberty of all a real possibility. It "failed," despite the liberal impulses in its theory, insofar as it was impelled by its inner dynamics to carry equality of social position beyond the point at which it turns from a precondition of liberty into a threat to its existence.

As constructive political ideas, both liberalism and socialism belong to history today. One need but look at the political parties that started their careers under these banners to see that both are largely relics of the past. Today we see liberalism and socialism giving way to a new, and as it were Hegelian, synthesis, in which they are *aufgehoben* in the triple sense of the German word, i.e., at the same time abolished, preserved, and raised to a higher level. Heimann's formula of "equal liberty," understood in our terms, expresses the new synthesis perfectly. A social-liberal policy today must aim at preserving and extending that equality of citizenship status which alone makes possible the liberty of all, but it would support equality no further; it would resolutely oppose all social leveling and uniformity, and as resolutely advocate institutional pluralism, social differentiation, and diversity. Probably this idea will fare no better in political practice than its historical predecessors. The Hegelian synthesis makes a pretty figure of speech, but such a neat balance of opposites is alien to reality. Thus no doubt social liberalism, too, will in the end be reduced to its polemical core, which is neither more nor less than a revival of the claim of human liberty in society. Equal citizenship is today largely no longer a goal, but an undisputed political given. What matters, therefore, is to concentrate once again on that goal for the sake of which the notion of equal citizenship was introduced in the first place. The aims of a social-liberal politics must above all be liberal, for equal liberty is above all liberty.

8

Market and Plan
Two Types of Rationality

That modern societies are becoming increasingly rational is a statement so true it can hardly be false—and thus it means very little. So long as one makes it clear that we are all "civilized" now, that there are no "savages" left anymore, one can quote Max Weber today without fear of attack in Accra, Minsk, or San Diego:

> What gives the life of "civilized" man . . . , as opposed to the savage, its specifically "rational" flavor is . . . (1) his general tendency to believe that the phenomena of his everyday life—a bus or an elevator, money, a court of law, military affairs, medicine—are in principle rational, i.e., that they are human artifacts accessible to rational knowledge, creation, and control (this view has certain significant consequences for the character of the "consensus"); and (2) his confidence that these phenomena function rationally, i.e., according to familiar rules, and not irrationally, like the powers that the savage seeks to influence with his magic, so that at least in principle one can reckon with them, calculate their effects, and base one's actions confidently on the expectations they arouse. (24: 473–74.)

Modern society is becoming more rational. It is becoming more calculating, notably in its economic processes, where profit is balanced against cost and experts in accounting and logistics abound. It is becoming more scientific, with more and more decisions based on theoretical and general knowledge, and more use made of techniques in both the narrow sense and the broad. It is becoming more organized, with staffs of administrative specialists processing all decisions before they reach those who will carry them out. It is relying more heavily on statutes, on codified law, and less on unquestioned traditions and the winning qualities of individuals. It is becoming increasingly subject to the control of those who live in it, more and more of whom help make its decisions because they know its laws. It may even be becoming more reasonable.

In science, at least, statements that cannot be false are useless; and if generalizations about "modern society" make any sense at all, it must be to those who have never suffered from any particular society, notably their own. But before we condemn our generalization about increasing rationality on methodological grounds, let us have another look at it. For it might just possibly be false, and hence of scientific interest. Have there not been some very different, even contradictory, trends?

So far as Weber's political concept of rationality is concerned, a hierarchic administrative system in which communication between equals can take place only through the intermediary of their common superior seems every bit as lacking in rationality as the bureaucratic "empire-building" satirized in Parkinson's laws. Here, as so often, the success of National Socialism in Germany gives rise to serious doubts. At least one interpretation of that phenomenon explicitly emphasizes its non-rational, even irrational aspects: the charisma of the Führer, the fanaticism of his followers, the seduction of the masses, the anti-scientific character of the ideology. Yet the same Hannah Arendt who clearly subscribed to such views in her *Origins of Totalitarianism* later went all the way to the other extreme. What has made her book *Eichmann in Jerusalem* so controversial is precisely her insistence that the evil, too, is banal, that it is part and parcel of the *rational* workings of a gigantic modern state bureaucracy.[1] Eugen Kogon, writing soon after the war, was

---

[1] Miss Arendt might not altogether agree with this interpretation of *Eichmann*; and indeed it might be argued that the "banality of evil" is a philosophical thesis rather than a sociological one. Be that as it may, I maintain that Miss Arendt was essentially trying to reconcile the existence of dispassionate rational patterns of administration and the associated individual roles with the perpetration of such a gigantic crime.

the first to describe the "SS-State" as a characteristic product of modern rationality (152).

Thus it is at least doubtful whether National Socialism and its cruel crimes can be cited to refute the thesis of the growing rationality of the modern world. Indeed, it would seem that rationality is simply a way of solving problems, not a way of discovering what they are or whether their solutions are morally defensible; otherwise it would be impossible to describe all modern societies in terms of a trend to rationality. What is rational, then, is always means, never ends. But—and these are the central issues to be discussed in this essay—do we really always mean the same thing when we speak of rational methods? And does rationality remain morally indifferent under all circumstances? Is it thus really true that while there can be a political theory of rationality, there cannot be a rationalist political theory? Is the category of rationality not suited to distinguish between different social and political forms?

If we set aside the question of whether the National Socialist regime was rational, there still remain two very different patterns of social organization, both of which might plausibly be described as rational. One is the liberal pattern. In liberal thinking, rationality is a quasi-economic term. It seeks a maximum yield at a minimum cost—for example, a maximum of individual happiness with a minimum of political decision. The social order rests on the assumption that this kind of rationality guides the individual as well, so that as a rule people will not systematically act against their own interest. It is further assumed that every increase in the rationality of the political process will necessarily increase the utility of this process for the people involved. According to this view, then, if social forces are simply allowed to take their course, they will produce the best possible political solutions at any given time.[2]

It is on this point that the critics of liberal rationality find it least

[2] Among contemporary liberal political theorists, Milton Friedman (*Essays in Positive Economics, Capitalism and Freedom*) probably comes closest to this undiluted eighteenth-century liberalism. Others—notably Friedrich A. Hayek (*The Constitution of Liberty*), Karl Popper (*The Open Society and Its Enemies, The Poverty of Historicism*), and Raymond Aron ("La Définition libérale de la liberté")—have moved, in varying degrees, toward the more complex notion of rationality (and of liberty) suggested in this essay.

persuasive. Indeed, for at least a century critics of various schools have assigned the quality of rationality to quite a different pattern of social organization. On the grounds that the liberal pattern leads to chaos, they urge that the powers of human reason be applied to the task of designing and building the just society, or, more modestly, to solving certain social problems. To these critics rationality consists in the consideration of every step along the way from a problem to its solution, and in the creation of suitable organizational conditions for keeping problems under control. Solutions do not come about by themselves, but only as a result of controlled and controlling action.[3]

Which of these two kinds of rationality did Weber mean when he referred to the increasing rationality of the modern world?[4] I suspect that he was ambiguous on this question, and I think this ambiguity is a factor in the political ambivalence of his work.[5] For if we distinguish in this fashion between two types of rationality, the peaceful uniformity of modern society immediately dissolves and gives way to two conflicting forms of social organization. Though these two forms may in fact coexist, they are incompatible in their principles, whose clash provides the substance of the central social and political conflict of our time. The organizing principles of the two forms may be summed up in the words *market* and *plan*. The

[3] Communists apart, probably the most extreme representative of this view was Karl Mannheim. In Mannheim's view, the second kind of rationality was in the process of supplanting the first: after an original phase of "horde solidarity," followed by a phase of its antithesis, "individual competition," mankind was now moving toward the great phase of synthesis, in which all men would share "responsibility in planning the whole course of events in the society in which [they] move" (153: 70). Other names one associates with this position are Harold Laski and Joseph Schumpeter. Strikingly, these are all men of an earlier generation; for contemporary economists and political theorists, "planning" (and even *planification*) has generally acquired a much more liberal meaning, one not incompatible with the suggestions offered later in this essay. We are thus witnessing a convergence of views.

[4] There is widespread agreement today that, to quote Mannheim (153: 52n), "Max Weber's whole work is in the last analysis directed toward the question: 'Which social factors have brought about the rationalization of Western civilization?'" For this reason, there is a considerable interpretative literature on the subject, from H. J. Grab (148) to Franco Ferrarotti (145). This literature is obviously relevant to our problems without being directly addressed to the question as we have posed it.

[5] See Wolfgang Mommsen, *Max Weber und die deutsche Politik* (154), and the discussion of this book in 144 and 151.

liberal society is organized on market principles; the non-liberal is organized according to plan. Whether we try to solve the problems of our world with market-rational or plan-rational methods is a serious question, with manifold implications and consequences.

The market is a place of exchange and competition, where all comers do their best to improve their own lot. The starting point of any market-rational attitude is the assumption that a smoothly functioning market is in fact to the greatest advantage of the greatest number. To this extent, the market-rational attitude is politically passive, a hands-off attitude in matters of legislation and decision-making. Decisions are of course made, but only for the purpose of safeguarding the functioning of the market, i.e., defining and enforcing the rules of the game. It follows that market-rational political theory concerns itself with the forms, procedures, and personalities of political competition, but leaves out of consideration the substance of this process, namely what the competing parties or candidates stand for. The holding of elections, their timing, the system by which votes are translated into seats, when and how parliament is constituted, how the president is selected—all these are rules of the game in the market sense, with their ultimate sanction, perhaps, in a constitutional court. What market-rational theory cannot as readily deal with are questions involving substantive norms: questions like whether workers must be represented to a certain extent in parliament, whether private property is permissible, and whether or not to allow private nursery schools.[6]

The plan-rational orientation, by contrast, has as its dominant feature precisely the setting of substantive social norms. Planners determine in advance who does what and who gets what. The ideal plan-rational orientation leaves no room at all for individual decisions, or indeed for conflicting decisions. Instead, the plan—assuming it is benevolent—successfully anticipates all needs, prescribes the means of satisfying them, and relates ends and means

---

[6] The examples all refer to German constitutional theory and practice. Private nursery schools were proscribed by the Weimar constitution, and continue to be proscribed under the Basic Law of the Federal Republic (Article 7). The other examples should be self-evident.

unambiguously to each other. In such an orientation, rules of the game are in principle as superfluous as substantive norms are in a market-rational approach; there is no game, but merely the controlled working out of predetermined processes.

The implications and consequences of the two types of rationality are hard to assess impartially, and I shall not even try to assess them here. Let us instead take a sociological approach and begin with a familiar question: Which of the two principles is more efficient? Can a pure plan-rational approach work at all? If we consider the plurality of interests in society and their contradictory character, and if we take into account the technical (if not fundamental) difficulty of finding out what needs exist and how best to satisfy them, the efficiency of pure plan rationality seems at best questionable. Another difficulty comes from conflict theory. My theories of social conflict may be wrong; but assuming they are right, it follows from them that plan-rational societies are immune to revolutionary upheavals only insofar as they allow leeway for market-rational considerations and institutions, and that they are in any case much less stable than market-rational societies.[7] We shall return to this point at the end of the present essay.

The difficulties of applying market and plan multiply when we consider the epistemological implications of the two principles. Plan rationality presupposes the possibility of certainty; whoever assumes this possibility takes a step down the path that all too predictably ends in the dogmatizing of error. Market rationality, by contrast, presupposes the fundamental uncertainty of our knowledge; the rules of the game keep all results reversible, for the game in question, the political process as a whole, has no end.[8] Friedrich Hayek has traced the epistemologies of the two kinds of "rationalism," as he calls them, to Hume ("critical rationalism," or market rationality) and Descartes ("constructivist rationalism," or plan rationality), and I accept his analysis without reservation (see 150).

---

[7] My theories of conflict are discussed in *Class and Class Conflict in Industrial Society* (7) and in several of the essays in this book. In *Conflict after Class* (143), I point out that if effective suppression of dissent is possible, or even if a combination of suppression and redirection of conflict is effective, some doubt is cast on conflict theory.

[8] For further remarks on this point, see the following essay, "Uncertainty, Science, and Democracy."

In political terms, the dogmatizing of error characterizes the total state; concentration on the rules of the game characterizes the liberal state. Both states claim, in theory and in practice, to serve the cause of freedom. Throughout the history of political thought, there has been a great controversy between the formal and substantive concepts of freedom, between freedom as a universal reality and freedom as a universal possibility. This controversy is directly related to the two kinds of rationality. The formal concept, which sees freedom essentially as the absence of constraint, corresponds to the market-rational orientation; the substantive concept, which sees freedom essentially as a state to be achieved (as Marx does, for example), has an intrinsic relation to the plan-rational orientation.

II

But the time has come to end such contrasts, for the distinction on which they are based, at least as it has been presented so far, is much too simple for the political analysis of any given society, or indeed for even the beginnings of a modern political theory. It is not just that reality is more complex than such simple types, that obviously no pure market-rational or pure plan-rational society exists. Nor is it merely that certain combinations of the two principles are possible: that even a market-rational purist may construct models of interdependence in order to study the remote effects of certain decisions, while a plan-rational purist may be moved to simulate the market to some extent by decentralization. (Combinations of this sort are so characteristic of contemporary states that most no longer even pay lip service to the stupid extremes of the typology.)[9] I mean something different and more fundamental here. For as soon as one brings the two types of rationality down from the thin air of conceptual debate and relates them to political reality, one encounters at least two difficulties of both political and theoretical significance. These difficulties are worth a moment's consideration.

[9] This statement must be taken with a grain of salt; in any case, each side helps keep the stupidest and most extreme version of the other side alive by suspecting the other side of aspiring to that extreme. In this respect, the word "totalitarianism" has done as much harm in the West as "capitalism" has in the East.

In characterizing market rationality and plan rationality, we have distinguished between rules of the game and substantive norms. The rules of the game are essentially formal: unlike substantive norms, they offer no way of telling one player from another. For example, according to the rules of the game every adult citizen has one vote, which he casts by ticking off a name on a paper ballot. But what if some adult citizen cannot read the names on the ballot? What do the rules of the game mean if tenant farmers get the idea that anyone who goes to the polls will lose his job? How do the rules of the game apply when a husband influences his wife to vote the way he votes? Such examples are legion, and not only in voting: how, for example, do the rules about "buying players" in professional football affect teams whose stadiums, and therefore incomes, are small? In short, in all social fields in which market rationality and plan rationality may compete, there are social structures that undermine the effectiveness of the rules of the game, arrangements by which certain players are in fact distinguished from others by being put at an advantage or a disadvantage. It follows that in order to make the rules of the game effectively valid, some compensating mechanism is necessary; and this mechanism can only be substantive norms. Rules of the game never exist by themselves, but always presuppose substantive norms.

A dramatic illustration of this process in recent history is the gradual supplementing of the legal and political rights of citizenship by social rights. This process has required many far-reaching normative adjustments on society's part, among them the development of social policy, the introduction of graduated taxes, and the extension of publicly supported education. The basic idea behind all these changes has been to create by normative means the equal starting chances that the competitive market model presupposes. There is no country in the world today where this process has been completed. Indeed, it may be a characteristic of this process that it can never be completed, that every new equality produces new inequalities.

It is obvious from this example that a market-rational politics presupposes certain plan-rational decisions, unless it is to remain an ideology of systematic privilege for those who are already in a position to participate. For wherever new conditions of participation must be created, the planned intervention of government is indispensable. This leads to an important question in liberal political theory—a theory, incidentally, that regards even such necessary interventions without enthusiasm—namely, when and to what extent must plan rationality be involved? Perhaps we might answer that the rules of the game require the protection of substantive norms whenever they permit any possibility of privilege or deprivation. The market has to be protected not only from monopoly but from the outsider's inability to participate, not only from charisma but from illiteracy, not only from the political power of nonpolitical institutions but from the political impotence of women. This is the old problem of the tension-ridden relationship between liberty and equality.[10]

In principle, then, a pure market-rational society that includes all citizens is impossible. It remains to discuss our second difficulty (which is more interesting, or at any rate subtler), namely that however plausible the distinction between rules of the game and substantive norms may sound, in practice it is very hard to make. Does not even the most market-rational political system involve systematic disadvantages to those whose information is inadequate through no fault of their own? Are there, for example, any rules of the game to compensate for the special position of French peasant smallholders as described by Marx in his *Eighteenth Brumaire*?

What is even more significant is that rules of the game themselves have a way of turning into substantive norms. Many an arrangement that started out as a rule of the game has ended up, thanks to the influence of social change, by favoring some people and penalizing others. No distribution of constituencies is entirely just in a modern, mobile society; some members of parliament inevitably

---

[10] The problem sounds abstract and remote. Yet considered in the terms used here, it can provide a fairly firm basis for a detailed account of political liberty in the modern world, extending to constitutional policy, education, social services, and other aspects of the social infrastructure of politics. For a further discussion along these lines, see the preceding essay; for a concrete application of it, see my book *Bildung ist Bürgerrecht* (142).

represent many more voters than others.[11] Or, to take another aspect of mobility, any highly mobile society will have a large number of citizens who cannot vote in an election because they have moved too recently to register in their new place of residence.[12] The example is of special interest because it shows how a single substantive norm— the right to mobility—may simultaneously serve as a condition of market-rational rules of the game and turn these same rules into differentiating norms.

Probably the most striking example of the transformation of rules of the game into norms under changing social conditions is provided by social policy. It seems clear that under the economic conditions of, say, the turn of the century, the effectiveness of the market-rational political rules of the game required security benefits for the unemployed, the disabled, the ill, the aged, and the poor.[13] But it may be argued that the methods chosen to provide this security, namely special legislation, presupposed economic conditions very different from those of the "affluent society," i.e., of a post-cyclical economy in a permanent state of expansion. In the affluent society, measures that were once a condition of the market-rational rules of the game strengthen the state without evident need, and thereby make it more plan-rational. Thus what was once necessary to the political competition of social forces now has destructive effects on that same competition.

It is not my intention here to advance a theory of the decay of market rationality. Rules of the game that have turned into substantive norms may, after all, be replaced by new rules of the game, and it is even possible to abolish social institutions. Only one conclusion may be drawn from our observation that such rules are not

[11] Most electoral laws specify that constituencies must be within a certain permitted deviation from a mean size. Often, however, this permitted deviation is rather large (in West Germany it is ±33⅓%), and invariably in a mobile society it favors the more sparsely populated sections of the country, i.e., the conservatives.

[12] Residency requirements vary, but it seems safe to assume that in highly mobile countries like West Germany and the United States, such requirements bar at least 5 per cent of all voters from any given election.

[13] At the same time, the social policy of that time seems to have been designed to decrease mobility by tying people's security to their place of residence; this was clearly one of the motives behind Bismarck's welfare policies. From this point of view, social policy counteracted market rationality as well as supporting it.

eternally valid but change their character in the course of time: that they should be constantly reexamined to see whether they are beginning to make the game harder instead of easier, or to differentiate among those whom they are supposed to provide with equal chances.[14]

At least with respect to society as a whole, the market must be constantly supplemented by the plan. Not only are market-rational rules effective only when their effects have been deliberately planned, but the planning behind them must be constantly reexamined with a view to whether it remains necessary to the operation of the market. Rules of the game, too, may turn into substantive norms, as many examples show. Such reflections must make the liberal sad, since they imply that pure market rationality works only in a vacuum and has absolutely no place in the real world. As a principle of a political theory that claims practical relevance, market rationality must invariably be supplemented by plan rationality.

III

There is no great accomplishment in getting this far. We are simply one step further along in an argument about the sociological foundations of political theory (which, as will be evident by now, is my subject here). Plainly there is some force that persistently interferes with the pure realization of market-rational principles, something that makes it impossible to play the market-rational game according to purely formal rules. This force can be identified: it is power, and the social consequences of power.[15] Because there is

[14] In this sense the present reflections, while not predicting or proposing the decay of liberalism, indicate once again why constant change is desirable. If the statement that one cannot enter the same river twice is obscure in its social application, observations such as these can help render it more precise: in a word, we need change, and conflict, if we want to remain free.

[15] A note about terminology is in order. In English, the distinction between *Gewalt* (violence, de facto control of others by the use of force), *Macht* (power in the narrow sense, de facto control of others), and *Herrschaft* (authority, institutionalized control over others) is somewhat inconvenient; as a result, "power" is often used both for the generic notion of control over others and for *Herrschaft*. I have conformed to this usage here. That is to say, unless otherwise indicated, "power" signifies a structured relation between people rather than a merely factual relation: the ability, by virtue of social roles, to make and enforce norms influencing the life chances of others.

power, i.e., because there are rulers and ruled, there are always inequalities of participation in the regulated game of the political process, and there are always people interested in translating the rules of the game into substantive norms that create or perpetuate privilege. Because there is power, the political process is not a game. Because there is power, this process is not a strictly market-like process; what it has of market rationality is restricted by plan-rational requirements and inevitabilities.

I should perhaps emphasize that these statements are so far mere assertions, and what many would call unproven assertions. Yet they seem capable of yielding reasonably satisfactory solutions to a good many problems, including those one encounters in applying the pure concept of market rationality to social phenomena. For if we see the creation of agencies of power as being, so to speak, the first rule of the game of human societies that is subject to the process of degenerating into a substantive norm, it becomes apparent that in all decisive questions there can be no such thing as equal chances of participation in the political process. Under all conceivable so-cial conditions, the market is a fiction; the game always takes place in front of city hall.

Whoever finds these remarks regrettable or depressing should re-flect that the market is but one of the many versions of the utopia of powerlessness, of which neither modern political theory nor modern political practice seems to tire. The market utopia is cer-tainly not undynamic; it is at any rate more dynamic than the har-monious *associatio,* the cooperative association, the *Gemeinschaft* of blessed and cursed memory, the barely evolutionary classless so-ciety, or the cybernetic idyll of pseudo-political feedback processes.[16] Something after all happens in the market. But the notion of the

---

16 The search for utopia will not die. But whereas in the past utopian models of society were the weapons of radical movements—the classless society of the Marxists, the people's community of the Nazis—they have today become the conservative ideol-ogies of a stagnant society. Contemporary Western countries are described as classless (Helmut Schelsky); cybernetics serves technocrats and their theorists (Karl Deutsch); democracy is described as the legitimate successor to the ancient idea of association (Carl Friedrich). To judge by utopia's sociological implications, this is the camp it belongs in; but that does not make the concept any more plausible. See the essay "Out of Utopia" above.

market shares with other utopias the impossibility of accounting for the necessity, the direction, and indeed the origin of change. What happens in the market is a constantly repeated game that is sufficient unto itself. Only a *deus ex machina,* the entrepreneur or the political leader, can initiate change in the market, and even then one cannot predict what direction change will take. At this point, the pure market theory of state and society comes close to pure determinism.

The structures of power in which the political process takes place offer an explanation not only of how change originates and what direction it takes, but also of why it is necessary. Power always implies non-power and therefore resistance. The dialectic of power and resistance is the motive force of history. From the interests of those in power at a given time we can infer the interests of the powerless, and with them the direction of change. Here is the nexus where norms are laid down, called into question, modified, and called into question again. Here is the source of initiative, and thus of the historicity—and that means the vitality, the openness, the freedom—of human societies. Power produces conflict, and conflict between antagonistic interests gives lasting expression to the fundamental uncertainty of human existence, by ever giving rise to new solutions and ever casting doubt on them as soon as they take form.

Such considerations lead to what one might call a sociologically refined concept of market rationality, a concept that resembles pure market rationality in name only. The game whose rules we have so often referred to is never a game of equals. To be sure, the inequalities between players take various forms, and there are ways of reducing them to minimum (as market rationality demands), but even in the most favorable circumstances the game remains a conflict. A market-rational theorist might concede as much, but go on to argue that whereas social norms are desirable to the extent that they merely regulate and channel conflict, they are undesirable to the extent that they interfere in the conflict, whether to support one party or simply to restore peace. Such an argument is no more than an extension of pure market rationality. It implies an equality of starting chances that does not exist even among the citizens of politically and industrially advanced nations. Indeed, applying market-rational principles to politics does not lead to a frictionless society, but to the orderly regulation of changes in the social structure. To say this is by no means to disparage the principle of market rationality, which has now become a metaphor; on the contrary, this may well be its noblest application. But it does lead to a much more subtle and complicated notion of a rational social order than the one suggested by market rationality in its pure form.

If we perform the corresponding operation on the notion of plan rationality, we find that the concept does not evaporate into a metaphor, but merely requires considerable refinement. Plan rationality clashes with social reality in a special way. As a claim to certainty, plan rationality always implies an absolute claim to power. But reality resists such claims. Resistance and opposition do not disappear just because the ruling groups want to see them disappear; the plan that does not tolerate contradiction does not for this reason remain uncontradicted. Thus, any real plan-rational behavior must conclude many a compromise with reality.

All such compromises, including arrangements for recruiting planners, for discussing matters of substance, and for generating criticism, are necessarily included in the plan itself, which thus takes on market-rational aspects. The generating of criticism—i.e., the planning of opposition to one's own power—is an especially absurd business that has provided pointless extra worries for such enlightened despots of the modern world as Atatürk and Nasser.[17] For plan rationality always creates a precarious state in which the planning of resistance is likely to accelerate rather than prevent revolutionary upheavals. Functioning plan rationality requires a dubious combination of terror and institutionalized market factors, a combination that can respond to unexpected changes while restricting the people concerned to the narrowest possible range of freedom. Whether such plan rationality in the social and political order can gradually give way to market-rational conditions is one of the great questions of our time, and one to which I see no clear answer.

[17] Both actually tried to organize opposition to their own policies—within limits, as one would expect.

Our sociologically refined market rationality seems clearly worth striving for. If it does not create absolute freedom—and the very idea implies the nonexistence of society—the metaphor of the market still guarantees more freedom than any other idea in the history of political theory. Its strength lies in its recognition of social conflicts, and thus of the fundamental changeability of any society. More than the most perfect plan, this approach makes social change controllable. To the market rationalists, change takes place all the time, but gradually; patterns and forms remain, and society is never overpowered or engulfed. To be sure, this kind of control is precarious: since the only chance of creating a perfect social order lies in a readiness to put down threats and bar innovations, a market-rational order is by no means substantively perfect. Nonetheless, the principle of market rationality, with its sense of the reality of social structures and the uncertainty of all human knowledge in matters of value as of fact, is more conducive than any other principle to an open society and a free people.

IV

Since these remarks have been very abstract, it may be useful to conclude by briefly indicating how they may be applied beyond the confines of sociological para-theory, political analysis, and political theory. Let us take West German society as an example. Economically, at least, the Federal Republic was founded on market-rational principles; in a broader social sense, however, its leaders have had no theoretical principles at all. Over the years, and especially since 1963, economic market rationality has been increasingly restricted, while in the social field plan-rational approaches have increasingly come to the fore. For Socialism has no monopoly on plan rationality; fascism, too, was plan-rational in essential respects, and so is the "formed society," based as it is on substantive norms.[18]

---

[18] The "formed society," *formierte Gesellschaft*, was Chancellor Erhard's attempt to emulate President Johnson's "Great Society." Although the term was never elaborated beyond a few general statements, it clearly referred to an organization of divergent interests and groups along the lines of a corporate state. Erhard's combination of liberalism in economic matters and anti-modern romanticism in social matters echoed such heroes of his as Wilhelm Vershofen and Wilhelm Röpke.

Where we might have expected a critical analysis of how the market-rational rules of the game operate in German society, and an attempt to create the necessary conditions for their operation (or to abolish these conditions where they are superfluous), we find ideologies of stagnation, i.e., attempts to avoid confronting the uncomfortable multiplicity and changeability of things social. The resulting authoritarianism is plainly dangerous, and to liberals intolerable. There will probably be no effective liberal opposition within the traditional parties. The question has accordingly been raised whether Germany might not do well to emulate France in this respect, and encourage the formation of small, exclusive political clubs that can formulate precise proposals and bring pressure to bear for their adoption.[19]

The application of our considerations of rationality to West Germany is comparatively obvious; the social and political problems of the Federal Republic are far from subtle. By contrast, the problems facing nations with highly developed liberal traditions and institutions seem to me much more significant. For everywhere today it is being asked whether the traditional democratic institutions as such can still accomplish what they once accomplished. Parliamentary debate, opposition, the mechanisms for generating political initiative, the principle of elections—all these are in crisis. What lies ahead?

In a situation of this kind it is useful to remember that the future of liberty is as little tied to the specific institutions of parliamentary democracy as its past has been. Parliamentary institutions are but one historical manifestation of the market-rational principle; and it is perfectly conceivable that they should lose their meaning in time and give way to new institutions designed to accomplish the same ends. Only the barest glimmer of such a radical change in political theory can as yet be detected, though the need for such a change may well be more urgent than our tired political leaders—

[19] A notable example is the Club Jean Moulin, which has brought together leading French civil servants, businessmen, and scholars to produce significant and effective policy proposals in a number of areas. The first of these, and the one most directly related to constitutional policy, was the volume *L'Etat et le citoyen* (141).

and their often no less tired ideologists—would have it. When the time comes, it will be necessary above all to remember that the principle of freedom lies in what we have called the sociologically refined concept of market rationality. With this concept it may become possible at last for modern society to find rational ways of recruiting people for political leadership, of developing political initiative, of institutionalizing resistance. Only one thing remains certain: that if the new rationality is to be compatible with human freedom, it must be market rationality.

9

Uncertainty, Science, and Democracy

It is an old saying that even if we know a lot, we know very little. Socrates occasionally made this point in his familiar remark that he knew enough to know that he knew nothing. The further we push back the open frontier of knowledge, the more clearly we perceive the vastness of the unexplored lands on the other side; and the more clearly, too, do we perceive how little we know of the realm on this side, well-ordered though it appears in our atlases and textbooks. Yet wise sayings of this kind can also become alibis. They are dutifully and solemnly intoned and then forgotten; no one sleeps any the worse because he has acted on assumptions that are hard to reconcile with wise sayings. In this essay I want to explore, at least in a preliminary way, what follows if we take Socrates' remark seriously, that is, if we attempt to draw consequences from it and act accordingly.[1]

First, since it is by no means a matter of course to speak seriously about our ignorance, we must ask what it means to say that certain fundamental barriers to our knowledge render it incapable of ever being sufficient. At the center of the following remarks is the further question of how we would behave if we acted on the assumption that we do not know anything, or at least cannot know how much we know. Since this is a very abstract statement, and even as such only

---

[1] It is perhaps worth remarking that Plato did not draw these consequences, at least not explicitly. Whether Socrates himself did so is hard to say. Our concern here is primarily with Socrates on trial (as Plato has drawn him), before sentence is passed.

moderately fruitful, let us make it more precise. Assuming that we can know nothing, how would we behave in two areas that may be seen as symbolizing, if not epitomizing, our life chances—the theoretical area of scientific knowledge and the practical area of political decision? In addition, of course, there are the areas of political theory and applied science, as well as areas of knowledge and decision that have nothing to do with science or politics. But it is my feeling (following Max Weber, who for good reason made these two "vocations" the subject of his famous Munich lectures) that in these two areas the existential modes of learning and decision-making take on an unsurpassed clarity.[2]

There is no need to specify the discipline to which an inquiry of this kind belongs (although some readers may be concerned about its obviously marginal character). Epistemology and the logic of science, political philosophy and sociological analysis, will be indistinguishably merged in the following pages. If I had to give the inquiry a name, I would call it a study in morals—perhaps, if such a thing exists, in the morals of knowledge. In theme and intent it is greatly indebted to two lectures: one by Karl Popper to the British Academy "On the Sources of Knowledge and of Ignorance" (168), the other by J. W. N. Watkins to the British Aristotelian Society on "Epistemology and Politics" (170). My reflections here, however, will take a somewhat different course from theirs.

II

What can we mean when we say that we know nothing? Although Schiller, in his essay "On the Necessary Limitations on the Use of

[2] The sociologist in particular is apt to think here of Max Weber, who so obviously suffered from the abrasive incompatibility of these two modes of human endeavor. For me, the peculiar moral character of the two realms of science and "practice" (a concept in which the areas of individual ethics and politics are somewhat imprecisely mixed) has been demonstrated most impressively by Josef König in his lectures on ethics at Hamburg University in 1949–50 and in later correspondence. König points out that a scientist has two consciences, one general, the other scientific, and thus embodies, as it were, the difference between the worlds of science and common sense. In this sense the scientist may be said to live a second life; and whether this second life is subject to moral laws analogous to those of the life of common sense becomes an important question. See also the following essay, "Sociology and the Sociologist."

Beautiful Forms," recommended in a burst of intellectual puritan-
ism that "the writer who is concerned about scientific rigor" use
examples very sparingly (169: 355n),[3] we shall try to answer our
question with an example, and not a very puritanical one at that.
In his *Treatise on Probability*, John Maynard Keynes (163: 25ff)
describes a legal action taken by a certain Miss Chaplin against a
Mr. Hicks as a result of a popular, if somewhat complicated, beauty
contest staged by the London *Daily Express* in 1911. Six thousand
girls from all over Great Britain accepted the paper's invitation to
send in their photographs. The *Daily Express* then divided the
country into fifty regions, published the photographs, and asked its
readers to select the most beautiful of their region's beauties. After
that, Mr. Hicks, a member of the paper's staff, was supposed to
interview the fifty regional winners and select twelve finalists. To
these finalists the paper offered not only the promise of a theater
engagement, but also the unmistakable suggestion that the winner
might hope to marry a member of the English aristocracy.

Our interest lies in the actions of the aforementioned Miss Chaplin, one of the fifty regional winners. Like the other semifinalists,
she was invited by Mr. Hicks to come to London for an interview.
An appointment was made for this purpose, but she was unable to
keep it, and as a result she was excluded from the final round of the
contest. Miss Chaplin considered her disqualification unmerited
and brought suit against Mr. Hicks for not giving her a fair chance
to present herself, claiming damages for the benefits his action had
cost her.

At this point we must consider how the situation confronting the
court in the case of Chaplin v. Hicks was affected by the particular
limitation on knowledge that I shall call "uncertainty." Obviously,
the court has first of all to find out why Miss Chaplin was unable
to keep her appointment. If this information is not obtained, the
court must proceed in a state of uncertainty. The uncertainty in

---

[3] Among the many unhappy dichotomies characteristic of German thought (form
and content, state and society, *Gemeinschaft* and *Gesellschaft*, culture and civilization)
is the distinction between "reason" and "imagination" that Schiller advocates here,
as if experience might sully the purity of the general and the necessary. It is hard for
the mind to find its way back from such dead ends.

question is of a simple and inexcusable kind: uncertainty about obtainable information that has in fact not been obtained. Perhaps one should not be too hard on those who fail to obtain readily available information, so long as they are acting in good faith. For example, it may be very expensive for a businessman to acquire information about all the markets in which his product might be sold. Even a court of law, having carefully weighed the potential benefits of presumably obtainable precise information against the cost of obtaining it, may sometimes settle for a supposition. Indeed, ignorance that is remediable in principle occurs quite often, although we may on the whole agree with John Locke: "He who judges without informing himself to the utmost of his ability, has no excuse for a false judgment." (95a: ii, xxi, §67.) But we have not yet come to the problem that concerns us. In fact, the court in the case of Chaplin v. Hicks did obtain the necessary information, and in due course concluded that Mr. Hicks had indeed unfairly denied Miss Chaplin sufficient opportunity to present herself.

The situation would be of rather more interest (to depart for a moment from the historical case) if Miss Chaplin had deliberately and successfully deceived the court about why she failed to keep the appointment. Uncertainty with respect to information that has been obtained but is in fact false is a worrisome possibility because we often have trouble determining whether something is true or false, a problem that brings us much closer to our main concern in this essay. Not only in wars but in economic competition and other non-military conflicts, spreading plausible but false information is a popular and effective strategy. But let us concede that the judges in the case of Chaplin v. Hicks were not deceived, and henceforth disregard the problem of false information without in any way implying its insignificance.

The court's decision that Mr. Hicks did not give Miss Chaplin a fair chance to be interviewed does not tell us anything about Miss Chaplin's claim for damages; indeed, the judges were much less sure of themselves on this point. The verdict refers to the difficulty of determining with "precision and certainty" Miss Chaplin's chance of being one of the twelve finalists. To judge her claim fairly, one would have to know not only the precise value of the benefits the finalists received, but also Miss Chaplin's properties in comparison with those of the other forty-nine semifinalists, not to mention the personal idiosyncrasies of Mr. Hicks—all in all, not a very simple task. This, however, is a situation we all find ourselves in frequently. We know what we would have to know in order to make an informed decision; the information is in principle obtainable, in the sense that we can imagine ways and means of acquiring it; but these imagined ways and means go beyond the technical possibilities of the time. Which psychological tests can give us "accurate" information about the preferences of Mr. Hicks? On what basis can one calculate the value of a theater engagement, or indeed of an aristocratic mariage? What we have here is uncertainty with respect to information that is obtainable in principle, but for the time being technically unobtainable.

The case was ultimately tried in two courts. The court of the first instance faltered in the face of this uncertainty, and confined itself to pronouncing Miss Chaplin morally in the right. The court of the second instance, by contrast, confronted the problem head on, in a way that on the surface seems plausible enough. It broke through the circle of uncertainty as follows: first, it established the value of the benefits to each of the twelve finalists at £400; and then, calculating Miss Chaplin's chances with the aid of probability theory, awarded her £100, i.e., about twelve-fiftieths of a finalist's share. Miss Chaplin was satisfied with the judges' decision, and so was Lord Keynes, the theorist of probability, but we cannot be.[4] Arbitrary decision and probability theory are substitutes for actually resolving the dilemma of uncertainty. Although the judges may have had no alternative, their decision merely conceals the epistemological problem that concerns us in this essay.

---

[4] This apodictic statement must be qualified. In science, there are many situations in which information is theoretically obtainable but for the time being unavailable for technical reasons. In such situations, the scientist must rely on what one might call "informed arbitrariness," i.e., a decision based on nothing more tangible than general expertise. What is more, this way of reaching decisions is not only permissible but extremely useful. Miss Chaplin's judges made such a decision when they established the value of the prize at £400. What is unsatisfactory is the implication, which Keynes apparently accepted, that all uncertainties may be resolved in this manner.

Often we do not know as much about something as we would like to know or might conceivably know, owing perhaps to our inertia, to inadequate means, to deception by others, or to technical difficulties. Sometimes, however, our uncertainty assumes a more fundamental and threatening character, notably when we want to know what is right. Is the value of the prize really £400? Does the decision in Miss Chaplin's favor accord with the facts of the case? There is a definite ambiguity in the little word "right" here. We cannot know whether certain information is right in the sense of being ultimately *true,* nor can we know whether certain decisions are right in the sense of being ultimately *good.* When the judges in the case of Chaplin v. Hicks (like all judges in the world) acted naïvely—i.e., made their experience and general expertise the standard of truth, and legal tradition the standard of goodness—they sidestepped the fundamental problem of uncertainty. That with increasing knowledge we recognize how little we know is not a quantitative statement about the relationship between known and unknown things. It does not mean that we might know much more if we made the effort. It means rather that there is some fundamental barrier to our knowledge in this matter of rightness, which we must get beyond if our knowledge is to be true knowledge; and that since we cannot get beyond this barrier, our knowledge must remain forever uncertain.

The term "uncertainty," as I am using it here, occurs primarily in modern economic and political theory (if we leave aside Werner Heisenberg's uncertainty principle).[5] The economist Anthony Downs defines uncertainty as "any lack of sure knowledge about the course of past, present, future, or hypothetical events" (90: 77). It would appear that this definition does not refer to a fundamental

---

[5] Apart from Heisenberg's work, the concept of uncertainty figures most prominently in those disciplines which directly or indirectly draw upon information theory, notably theoretical economics. For some time, eminent economists have been using their tools to cast new light on traditional problems of political theory (Arrow, Downs, Friedman, and others in the United States, Giersch and Liefmann-Keil in Germany); in their work the concept of uncertainty is even more important. Not surprisingly, the term also plays a part in experimental psychology; see Wendell R. Garner (160).

limit to our knowledge of truth and goodness, a limit that in principle makes it impossible for us to decide ultimately what is true and what is good. Indeed, the economic concept of uncertainty is very sweeping (not to say imprecise) and applies above all to situations in which the cost of information can be calculated, or at least estimated. Modern economists, too, would thus concur with Lord Keynes's satisfaction with the Chaplin decision. Perhaps we may even go a step further and assert that economic and political theorists shrink from the assumption of a fundamental limit to our knowledge because such an assumption makes formalization and quantification difficult, if not impossible.[6]

But does such a limit really exist? Here an important modification in our argument is necessary. On the basis of our discussion so far, it would be frivolous to assert more than a suspicion of uncertainty with respect to the truth of the true and the goodness of the good. We can suspect that our questions about the rightness of our knowledge evade answering in a sort of infinite regression. Miss Chaplin has been robbed of her chance to be a finalist. Did she really have such a chance? Was she as beautiful as the other finalists? Are there reliable ways to establish Mr. Hicks's criteria for judging beauty? Supposing there are, would they mean anything today, considering the time that has elapsed since the contest? Given such a series of unanswerable questions, it is not implausible to suspect that our knowledge and our decisions always occur in the context of uncertainty; that even if we want to know something precisely or do something right, we cannot because the truth of the true and the goodness

---

[6] Thus Downs (90: 78) says explicitly: "Uncertainty refers to particular events; it is not a general condition." This corresponds to the definition of the term in information theory. If I am not mistaken, the assumption of an uncertainty from which one cannot buy oneself free would be most unattractive to any theorist in the social sciences who is bent on formalization. The starting point for formalist theory (as Milton Friedman has remarked with reference to economics) is invariably the assumption that everything, without exception, has its price. However, the two assumptions are not unreconcilable, and it cannot be argued either (1) that formalization is useless, or (2) that social scientists can confidently dismiss the hypothesis of irremediable uncertainty. (For a start toward reconciling the two assumptions, see Giersch, 161: 324–25, 335–36.) On the contrary, I should think that any meaningful theory of economic, social, foreign, or general policy would have a chance of success only if it took this radical point of departure.

of the good are in principle beyond our grasp. "We cannot know," as Popper says; "we can merely guess." (168: 69.)

This is the *suspicion of uncertainty*—a suspicion well founded in our everyday experience and reflection, but of course open to discussion and objection. Let us now take the decisive step of the argument and consider what a fundamental uncertainty with respect to the true and the good would imply for our behavior. Let us assume that the condition which has been so far presented as possible, perhaps as probable, is a fact; that is, let us convert the suspicion of uncertainty into a hypothetical *principle of uncertainty* and see what happens. Neither implicitly nor explicitly are we asserting that uncertainty is a proven aspect of the human condition. We intend simply to experiment (so to speak) with this notion, which our discussion so far has shown to be not entirely implausible.

This is to begin with an apparently very abstract, indeed non-Euclidean, undertaking: to examine the consequences of a mere hypothesis.[7] In order to alleviate suspicion on this score immediately, the general answer to our question must be given here, although of course it will gain meaning and sharpness only in the course of the argument. What can we do, what should we do, if we must live our lives in a state of uncertainty with regard to the true and the good? Unless we want to abandon all hope of doing anything at all,[8] we obviously have no choice but to emulate the statistics-minded judges in Chaplin v. Hicks: to make a decision, to make up our mind. But since, according to our hypothesis, we can never be sure what is right (what is true, what is good), any decision we make may be wrong, and—what may be even more important—no decision can be demonstrably and finally right. But if no knowl-

---

[7] The procedure seems to me preferable to operating with the category of "pragmatic implication" (as Popper and Watkins do), important though that category is. The non-Euclidean point of departure—how should we behave if we assume a fundamental uncertainty, without bothering for the time being to ascertain whether our assumption is valid?—makes it easier to single out the point on which the entire argument hinges. This is done in section V below.

[8] This stipulation is not meant frivolously. The difficulties to which the principle of uncertainty leads us in personal ethics become apparent at this point. Can there be any ethics without certainty? Can there be life without certainty? It would be superfluous to invoke here the long history of philosophical ethics.

edge is indubitably true, no decision finally right, and if one does not intend to elevate error—the untrue, the ungood—to the status of principle, it follows that the way must remain open to various ideas of the true and the good, and in particular to contradictory ideas. The only adequate response to the human condition of uncertainty, and thus the supreme moral consequence of our assumption of the principle of uncertainty, is the necessity of maintaining a plurality of decision patterns, and an opportunity for them to interact and compete, in all spheres for which the assumption of uncertainty holds. Uncertainty demands variety and competition. From the assumption of a fundamental uncertainty about what is right, there follows the necessity of conflict. We shall now illustrate this thesis in the realm of the true, i.e. science, and the realm of the good, i.e. politics, before once again questioning our assumption as such.

III

In Popper's lecture "On the Sources of Knowledge and of Ignorance," he distinguishes among various theories of truth that have figured in the history of thought. He is particularly critical of a theory that he calls the "manifestation theory of truth," and its converse, the "conspiracy theory of error"—in short, of the epistemology of the classical empiricists. In the view of Bacon and Hume, every man has the capacity to attain true knowledge, whether by his senses or his reason. If truth nevertheless does not always make itself "manifest," certain external disturbances must be to blame. The other side of the "epistemological optimism" of the empiricists is their belief in the "kingdom of darkness," in "the work of some mischievous power, the source of impure and evil influences which pervert and poison our minds and instil in us the habit of resistance to knowledge" (168: 39). Popper impressively describes the contradiction between this theory and the liberal and enlightened political effects that accompanied its application in the seventeenth and eighteenth centuries, especially the eighteenth.[9] At the same time,

---

[9] This discussion of the "disastrous consequences" of the empiricists' theory of knowledge is preceded by the following remarkable paragraph: "Thus the optimistic

he develops a more consistent liberal epistemology in his own "approximation theory of truth." According to this theory, truth is sought by a "method of conjecture or hypothesis"; certainty is beyond our reach, even potentially, so that our actions and questions are primarily directed toward correcting errors. This theory bears an obvious relation to the principle of uncertainty postulated here (which is more general insofar as it also permits what Popper calls the "illusion theory of truth"); and in the following remarks we remain very close to Popper's position.

What does uncertainty mean in the sphere of scientific knowledge? It means first of all that there neither are nor can be any true —i.e., finally proven—statements. In this respect the "law" of gravity is no different from a cautious historical generalization about the course of revolutions. Every scientific proposition may be false. Even in the unlikely case that a proposition covers all relevant events that have occurred in the past,[10] the future remains open; the law so far unrefuted, the theory not yet disproved, may be refuted or disproved tomorrow. It follows that any scientific proposition which has become a dogma must be false. The relative truth of science depends on the possibility of refutation. Only so long as science remains a process of constant critical examination of relations held to be valid is it possible to avoid the extremes of error. The triumph of science is not in ultimate knowledge, which is un-

---

epistemology of Bacon and of Descartes cannot be true. Yet perhaps the strangest thing in this story is that this false epistemology was the major inspiration of an intellectual and moral revolution without parallel in history. It encouraged men to think for themselves. It gave them hope that through knowledge they might free themselves and others from servitude and misery. It made modern science possible. It became the basis of the fight against censorship and the suppression of free thought. It became the basis of the nonconformist conscience, of individualism, and of a new sense of man's dignity; of a demand for universal education, and of a new dream of a free society. It made men feel responsible for themselves and for others, and eager to improve not only their own condition but also that of their fellow men. It is a case of a bad idea inspiring many good ones." (168: 45.) Perhaps it is unreasonable to demand that history be logically consistent; still, many questions come to mind if we accept Popper's opening sentence as true.

[10] It can be argued that scientific theories with respect to past events are subject merely to a technical uncertainty: i.e., that it is technically impossible for us to carry out the fantastic labor, implied by any inductive theory, of scrutinizing all events relevant to a given case. The fact of a future, of events that cannot be examined at a given time, may therefore be crucial to the notion of a fundamental uncertainty.

attainable; it is in the refutation of theories and laws formerly held
to be valid, and the consequent formulation of better theories and
laws. Mutual criticism is thus the supreme principle of the ethics
of scientific discovery.

Two examples, which are taken from the social and historical
sciences but which might as easily have come from other disciplines,
may illustrate how deeply the "conspiracy theory of error" and the
"manifestation theory of truth" affect our understanding of scientific method, and how much weight is given to these theories by the
professional scientist. Ever since Max Weber insisted that the social scientist take pains to distinguish value judgments from scientific judgments, "objectivity" has been a watchword in the training
of social scientists. The demand for "objectivity" was spelled out
most plainly in what Max Scheler and Karl Mannheim called the
"sociology of knowledge," which soon became, quite apart from its
substantive value with respect to the social aspects of artistic and
scientific production, a method for the self-purification of social
scientists. It is only natural, therefore, that Jay Rumney and Joseph
Maier in their sociology textbook should urge the sociologist "to
train himself in attitudes of scientific objectivity"—i.e., "to observe
and explain the social facts without regard to his own interests
and wishes"—in which effort "psychoanalysis and the sociology of
knowledge" may be very valuable (19: 27–28). Indeed, such demands are widespread; to speak of the "objectivity" that the scientist in particular has to display is a commonplace in the self-criticism of social scientists.

Nevertheless, such demands clearly presuppose the "conspiracy
theory of error." If we err, according to this theory, we err because
our thinking is distorted by evil spirits—by neuroses and secret
desires, social interests and biases, idols and ideologies. We must
therefore banish these spirits, purify ourselves, and keep ourselves
under constant critical observation. By contrast, the principle of
uncertainty leads to very different conclusions. We are always liable
to err, never certain of truth. This situation is basic; neither psychoanalysis nor the sociology of knowledge can change it. Our only
protection from bad science and from the dogmas of false science
lies in the mutual criticism of practicing scientists. Science is always

a concert, a contrapuntal chorus of the many who are engaged in it. Insofar as truth exists at all, it exists not as a possession of the individual scholar, but as the net result of scientific interchange.[11] Although criticism and discussion, the refutation of long-accepted theories and their replacement by new ones, cannot banish error, they can prevent error from becoming dogma, as morning exercises in objectivity cannot. Harmless as self-control and self-criticism may be, they are poor guarantees of the progress of knowledge compared with the mutual criticism and correction, the friendly antagonism, of the *universitas scholarium*.[12]

The same criticism applies to a second widespread error, one made especially in the historical sciences and one that paralyzes the progress of scientific knowledge in a special way. As in the assigning of doctoral dissertations, so in choosing the subjects of scholarly works, it has become a generally accepted principle that each scholar should stake out his own little garden plot on the huge site of scholarly problems, and immediately erect a fence around it so that no one else can get in. Research often seems to establish what amounts to a property right in a problem—and shame to the scholar who dares intrude on another's carefully fenced-in domain. Since there are plenty of problems to go around, and since this sort of partitioning of the terrain is obviously a comfortable arrangement for all the parties involved, it has won widespread acceptance.[13]

Yet this arrangement, too, makes sense only if one accepts the

[11] From the perspective suggested here, even the customary identification of science with the "search for truth" may be misleading. To be sure, the formula is not really wrong. But insofar as it evokes the notion of a lonely search for a truth that the individual seeker may gain possession of (or even that the individual as such may approximate), the phrase leads to a disastrous scientific ethics. If I am not mistaken, such notions are especially widespread in Germany. More important than the education of young scholars for "teamwork," it seems to me, is education for openness and receptivity to criticism.

[12] Popper likes to distinguish between the "optimistic epistemology" of the empiricists (see n. 9 above) and his own "pessimistic" notion of the impossibility of certainty. In terms of the ethics of science the situation is nearly the opposite: whereas it seems futile to hope that all scientists will become "objective," it seems quite possible to maintain an atmosphere of mutual criticism.

[13] One sign of this attitude is the frequent reference to the "subject matter" of scientific disciplines, as if there were a preordained harmony between the articulation of the world and the encyclopedia of scientific disciplines. Science has only tasks and problems; and from this point of view, its "subject matter" is indivisible.

"manifestation theory of truth." It assumes that the garden, once cultivated, can never be planted in a different and better way, and hence that no one else need give a thought to what its "owner" does with it. Here again, the principle of uncertainty yields a very different and probably much more fruitful view. From this perspective, the fencing-in procedure is simply yet another way of giving error the status of dogma. Anyone who claims a "subject" entirely for himself, thus removing it from outside criticism, arbitrarily postulates the certainty of the uncertain. The principle of uncertainty requires exactly the opposite procedure: dealing again with the very problems that have been dealt with before by others. Every theory is an invitation to criticism and refutation. Where this lively contest gives way to fence building, scientific progress ceases. Many scholars may dislike seeing their research permanently exposed to sharp criticism from their colleagues. And indeed in the modern scientific world, where all interested parties know one another personally and nobody wants to make enemies, serious and businesslike criticism has become rather rare. Suffice it to say that the price for such comfort and convenience is always inferior scientific research.

An attitude like the one sketched here involves taking a stand both against and for the much-discussed specialization of modern science: against a specialization that results in everyone's having his own special subject to the exclusion of outside criticism, but for a specialization that helps promote competition among scholars in solving scholarly problems. But then specialization is not the most important problem of modern science. In my opinion, it is more important to remember that if the principle of uncertainty holds, science is not a private affair, not an occupation that can be pursued alone in a quiet attic. Science requires publicity and thus commitment. It is a *politicum* in the broadest and best sense of the word, even if only a few experts understand its statements. Science without publicity is like a dead planet, one without the atmosphere necessary to sustain life.

At this point, the principle of uncertainty can be seen as yielding certain rules that should both govern the scientist's behavior and serve as the orienting principles of his second, or scientific, con-science.[14] If we do not know but can only guess, then mutual criti-cism is an indispensable defense against the dogmatizing of error; and it follows that the individual scientist must be receptive to new and better solutions to "his" problems. But more important than individual attitudes (which decide the quality of the individual scholar, but not the future of scientific research) are the institutional provisions made for the critical concert of science. Preeminent among these are the public presentation and discussion of all the results of scientific research in an atmosphere free of threats or co-ercion from any public or private agency. This in turn demands a multitude of social and political institutions. We shall presently return to the political ones; among the social ones are universities and colleges, congresses and professional organizations, journals and publishers. If this inference from the uncertainty principle is correct, what follows from it for our understanding of the history of the sciences should be obvious. In any case, these remarks merely touch on a question that would justify a longish study by itself.[15]

It should be apparent, though it has not been made explicit, that the "science" we have been speaking of is by no means identical with the traditional notion of *Geisteswissenschaften,* i.e., the hu-manities or moral sciences. The principle of uncertainty and the consequent moral necessity of debate may be applied to all scien-tific disciplines: to the theories of the nuclear physicist, the models of the economist, the interpretations of the art critic, the presenta-tions of the historian, even the conjectures of the philologist (though

14 I shall not even touch here on the logical consequences of the principle of un-certainty, which have been convincingly developed by Popper and his disciples. It seems more important to me to explore the comparatively neglected areas of the ethics and politics of scientific research.

15 Perhaps the developments mentioned by Popper (see n. 9 above) are not so much good consequences of a bad idea as intellectual consequences of certain social developments in the direction being urged here. But this remark, like the entire para-graph above, calls forth more questions than it settles. Why did these institutions emerge? What threatens them at different times? What is the effect, for example, of the militarily relevant areas of modern natural science? Is there a rank order of the institutions that participate in the public dissemination and discussion of scientific knowledge? These and many other questions raised in the context of these reflections I hope to deal with one day in a projected study on *The Ethics of Uncertainty.*

in this last case, unlike the others, there remains the possibility that a newly found papyrus will reveal the *Ding an Sich*). In all disciplines, vigorous mutual criticism and progress through the refutation of old positions are the necessary moral consequences of working in a context of fundamental uncertainty. All disciplines, therefore, are subject to those conventions—or more correctly, those moral laws and institutional arrangements—of which we have spoken here.[16]

IV

What I have called institutional provisions for the concert of science naturally include certain political institutions. Exercises in objectivity with the help of psychoanalysis and the sociology of knowledge, fenced-in research gardens, the dogmatizing of error— all these can also flourish under authoritarian and indeed totalitarian conditions. A critical science cannot. "Inner emigration"— the privatization of a "truth" that is allegedly still thought but is no longer uttered—is not only an extremely dubious moral and political program; it also makes scientific criticism impossible. Modern totalitarianism implies, moreover, the conversion into dogma of certain cynical or utopian points of view, and with it the prohibition of criticism and the impossibility of science.[17] The critical institutions essential to the progress of scientific knowledge are possible only within a political order that permits conflict. In this sense, the ethics of scientific research, as derived from the principle of uncertainty, are incompatible with any form of constraint. In

16 These remarks are not intended to blur the distinction between the historical and theoretical disciplines. Insofar as the historical disciplines need not test their statements against future events, one might even argue that their uncertainty is always technical in nature, so that only a problematic analogy can relate them to the ethics of uncertainty. In many contexts, this rigorous distinction is relevant. But in fact the technical difficulties in the way of ultimate verification are likely to be so great in most historical disciplines that there seems no point in exempting them from the conventions of the theoretical disciplines.

17 If science nevertheless thrives under conditions approximating totalitarianism— as it does in Poland, and to some extent in the Soviet Union—this is because it creates its own public, limited in membership but internally free. This also means that in fact there have been only approximations to the total state, never a state truly total.

this sense, too, modern science and liberal political conditions are inseparably related.

But this is irrelevant, or at least not directly relevant, to our attempt to derive consequences from the principle of uncertainty that apply equally to the two apparently widely separated spheres of science and politics. Here we are not so much concerned with the direct interdependence of the two spheres as we are with the strange congruence between the conventions of science and the rules of the game of representative government—a congruence such that either might serve as a metaphor for the other. This metaphorical relation between science and representative democracy helps explain the common advance of both in the Anglo-Saxon countries, the difficulties of both in Germany and France, and, in general, the power that each has to shape the other.

But these remarks anticipate conclusions that have yet to be demonstrated. The starting point of our reflections in the realm of politics is not uncertainty about truth, but uncertainty about goodness, or (to give goodness in the social sphere its traditional name) about justice. We are assuming that nobody knows or can know what form of social order is ultimately satisfactory, good, just.[18] If this is the case, it follows that the bad society, the clearly unjust society, can be avoided only if and so long as the conflict between different conceptions of the just society is kept alive. Uncertainty requires competition, social and political conflict, and institutions that provide suitable conditions for this conflict. Starting from the principle of uncertainty, we arrive at the significance of the institutions of representative democracy.

Obviously, there are quite different political epistemologies. In politics, too, there is a "manifestation theory of justice" and a corollary "conspiracy theory of injustice"; indeed, it seems likely that

[18] Even the remark that goodness in the social sphere is traditionally called justice poses problems. The tradition of which we are speaking here is not that old; and both concepts, "good" and "just," have been applied both to the individual and to society. Nevertheless there is a relationship between the two concepts, a relationship that I have tried to express in the word "satisfactory." This question has been explored further in Josef König's lectures on ethics and in Chapter II of my dissertation (partially published in 158), which was greatly influenced by these lectures.

Popper took at least the latter concept from politics in the first place. What is of interest here is the consequences of any such manifestation or conspiracy theory. To the belief in the insight of the few who have succeeded by virtue of charisma or tradition in finding their way past all obstacles to the knowledge of justice, there corresponds the theory of the authoritarian state. "The state"—to cite this theory's crown witness, Hegel—"is the actuality of the ethical ideal. It is ethical mind *qua* the substantial will manifest and revealed to itself, knowing and thinking itself, accomplishing what it knows and insofar as it knows it." (162: §257, p. 155.) But who is the state if not those who direct it? Thus there are some to whom the moral ideal—αὐτὴ ἡ δικαιοσύνη—is manifest and who are therefore called upon to elevate their certainty to the status of public law.

That a conspiracy theory is the corollary of this manifestation theory is ironically, almost tragically, apparent from Ferdinand Lassalle's famous formulation: "The development of the human race to freedom [is] the true, moral nature of the state, gentlemen, its true and higher mission. So much is this the case from the beginning of time, through the very force of events, it has more or less been carried out by the state without the exercise of will, unconsciously, even against the will of its leaders." (166: 55.) Justice is manifest. If it nevertheless goes awry, the malevolence of its administrators is to blame, and even this is limited in its effects by the certainty of goodness in the state. Lassalle goes on to urge the "working class" to bring about complete harmony between the state's "moral nature" and reality.[19]

Given the assumption of fundamental uncertainty, such claims as Hegel's and Lassalle's lead to the elimination of discussion and thus to the dogmatizing of error. Nevertheless, we know that this form of the belief in the possibility of certainty is less harmful than the terroristic form taken by modern totalitarianism, in which mere opinion is transformed arbitrarily and often cynically into dogma.

---

[19] The great difficulties encountered by any theory of certainty that calls for political reform should by now be apparent. The idea that there can be certainty with respect to justice is necessarily conservative in its political consequences (which is not to argue that conservative thought necessarily implies a belief in certainty).

Totalitarian ideologies are always ideologies of certainty. Many of them may accordingly be described as utopian: as a grasping for the unreachable, or rather as an assertion that the unreachable has been grasped. In practice, however, this distinction is not useful; a utopian ideology soon becomes indistinguishable from that cynical totalitarianism which is indifferent to whether a program is right or wrong, good or evil, so long as a single concept of what is right prevails and the regime succeeds in suppressing all resistance. National Socialism is perhaps more inclined to the cynical variety of so-called certainty and Bolshevism to the utopian variety; but in practice both lead to the elimination of criticism and opposition, and thus to the entrenching of error.[20]

Watkins, in his lecture on "Epistemology and Politics," remarks, "I hold that political disagreement is pragmatically implied or presupposed by democratic institutions: they would be pointless or absurd if it were missing." (170: 85.) Our argument has traveled the same road in the opposite direction: we started off with the principle of uncertainty and ended with the necessity of competition between various conceptions of justice. Since nobody can know precisely what constitutes the just society—the ultimately right order of social and political affairs—the only satisfactory course is to keep alive the interplay of divergent concepts of justice. This is done by democratic institutions, or rather (to avoid confusion with the totalitarian democracies) representative institutions, i.e., political institutions in which the inevitable variety of proposed solutions to given problems may find representative expression. In this sense the institutions of representative democracy are attempts to domesticate conflict in recognition of its fruitfulness in a world of uncertainty.

If one pursues this interpretation to the details of representative institutions, many important questions arise. For example, what if there is no established consensus about the form of conflict? Do we not have to assume with Watkins that democracy presupposes not

---

[20] It may be remarked here that totalitarian regimes are by no means as "rational" as they are occasionally said to be. In such regimes the chance of error is always greater, the chance of correction smaller, than in representative democracies. For a discussion of this problem, see the preceding essay, "Market and Plan."

merely disagreement, but "disagreement without distrust" (170: 88), i.e., disagreement without criticism of that fundamental set of ground rules that we call a constitution? How can representative institutions be effectively protected from the many threats to which they are exposed in modern society—radicalisms of left and right, the encroachments of the mass media, the widespread indifference of the represented, the dwindling of the role of parliaments, the signs of a new conservative authoritarianism, and other tendencies? What form should political competition take in an era that has grown tired of comprehensive political ideologies, or, more precisely, that no longer provides the social basis for such ideologies? These are questions of political theory, a field that is wrongly neglected today.[21]

A given principle may be the inspiration of very different political structures under different historical circumstances; parliaments, for example, are not necessarily the only form of representative institution. But whatever specific political forms may be generated by the social conditions of the present, conditions so different from those of the heyday of liberal thought, it seems to me important to remember the standard against which political institutions should be measured. If we proceed on the assumption that nobody knows the final answer to our persistent questions about the good and just society, we must see that it remains possible for people to give different answers to these questions. To put this principle in a more provocative way, the free society is the highest goal of politics because we cannot define the just society.

It would certainly be possible to defend this formulation. But it

---

[21] The decline of political theory would require an essay of its own to describe. "For the moment, anyway," the editor of a much-discussed collection of essays declared a few years ago, "political philosophy is dead" (164: vii). Although the same writer has since qualified this assertion—"The mood is very different and very much more favorable than it was six years ago" (165: vii)—it remains a regrettable fact that political theory has disappeared from political behavioralism on the one hand, and from public law on the other. A really significant recent study of political theory, Friedrich Hayek's *Constitution of Liberty* (149), which is based on the same point of view as this essay, has had many reviews but little response—except from Raymond Aron (140). After the ethics of science, political theory is the second "gap" in contemporary thought to which I hoped this essay might call attention.

seems subject to one serious misinterpretation, namely that the free society, and the ethics of uncertainty in general, are a disappointing substitute for a certainty that is beyond our reach. This is emphatically not what I mean here. With respect to science I have tried to show not only that critical debate is the sole adequate procedure in view of the fundamental limitations on our knowledge, but also that it is the only way to guarantee the progress of scientific knowledge, or at least to protect it against retrogression and stagnation. The analogous point holds in politics: without discussion and conflict, every society is condemned to stagnation. The contest between divergent concepts of the just society is itself the motor that moves the real world closer to that unattainable goal. The problem discussed so seriously by Kant in his "Idea for a Universal History with a Cosmopolitan Intent" can only be mentioned in passing here:

> It must always remain puzzling that earlier generations seem to work so hard merely for the sake of later ones, erecting scaffolds from which to raise nature's intended edifice to new and greater heights; and that only the latest should be fortunate enough to live in a building on which a long line of their ancestors (whether intentionally or not) have labored without ever knowing the happiness their efforts made possible.

But I accept Kant's "Fourth Proposition" without reservation, that "the means by which nature brings about the development of all its endowments" is the "antagonism of the same in society, insofar as this ultimately becomes the cause of a regular order of the same." (104: 209–10.) Thus freedom as freedom for conflict is by no means a second-rate substitute for justice; indeed, as a condition of the possibility of progress, it is also a necessary precondition of the just society, or whatever approximation to it can be achieved. In the world of uncertainty, freedom *is* justice.

V

There is no lack of examples to illustrate this principle. One might almost make it an ethical precept in the individual sense as well: to wit, wherever you do not know precisely what is right, be receptive to criticism and correction, for the danger of error is always increased by dogmatism.[22] This holds in private life as it does for social institutions. It holds, moreover, even where one might think that the principle of uncertainty, in the sense of the assumption of certain basic limitations on our knowledge, is invalid—i.e., where uncertainty seems to reflect nothing more profound than technical difficulties, as happens, for example, in the criminal trial. The example of the criminal trial is at once so important and so striking that we shall use it here to summarize these reflections.[23]

In a way, the criminal trial combines scientific knowledge and political decision. A criminal case is supposed to be cleared up *and* judged—a case about which there is uncertainty to begin with. If we dismiss from consideration the arbitrary, terroristic (and in that sense totalitarian) approach to "solving" this dual problem, there remain in principle two possible approaches. One can work on the assumption that certainty is possible in matters of fact and of value. This assumption leads on the one hand to the creation of the "most objective authority in the world" (as a prominent German criminal lawyer, without intentional irony, has described the prosecutor's office in German law), and on the other hand to confidence in a codified set of laws. Or one can work on the assumption that certainty is not possible in either matters of fact or matters of value. In this case, the "accusatory" criminal procedure will take the place

[22] This principle is related to another ethical precept (also borrowed from Professor König's lectures), to the effect that since not every dilemma can be solved, we do well to resign ourselves to living with many an unsolved dilemma. Once again we have to keep in mind a question raised before (n. 8 above), namely, whether fundamental uncertainty is bearable for the individual.

[23] The criminal trial makes a fascinating example partly because it ranks high among the symptomatic institutions of any society; thus Frederick Maitland wished that a good fairy would give him the opportunity to see a murder trial "in every age of history of every race," "because I think that it would give me so many hints as to a multitude of matters of the first importance." The possibility of comparative social analysis on the basis of the criminal trial has been mentioned by Watkins (170: 85ff) and in a speech by James B. Conant (157: 8ff). Conant took the title of his speech from the "pamphlet 'Two Ways of Thinking' by the famous English jurist Lord Macmillan" (157: 9), which deals with the same subject. In my Sidney Ball Memorial Lecture at Oxford, I attempted a somewhat more elaborate comparative analysis of the social structure of criminal trials (159).

of the "inquisitory" one. That is, justice by decree will give way to adversary procedure, in which prosecution and defense figure as agencies of equal rank; and the *codex iuris* will give way to the more flexible procedure of jurisdiction by precedent. Obviously I am describing the difference between the Anglo-Saxon (incidentally Germanic) legal tradition and the Continental or Roman tradition; and indeed a contrast between Anglo-Saxon and Continental (especially German) procedures is implicit throughout this essay.[24] To say this is not to suggest a historical or comparative argument for or against any position; intellectual history is a bad means of proof. Rather, let us see where abstractions take us. We have reached a point now at which we can free our so far wholly hypothetical reflections from their logical supposition and convert them into a thesis.

Throughout we have proceeded on the assumption that one aspect of the human condition is a fundamental uncertainty with respect both to knowledge and to decision. To begin with, there is no particular reason to consider this assumption correct; at least we have not advanced any such reason. (Moreover, it is clear that any attempt to argue the correctness of the assumption that we cannot know what is correct leads to the famous paradoxes of Descartes and Fichte, i.e., to the "absolute ego" or some other initial position of certainty.) From the assumption of uncertainty follow definite moral precepts: conventions of science, rules of the game for politics, and various codes of private and public behavior. The argument can be summarized rather crudely as follows: the ethics of uncertainty are the ethics of liberty, and the ethics of liberty are the ethics of conflict, of antagonism generated and institutionalized.

I now propose to make these derivations from the uncertainty principle the pragmatic foundation of the principle itself. If the ethics of uncertainty are the ethics of liberty, and if we think that the ethics of liberty are both the most appropriate to human dignity

---

[24] The difference between the two traditions in the context relevant here turns on the position of Hegel. To the present day Continental philosophy stands in Hegel's shadow, whereas Anglo-Saxon philosophers regard not Hegel but Kant as the "last philosopher."

and the most fruitful among the competing moral propositions, then it seems to me necessary to accept the assumption of uncertainty. Thus the question is not whether or not one thinks we may achieve certainty with respect to the true and the untrue, the just and the unjust; the question is, rather, whether or not one desires a free, dynamic society and a science corresponding to it. In making this moral-political decision one automatically solves the epistemological problem discussed here.

Thus the chief result of our reflections is what might be termed a basic clarification, which can be expressed in two ways. On the one hand, I have tried to show what would follow if we assume that we are living in a world of uncertainty. On the other hand, this demonstration enables us to locate the point at which it is decided whether or not this assumption holds. For behind any assertion of the principle of uncertainty there must always be a practical decision. I hardly need emphasize that my own concern goes beyond this conclusion, and that for my part I have long since chosen the path of uncertainty. This essay alone contains several invitations to combine a commitment to science and representative democracy with insight into the uncertainty of the human condition, and on the basis of the resulting syndrome to expound the ethics of uncertainty in the two spheres of knowledge and decision-making.

It may be objected that my enthusiasm for such an undertaking betrays, if not a belated representative of enlightened liberalism, in any case an unsubtle pre-Hegelian theorist. Such descriptions decidedly hit the mark, but I regard them as a confirmation rather than an objection. There is only the slightest difference between my views and the traditional liberalism of the enlightenment (if we leave aside the matter, merely hinted at here but very important, of reconsidering old principles in the light of changed conditions). Popper rightly emphasizes the contradiction between classical liberalism and its empiricist epistemology; and Watkins is also right in remarking that "classical empiricism and parliamentary democracy are incompatible in virtue of their clashing implications and presuppositions" (170: 97). The epistemology that accords with the dynamics of scientific progress and representative democracy is not empiricism or sensualism or rationalism, but (if labels are needed) what might be called *institutional liberalism*. Because we cannot recognize what is true and what is just, we need competition in science and politics, and competition thrives only if it is built into certain institutions. The institutions of critical science and representative democracy are conditions of progress in the realm of freedom, and thus the very goal for whose sake science and politics are carried on.

10

Sociology and the Sociologist
On the Problem of Theory and Practice

No despot to date has kept a court sociologist, a specialist with the duty, after the daily weather forecast, of charting the location and direction of the winds of change on a map of his country. Sociologists are relatively rare even in the more modest role of adviser to the temporarily powerful and those in lesser positions of power. For sociologists—or so one might think—this state of affairs is disheartening and consoling at the same time. It is disheartening because it is a fair judgment of their usefulness; a court sociologist would have an even harder time keeping up with an intelligent journalist than the BBC's Meteorological Service had some years ago with a weather-sensitive village chemist whom it was foolhardy enough to challenge to a weather-prediction contest. It is consoling because it spares the sociologist the troubles that give sleepless nights to his colleagues in nuclear physics and cell biology. But is this apparently tranquil state of affairs the true one? Is it even the most desirable one? Given the long and exhaustive discussion of the relationship between theory and practice in sociology, is not the sociologist better equipped than others to face problems involving this relationship? And finally, quite apart from what a despot might require of him, does he not already find himself in a dilemma in which his problems unexpectedly turn into questions, his questions into problems?[1]

[1] For the distinction made here between "problems" and "questions," as for the distinction between a scientific conscience and a moral one, I am indebted to Josef

Let us begin by examining this distinction between questions, which are of our making, and problems, with which life confronts us. To answer a question or not is our free decision; if we like, we can postpone a question or forget it. Moreover, how we answer a question is a matter of agreement on certain rules that hold only for those who have committed themselves to the enterprise of answering questions. By contrast, it is a condition of our existence that we solve problems; we can neither postpone a problem nor forget it, for unlike the failure to answer a question, the failure to solve a problem is itself a resolution. How we solve a problem is also a matter of rules; but the rules in this case, whatever the source of their binding character might be, hold in principle for all men. Finally, questions and problems relate differently to time. Questions, science, theory, are as such timeless, i.e., conceivable apart from the dimension of time. Rules may obtain—rules of argument, for example—by which certain answers to questions are projected very far, if not indefinitely, into the future; in this sense theory is like a game. If in fact theory, especially when it becomes empirical, encounters limitations of time, this is because in reality it cannot be as cleanly distinguished from practice as its concept may suggest. For so far as practice, life, problems, are concerned, in a certain sense we never have time. The rules for solving problems must enable us to give an answer in time; indeed, timeliness is a part of correctness.[2]

If we begin by taking the encounter of theory and practice, question and problem, as itself a question, we may come up with some explanations as well as some difficulties. An example may help us

König's lectures on ethics at the University of Hamburg in 1951–52. In German as in English, the terms "question" and "problem" are often used interchangeably, and they are so used in the preceding essays. In this essay, however, it has seemed appropriate to translate the German *Problem* always as "question," and the German *Frage* as "problem."

2 In this sense the connection made by Aristotle between the "theoretical life" and "leisure" is inescapable. His rank order, however, is open to question: "But leisure seems to carry within it its gratification, and happiness and the blessed life. This is why it does not belong to those who work but to those who have leisure. For he who works, works because of a goal which is not yet reached, but happiness is a goal and by general conviction it is not connected with pain, but with pleasure." (97: 1337b.)

here. Henry Christelow is a character in Robert Robinson's intriguingly titled detective novel *Landscape with Dead Dons* (188). Christelow, a don of an imaginary Oxford college, has spent many years of his life forging a manuscript that can convincingly be attributed to Chaucer. His motive in this enterprise is not to sell the manuscript at a profit, but by producing an edition of it, complete with learned commentary, to establish his reputation as a scholar. He is on the point of success when an unfortunate colleague named Manchip discovers the forgery (if it can be called that), which he regards as a successful "academic joke." Christelow does not share his opinion; he lures Manchip to the college roof, stabs him, and adds the corpse to the row of Renaissance statues along the edge of the roof. The macabre addition is soon noticed, and with the search for the culprit the drama of detection takes it course.

Our concern here is not with this drama but with the action just described. Christelow has done two things: he has produced a Chaucer manuscript, and he has murdered a man. The first deed is plausibly characterized by a colleague as "not strictly ethical," but the difference between the two crimes is not merely one of degree. The conventions violated by the production of a false Chaucer manuscript are esoteric rules in the world of theory. So long as Christelow does not try to sell the manuscript or otherwise use it for criminal purposes, no court of law can try him. The deed may weigh on his scholarly conscience, but morally it can be laughed off as an academic joke. The murder, by contrast, is in no sense a joke. As a breach of exoteric (i.e. moral) norms, it becomes a burden on the general conscience. It is a practical matter in only too manifest a sense.

Even in theory, however, the world of problems and the world of questions are not easily kept separate. Christelow, for example, may have regarded forging a Chaucer manuscript as the answer to a question, as an exercise in theory; but since this enterprise involved his scholarly reputation, Manchip's discovery posed a problem for him that required an immediate solution. Scholarly vanity is probably not the only connecting link between theory and practice. One might argue, for example, that any breach of conventions jeopardizes the reliability of all agreements on rules.[3] By this reasoning, Christelow's readiness to forge a manuscript indicates his potential readiness to commit murder; if esoteric conventions are broken, exoteric rules may be broken next. Whatever the merits of such an argument, it is no accident that both human vanity and the bogey of anomie raise sociological questions. Indeed, the whole relationship between theory and practice, considered as a question, concerns the sociologist more immediately than most of his colleagues because it is itself the subject matter of his research and his theories.

II

How do the answers to questions of theory in fact affect the solutions to problems of practice? Neither this formulation of the question nor the detective story paradigm touches the heart of the sociologist's commitment in this matter. There is a *question* of theory and practice; by virtue of his competence in his field, the sociologist should be particularly well qualified to help answer it. But there is also a *problem* of theory and practice. Science has certain effects, and the scientist must take a position with respect to these effects; the dilemma is nicely symbolized by the picture of interned German nuclear physicists hearing the news, over the radio, of the bombing of Hiroshima. If sociology has as its subject matter the encounter between theory and practice, it is important to find out how the sociologist solves the problem posed by this encounter. Does it help him to be a person who does sociological work? More precisely, in view of the problem of theory and practice, is it enough for the sociologist to regard himself as a person who works at sociology and nothing more? Again an example may be helpful, this time a less playful one.

In early 1964, Project Camelot, the biggest and possibly the most influential research project in the history of sociology, was launched with a grant of four to six million dollars from the Special Opera-

[3] F. Kambartel would argue this way; see 184.

tions Research Office (SORO) of the United States Army.[4] The
project, which was budgeted for three or four years, had one aim:
to find the causes of internal upheavals and revolutions in the developing countries, especially in Latin America. Behind this gigantic enterprise—its budget far exceeded the total budget of its
sponsor, SORO—was the realization, in the words of one of its
scientific directors, Jessie Bernard, "that neither cold nor hot war
was an appropriate way for dealing with the problems of international relations," and that "political rather than military solutions
were needed" (174: 24). But there were other motivations as well.
A circular letter of late 1964, designed to attract scholars to the
project, mentioned the desire to "identify with increased degrees of
confidence those actions which a government might take to relieve
conditions which are assessed as giving rise to a potential for internal war." The letter also contained this assertion: "The U.S.
Army has an important mission in the positive and constructive aspects of nation-building in less developed countries as well as a responsibility to assist friendly governments in dealing with active
insurgency problems." (See 182: 4.) The originators of Project Camelot did not like the term "counterinsurgency"; they defined their
goals as "insurgency prophylaxis."

The late Rex Hopper, a well-known expert on Latin American
affairs and theorist of revolution, became the director of the project.
Numerous other sociologists were taken on in more or less permanent positions, which involved consulting, attending conferences,
and carrying out special missions in the countries selected for investigation. One of those invited to participate was the Norwegian
conflict theorist Johan Galtung, who happened to be in Santiago de
Chile at the time. Galtung peremptorily declined the invitation,

---

[4] The project had its prehistory. Irving Louis Horowitz reports that "Project
Camelot was conceived in late 1963 by a group of high-ranking army officers connected with the Army Research Office of the Department of Defense" (182: 4). William J. Goode says in a letter of autumn 1966: "I first learned about this project (it
then had no name) some five years ago from my friend Rex Hopper." (179: 255.) The
name "Camelot," i.e., the allusion to King Arthur's realm, was carefully chosen, as
the director of SORO, Theodore Vallance, made clear to the House of Representa-
tives: "It connotes the right sort of things—development of a stable society with
peace and justice for all."

observing that he considered the army better suited to disrupting peace than to promoting it, and in any case not a suitable sponsor for such research. Galtung's arguments became known in Santiago at the same time that a sociologist from Pittsburgh, Hugo Nutini, a Chilean by birth, was discussing preliminary plans for a Project Camelot study with the Rector of the University of Chile, also in Santiago. Whatever path the spark may have taken, it set off the explosion subsequently known as the "Chilean debacle": angry newspaper stories, demonstrations against American espionage disguised as research, diplomatic protests in Washington by the Chilean government, an investigating committee of the Chilean parliament. Overnight Project Camelot had brought about almost exactly the sort of outburst that it was supposed to help prevent.

Other Latin American nations joined in the protests after the list of countries to be investigated became known.[5] The press campaign extended to Washington, where Senators Fulbright, Morse, and McCarthy called for a Senate investigation. At the same time a quarrel over jurisdiction broke out between the State Department (which felt neglected, if not deceived) and the Department of Defense (which had commissioned the project). On July 5, 1965, President Johnson wrote a letter to Secretary of State Dean Rusk stating that in the future all research projects abroad sponsored by U.S. government agencies must be screened first by the State Department for possible adverse effects on America's foreign relations.[6] On July 7, during a Congressional hearing on Project Camelot, the Department of Defense abruptly canceled the project.

Presumably this was the end of Camelot as a research project;[7] it was not the end of the Camelot affair. Argument over the pros and

[5] The countries were Argentina, *Bolivia*, Brazil, *Colombia*, Cuba, the Dominican Republic, *Ecuador*, El Salvador, Guatemala, Mexico, *Paraguay*, *Peru*, *Venezuela*, and, outside Latin America, Egypt, *Iran*, Turkey, Korea, Indonesia, Malaysia, *Thailand*, France, Greece, and Nigeria. (Italics indicate countries selected for field research and surveys.) If one considers the history of internal unrest in these countries, especially those outside Latin America, since Project Camelot was launched, one cannot quarrel with SORO's selection.

[6] Much of the ensuing debate among sociologists involved this letter, which many thought portended government "censorship" of research.

[7] D. L. Johnson reports (183: 206): "The hastily canceled project in Chile was resurrected, in varied form, a short time later in Colombia and Peru." Johnson

cons of the enterprise and its sudden death has scarcely abated since July 1965. Several American sociologists have published long critical reports;[8] and other comments, some quite emotional, have appeared in the letters columns of such widely read journals as *The American Sociologist* and *Trans-Action*. "Our scientific integrity has been compromised, and we must act to redeem it," a group of five social scientists wrote to *The American Sociologist* (177: 207). Students of Latin American affairs in particular complained that for decades all studies by North Americans would carry the taint of espionage: "Camelot-like projects are distasteful to Latin Americans and to anyone with a sense of dignity." (183: 207.) Angry sociologists have accused Project Camelot of both scientific and ethical irresponsibility—apparently both consciences are involved here! Only a few have managed to view the debate with some detachment, among them Irving Louis Horowitz (182) and William J. Goode (179). Each in his own way has pointed out the paradoxes inherent in the discussion: that the project was canceled for the wrong reasons, namely to preserve American prestige and avoid embarrassing the ruling Latin American regimes; that Camelot involved subjects of research for which sociologists had time and again sought support; that the critics of Camelot were themselves noisy advocates of intervention in the social structures of other peoples. One letter writer, Richard Kurtz, focused on the question for whose sake I have here discussed Project Camelot: "If we, as sociologists, are not sensitive to the practical application of our own conclusions, who can be expected to possess such sensitivity?" (185: 85.)

III

Not one of the letter writers, however, refers to the old, indeed almost classical, sociological discussion of the subject; indeed, one might almost conclude that every one of them has discovered the

---

based his statement on an item in the *New York Times* of February 7, 1966. In any case the more recent discovery of the extent to which research projects, foundations, journals, etc., have been financed by the CIA shows that Camelot is but an example of a far more general problem.

8 See 180, 182, 189, and 191.

question anew. Hans Albert, Helmut Schelsky, and Jürgen Habermas are not mentioned, nor are such intellectual equivalents of theirs in the Anglo-Saxon world as Karl Popper, Reinhard Bendix, and C. Wright Mills.[9] Perhaps the letter writers do not know these names, especially the first three. (Provincialism in the sense of cheerfully accepting a limited horizon is not, after all, a German monopoly.) But there may be another reason for the discontinuity. Theory, the scientific answering of questions, is according to its esoteric rules cumulative; a scientist who is ignorant of the theoretical tradition may incur professional reproach for merely repeating what has long been known. Practice, on the other hand, the solving of problems posed by real life, does not recognize rules based on the accumulation of experience; it is not even clear whether we *can* learn from history, to say nothing of whether we *must*. Thus even in the "scientific civilization" people, including scientists, are scarcely better than their forefathers at solving life's problems. One would have to be a weak proponent of rationality, however, to accept this condition simply as given.

Schelsky and Habermas both consider "scientific civilization" an apt term for our society, in which (in their view) scientific progress has fundamentally changed the relationship between theory and practice. They are in less agreement about what happened before the present era. Schelsky, who likes the modern world, believes that the new condition has rendered the great ideologies obsolete, and with them "sociology as a comprehensive revolutionary and conservative policy": "general sociological prescriptions for explaining the times and changing the world" are now no longer possible (20: 115, 118). Habermas, by contrast, is rather unhappy with the modern world and therefore condemns it, in characteristically Hegelian fashion, to the state of antithesis. The old world was at least thesis, or undeveloped truth; it was the world of the liberal idyll, of the

[9] The equation is fully justified only in the case of Popper and Albert. Still, Bendix's *Social Science and the Distrust of Reason* (173) is in some ways comparable to Schelsky's approach, and parts of *The Sociological Imagination* (186) call to mind Habermas's concept. Possibly the difficulties of comparison prove that the methodological dispute has become more explicit in Germany than elsewhere.

functioning public, of enlightenment. "Reason had not yet abandoned the will to reasonableness." (1: 232.)[10]

Habermas and Schelsky do agree, however, on the function of present-day sociology. As Habermas likes to put it, sociology as an "empirical-analytical science" has become a "productive force of an industrialized society" (1: 232). Schelsky means the same thing when he speaks of the "functional science of 'sociology' " and its "empirical-rational basis" (20: 119). It is readily apparent, moreover, that both men view such a sociology without enthusiasm. Habermas regards empirical sociology, so far as its relation to practice is concerned, as an instrument of "planning bureaucracies," in whose hands it will necessarily be fragmented to comply with "the rigid division of labor between analysis and decision, diagnosis and program" (1: 226). Since the only concern of such bureaucracies is to achieve certain technical goals, "all other practical applications [of sociology] can be dismissed in the name of value-free science" (1: 241). It is no accident that Habermas quotes Schelsky at this point: separated as "the system of social action" is from all "anthropological and philosophical theories that are related to the unity of the person," it "no longer permits the same mind to think in both diagnostic and programmatic terms, or to deal at the same time with matters of value and matters of fact" (20: 124). Schelsky is not quite so angry as Habermas with "sociology as a science of planning," but both deplore the separation of theory and practice that they claim has been caused by the development of a value-free empirical science of sociology.

Now one might well be inclined to agree with these rightly renowned critics; but if we apply their criticism to Project Camelot, which can clearly be taken as symptomatic of the condition they deplore, we encounter two preliminary difficulties that are worth exploring. Critics of an empirical science of sociology often describe it as a gigantic body of applicable social knowledge that is available to any interested party. It is more rarely asked whether this em-

---

10 Cf. also 181. In his evaluation of the Enlightenment Habermas differs from T. W. Adorno and Max Horkheimer (171), who regarded the Enlightenment as the antithesis, as Hegel did "civil society" and Marx "capitalist society"; Habermas, by contrast, distinguishes between the Enlightenment and positivism.

pirical science of sociology even exists. One of the more puzzling aspects of the Camelot affair is the subsequent discussion of the practicability of the project. Thus Charles Tilly accused those involved in the project of overrating its potential scientific achievement in their representations to the government; Harry Eckstein's reader *Internal War* had only recently shown that in this field there were "almost no established uniformities and no agreement whatsoever on theory, method, or likely hypotheses" (190: 84).[11] The accused, far from rejecting the charge, used it to justify their actions: precisely because there was no way of satisfying the sponsoring organization's desire for an empirically confirmed theory of revolution with clear implications for the maintenance of social stability, they considered their participation in the project above reproach. "Most of the men viewed Camelot as a bona fide opportunity to do fundamental research with relatively unlimited funds at their disposal." (182: 6.)

Wolfgang Zapf (192) has shown that in fact we know a good deal about the conditions of social stability and the possibility of social change, but it would clearly be wrong to speak of a theory, or indeed an instrument, of social engineering. So far the much-scorned empirical-analytical science of sociology consists at best of approaches, and often enough of mere programs. But in this case we must reconsider Schelsky's and particularly Habermas's criticisms. If in fact no "functional science of 'sociology'" exists, criticism of the concept amounts almost to a ban on scientific inquiry, i.e., a call to cease looking for solutions that as yet no one has found. It would be quite unjust to charge Habermas with deliberate obscurantism; but he (and even more T. W. Adorno) must face this implication of his criticism, so long as the object of contention is no more than a promise, and for many a hope.[12]

---

[11] Horowitz had already pointed out that curiously enough, "by never challenging the feasibility of the work, the political critics of Project Camelot were providing backhanded compliments to the efficiency of the project" (182: 45).

[12] Two questions (a question and a problem perhaps?) come together here. The first and simpler question is what to make of the implicit obscurantism of Habermas and Adorno (171). Both have conducted empirical research themselves, so that their implied support for placing limitations on scientific inquiry is clearly present only

Our other preliminary difficulty has to do with the notion of a value-free science. It is true that posthumously Max Weber has defeated his opponents in the Verein für Sozialpolitik; today, the separation of science and value judgments is the universal property of scientific methodology. But Weber's Freiburg inaugural lecture has not been forgotten either. It is not only the critics of Weber's early nationalism who invoke it, but also those who have fewer methodological objections to it than its author had twenty years later—and in this respect Weber was fortunately much less successful than some of his critics assume.[13] The debate over Project Camelot provides ample and in some ways surprising proof that many sociologists do not regard the postulate of a value-free science as a license to conduct research irrespective of its implications. Every one of the Camelot critics would have to be described as a committed sociologist; and although this may not seem astonishing, the director of the project deserves the same description. Goode reports an episode that should provide food for thought, especially for critical sociologists. At one Camelot conference, where "a RAND type of social scientist was giving his paper," Goode passed a note to Hopper protesting the idea of "containing" revolutions: "The better question was, I urged, how can we facilitate them?" Hopper replied in an answering note: "Yes, but in the light of our current sociological knowledge, isn't it more likely that we shall discover the best way of 'containing' revolution is simply to correct the abuses that generate a high revolutionary potential to begin with?"

---

de facto, and not by intention. One might argue, of course, that this implication does not detract from the effect of their argument. The other question, a much more difficult one, is whether there are legitimate limitations on our knowledge. Should we permit research whose results may be used to destroy mankind? (And, on a more harmless level, should we permit secret research?) The question is perhaps best answered by an appeal to history. Efforts to limit scientific inquiry have been uniformly ineffective since Galileo's time and long before; man's propensity for theory is indomitable. That is why the problem of theory and practice exists.

13 The substantive discussion of Weber's nationalism began with Wolfgang Mommsen's book *Max Weber und die deutsche Politik* (154); for its continuation see 144 and 151. For the methodological debate over "social science and objectivity," see 10: 39ff. Though I still regard my own contribution to this debate (Chapter 1 above) as essentially correct, it does not seem to me now to go far enough. This essay is an attempt to get beyond my earlier position.

(179: 255–56.) In other words, does not the practical application of the sociology of revolution mean more humane conditions of life for millions of men? Not only is there no functioning science of sociology as yet, but those who promote such a science are often sufficiently aware of values to give their critics cause for joy rather than scorn.[14]

What, then, is the "scientific civilization," and what relationship does it entail between theory and practice? There are at least two concepts of a "scientific civilization," of which only the second stands up on close inspection. We may begin by dismissing the first, the image of a world steering itself decisionlessly by the rules of a technical rationality—the technocratic utopia. Schelsky and Habermas occasionally find it gratifying to fight this chimera: "Even decisions are finally made in a self-regulating process of adaptation by learning automatons according to the laws of rational behavior." (1: 251.)[15] But the vision of the computer-directed world is in fact nothing but the wishful or fearful dream of the unpolitical. Even in the world of today and tomorrow the much-discussed intrinsic force of things is nothing but more or less reasonable decisions behind the mask of necessity; only those who do not know what decisions involve and how they are made can confuse the mask with the face behind it.[16]

The other concept of a "scientific civilization," however, is not a mask. More and more people are discovering that an apparent detour to ask questions in fact helps them in solving their problems. Practice may profit from theory, even if it is the practice of war from the theory of nuclear processes. Moreover, even where theory

[14] There are other attitudes, of course. Thus Jessie Bernard argues (174: 25) that basically it does not matter for whom the sociologist conducts his research, for in any case both "good guys" and "bad guys" can use his findings. But on the whole Talcott Parsons is certainly right that "the majority point of view [of sociologists] tends in the United States to be somewhat left of center." This Parsons accepts, but he deplores the "involvement of too large a component too indiscriminately in the politics of the left" (187: 64). There can be no doubt today that in research such attitudes tell.

[15] Schelsky explicitly develops the theory of the "technical state"; see 21, especially pp. 455ff.

[16] In that sense the technocratic utopia is a welcome ideology to a ruling class that likes to remain invisible. Here is one of the dangers of praising, as is done in the following argument, a "decided reason."

does not yet exist, the idea of its possibility is inherent in practice. The President of the United States, seeking stable political relations with his country's neighbors far and near, comes to feel (if belatedly) that it is not adequate or even useful to put down foreign revolutions by the use of an expeditionary force; instead he raises the question of the causes of revolution, which he seeks to answer by consulting experts or commissioning research. In this way it comes about that the great practical problems are themselves created by theory, and in that sense "made," contrary to their original concept, as Schelsky has demonstrated in an impressive catalog:

What does it mean that more and more people suffer and even die from diseases that man himself has created in the course of building his civilization? What does it mean that the material needs of man in our civilization are more and more separated from natural products and more and more frequently satisfied by artificial products? What does it mean that indirect information, instead of personal experience, is increasingly becoming the immediate reality of modern man? (21: 440ff.)

It is not cultural criticism that guides the pen here, but the modern problem of theory and practice, which Horowitz justly calls "the heart of the problem of Camelot: What are and are not the legitimate functions of a scientist?" (182: 47.) Since we are not concerned with the scientist in general, but with the expert on the question of theory and practice, let us modify Horowitz's wording. What is the social role of the sociologist today? What should it be?

IV

The three sociologies have each answered this question in their own way,[17] and in doing so they have each sought to establish a new connection between theory and practice. The simplest answer is that of the empirical scientists. Like Popper, Albert sees scientific theories primarily in terms of their application in the form of tech-

[17] For further discussion of the distinctions between these types, see my review of the book by Schelsky to which I have here referred (20), which bore the title "The Three Sociologies" (176).

niques. In this view, the more practical the questions that give rise to a theory, the better the theory. Popper quotes Friedrich Hayek with unequivocal approval: "Economic analysis has never been the product of detached intellectual curiosity about the *why* of social phenomena, but of an intense urge to reconstruct a world which gives rise to profound dissatisfaction." (155: 56.)[18] Moreover, in this view, the application of the answers to questions stimulated by practical problems should remain within the bounds of a "rational politics" of "piecemeal engineering." One of the practical effects of social science is that it generates illuminating criticism: "The use of social-science knowledge for social criticism may thus precede its technical application, by revealing in the first place those social facts and contexts from which then the tasks for political activity and thus for the application of social-technological statements and systems emerge. Thus social science itself becomes an agent of social change." (172: 70.) But the goals of social technology, the causes of dissatisfaction with the world, the directions of desired change, all these have nothing to do with theory; they originate in the "noncognitive realm" of decision-making. The sociologist of this persuasion might simply urge the Camelot scholars to be clear about the project's goals, and perhaps add, "For my part, I am against it."[19]

Schelsky is not content with a conclusion that goes no further than the "direct translation of sociological insights into practical plans and social techniques" (20: 123). He rightly emphasizes that in this formulation the dilemma of theory and practice is not resolved but merely stated. His own resolution of it is both old and new. The sociologist, and sociology, should entirely free themselves from the ultimately simplistic circle of scientific research and prac-

18 Popper adds at this point: "And some of the social sciences, other than economics, that have not yet adopted this outlook, show by the barrenness of their results how urgently their speculations are in need of practical checks."

19 Habermas could scarcely invent a better exemplar of this attitude than William Goode. A vociferous defender of Project Camelot, Goode nonetheless refused to take part in it; he simply did not like it. "Without question, I felt uneasy about doing any research *for* anyone, and especially for the Department of Defense. I have long asserted that 'applied' research can contribute to 'pure' knowledge, but temperamentally I don't like to work for a client. Besides, I have the usual liberal's aversion to the military. Perhaps, too, without being aware of my own pettiness, I did not wish to join a project I would not direct." (179: 255.)

tical application and should instead develop a Kantian "disinter-
estedness." In short, they should come to terms with reality by de-
parting from it completely: "Today, the most important achievement of sociological analysis for social action no longer consists in
stating what has to be done and how to get it done, but rather in
explaining what is happening in any case and cannot be changed at
all." (20: 125–26.) Schelsky refers to Kant, but his skepticism reminds one of Hegel: so far as "giving instruction as to what the
world ought to be" is concerned, Hegel says in the Preface to the
Philosophy of Right, "philosophy in any case always comes on the
scene too late to give it. As the thought of the world, it appears only
when actuality is already there cut and dried after its process of
formation has been completed. . . . The owl of Minerva spreads its
wings only with the falling of the dusk." (162: 12–13.) This is clearly
a very compressed presentation of Schelsky's (and Hegel's) position.
Indeed, Schelsky explicitly sets out to understand "sociology itself
as a part of the system of social action" (20: 131),[20] but his approach
does not bring him any closer to the Camelot scholars. All he can
do is tell them that they and their problems are symptomatic of a
scientific civilization. The sociologist as an interpreter of reality in
Schelsky's sense regards even his own disinterested reflections as
fettered.

   Habermas takes to task both the Kantian Albert and the Hegelian (or perhaps, rather, Fichtean) Schelsky. The Eleventh Thesis
on Feuerbach is closer to his heart than the antinomy of knowledge
and decision, or the sleepy distance of the owl of Minerva: "Philosophers have but interpreted the world in different ways; what
matters is to change it." (130: 595.) However, the Thesis itself requires interpretation:

   In the concept of an ideological criticism in which reason plays
   an active part, learning and decision-making are related dialectically. On the one hand, the workings of a change-resistant and

----

   [20] A certain ambiguity is characteristic of Schelsky's position. On the one hand, he
accepts the application of analytical science; on the other hand, he makes his acceptance contingent, at least for himself, on the acceptance of his highly personal "transcendental theory of society."

dogmatic society can be revealed only to the extent that learned inquiry is guided by the anticipation of an emancipated society in which all men are autonomous. Conversely, the interest in emancipating society requires an insight into processes of social development, because in them alone does it take objective form. (1: 239.)

From the point of view of Habermas the critical theorist, Albert and Schelsky make the same mistake: they call for—or at least tolerate—an area of political decision-making in which reasonable reflection plays no part. Schelsky regards the practical effects of technical rationality in excessively scientific terms; he accordingly fails to perceive that things not only happen, but are made to happen, and that making them happen requires the effort of thought.[21] Albert reduces the relationship between theory and practice to a mere matter of decision-making, an explanation that is none the more persuasive for his profession of faith in rationalism.[22] Neither Schelsky nor Albert considers the motive forces and directions of action; theory and practice stand side by side unreconciled, to the particular detriment of practice. According to Habermas, the task of critical theory is to "regain and assert on a new basis of reflection . . . the convergence of reason and decision that the great philosophers still consider self-evident" (1: 256). The formula in which Habermas prefers to summarize this task is "decided reason."

It is clearly doubtful that the Camelot scholars would find much assistance in a solution of this kind. Habermas likes complicated, often obscure formulations and those metaphorical assertions that frequently hide under the name of dialectics. His comprehension of the goals, the prospects, and the limits of empirical science is impaired by a cordial antipathy to it. Traces of personal pessimism, such as a nostalgia for the wholesome world of theory and practice

21 Cf. Habermas (1: 228): "If therefore sociology can be ascribed any task beyond the pragmatic tasks of an empirical-analytical science of planning, it is this: instead of explaining what is *happening*, to make us aware of what we are doing, i.e. planning and building, irrespective of whether we are doing it consciously or blindly and without reflection."

22 Compare Habermas on Popper (1: 252): "His motive is enlightenment, but with the resigned reservation that rationalism can be justified only as a profession of faith. . . . To adopt a rationalist attitude, I have to make a decision."

reconciled, at times limit the relevance of his conclusions. Habermas comes close, if not to Schelsky, then to Hegel, in asserting that a critical sociology in his sense is "possible only as historical sociology" (1: 229). None of these objections, however, affects his basic idea: namely, that in a world destined by the principles of its construction to witness the permanent clash of questions and problems, we will fall far short of our human responsibilities if we leave the problems to themselves, or to mere decision-makers, and turn all our reasoning powers to the answering of questions. The positivist separation of knowledge and decision, of procedures for answering questions and procedures for solving problems, is itself premodern; it originated in a time when speechmakers could still celebrate the idyllic relationship of mind and power, when the ivory tower of the university could be contrasted with the hard reality of, say, government, when professors could be patronized by men of action. Today, questions and problems are so closely intermeshed that neither the theorist nor the practitioner can avoid reasoning about them in a single context and with equal intensity. Decided reason is not the worst principle to bring to this task, so long as action, i.e. reasonable decision, is not forgotten.

V

These, however, are pretty words which tell us little about sociology or the sociologist. There is, to begin with, the science of sociology—often defined, often praised and scorned, but still largely at the program stage, a matter of prospective knowledge. If one thinks of this prospective knowledge—as I do—as scientific in the strict sense of the term, one works in sociology with the same presuppositions and conventions that govern all other empirical-theoretical disciplines. A descriptive account of the world of our experience, much as it may occupy us in our theoretical work, is merely material toward the formulation of general propositions (laws, theories) that postulate necessary connections. Theories may be understood as prohibitions; if they are correct, certain things will not happen. Thus to test a theory empirically, one looks for an event that was not supposed to occur. If one finds such an event, the theory must be modified or replaced; if one does not find it, one can work with the theory for the time being, not only in solving problems, but also in changing the world, in social technology.

All this is simply to recapitulate the familiar esoteric rules of scientific inquiry.[23] Their apparent limitations, however, are no reason for triumph on the part of those who do not accept sociology as an empirical science. Indeed, the critical potential of sociology thus understood—and therefore, at least to the same extent, its practical potential as well—is much greater than its detractors believe. In the first place, there are the fundamentally critical implications of rules that seek progress in the refutation of the accepted. Second, there is Hayek's contention that the great theories of social science were all stimulated by burning practical problems: by the struggle between capital and labor, by the formation of colonial empires, by the Great Depression, by the development of underdeveloped countries, by the threat of nuclear war, and by many smaller though hardly less exciting problems. Third, there is the critical effect of sociological knowledge, to which Albert rightly refers. Where ideologies distort people's view of reality, even scientific description may create useful unrest. This is why sociology, long denounced as a "bourgeois science," is only slowly finding a place in Communist countries; this is also why many people in the German Federal Republic regard sociology as "leftist" and hence subversive.[24]

A fourth factor in the critical potential of sociology as an empirical science is its conventions, which make publicity and debate

[23] These ideas are presented here in a highly schematic manner. Readers familiar with scientific methodology need hardly be told that this view of empirical science derives from the work of Karl Popper (18), as does the almost impracticably rigorous notion of general propositions, which excludes both empirical generalizations and probability statements.

[24] The much-discussed subject of the "critical and conservative tasks of sociology" (thus Habermas, 1: 215ff) is more complicated than it appears at first sight, as Schelsky in particular has pointed out in his remarks on "the allegedly restorative effect of empirical research" (20: 58ff). For the international discussion, see Leon D. Bramson (175) and Gerhard Lenski (107).

mandatory. Horowitz has rightly pointed out (in connection with Project Camelot) that it is to some extent simply bad scholarship to interpret all kinds of internal unrest indiscriminately as a "breakdown of the social order," requiring action to restore the status quo. Although in fact, as Horowitz observes, Project Camelot "was not canceled because of its faulty intellectual approaches" (183: 47), his point is clear: scientific debate ranks high among the moral commandments of scientific inquiry. Both the international debate on the merits of functionalism and the German "methodological dispute" show, moreover, that sociologists take this commandment seriously. A fifth and final critical effect of sociology as an empirical science is its openness to all views. This Habermas denies; despite much evidence to the contrary, he consistently charges empirical sociology with dogmatism, inventing for this purpose a "type of science admissible only on positivist premises" (1: 243). But while dogmatic positivists may be almost as numerous in sociology as dogmatic Hegelians, the chief methodological characteristic of sociology as an empirical science is precisely its aversion to dogma. There may be many roads to sociological knowledge other than testable theory, and we do well not to refuse any of them the name of sociology while according it to a "sociology that is nothing but sociology."[25]

Rich as the country of sociology with its open frontiers may be in potential, however, and far as its light (or at least that of its hopes) may shine beyond these frontiers, its glories do not extend to practice. Sociology is theory, and no amount of "decided reason" will set it to dealing actively with the social and political problems of our time. The verbal radicalism of those who like to see sociology and socialism confused—the silly talk, for example, of theory that itself becomes practice—is pseudo-practice, the wishful thinking of people rendered politically inactive by frustrated ambition.[26]

[25] This phrase is used by René König (4: 7) to distinguish empirical sociology from the "philosophy of history and society" and from "social ethics, social reform, and social policy."
[26] Habermas in this sense attacks Marx's attempts to assign dialectical sociology "the critical task of becoming a practical force" (1: 223). Here, however, I am thinking primarily of the lesser dialecticians.

But between the world of theory and the conceptually distinct practical world of action, there is someone who must not be overlooked: the sociologist. Theodor Geiger called the definition of sociology as "what sociologists are doing" a "daring *bon mot*" (178: 45). But the *mot* may well be not so much daring as overmodest. For the boundaries of sociology as theory need not be the boundaries of the sociologist; the sociologist may be more than a person who does sociology, and if the argument developed here is correct, he must be more. The social role of the sociologist cannot reasonably be defined by the business of sociology alone.

The concept of role is used rigorously here. To say that the sociologist has responsibilities beyond the boundaries of his science is not simply to say that in another role the sociologist is a citizen. Such a social division of labor between theory and practice—between "science as a vocation" and "politics as a vocation"—implies that the citizen's actions and the sociologist's knowledge come from entirely different sources.[27] The citizen is moved by passions, unmediated interests, intuitions, beliefs, or manipulated motives, whereas the sociologist, unaffected by such vulgar promptings, patiently works out the remote details of his theories. To think this way, one must hold the potential of theory to be very small and the efficacy of practice to be very great. Today the sociologist knows that advances in the social sciences do not leave people's interests, intuitions, and convictions unchanged; and, conversely, that many efforts to solve practical problems without a detour (as it may seem) by way of theory end up in the "solution," usually disastrous, of no solution at all. In these circumstances, there is little point, at least in the social sciences, in making an absolute distinction in role between theorists and practitioners, and hence between scientists and politicians. It is no longer possible for despots, or even chancellors, to keep a court sociologist—not that they ever tried or that a sociologist would have been much help to them if they had. Indeed, theory and practice have come so close together that theorists and men of affairs occasionally exchange roles: the social sci-

[27] Max Weber has to be understood in this way, especially in the two famous speeches to which I have alluded here.

entist becomes a cabinet minister, the politician a university professor. Although such role exchanges sometimes yield rather odd results, they do prove that "decided reason" forces the theorist and the man of affairs to consider problems and questions with nearly equal intensity.

The exchange of roles is symptomatic rather than typical; the two roles still typically generate different perspectives and conditions of life, though the differences are small. The sociologist begins with a question: Why are there so few working-class children in German universities? The politician begins with a problem: How can we change the German educational system so as to do justice both to the rights of citizens and to the needs of a modern society? Each is acquainted with the other's findings. The politician knows that the theory of social stratification leads from students to the phenomenon of the social distance of certain groups from the university, i.e., to the problem of social obstacles to information and motivation. The sociologist, having worked out a description of a society in which all men are free to develop their talents, does not shrink from considering what might be done to bring about such a society. When the two meet, they do not meet as man of ideas and man of action, the first to be paid a modest honorarium and released after presenting his findings, the second to be given full charge of the field of action. Rather, they discuss questions and problems with equal interest. Both need an answer to the question of whether information, affective orientation, or simply the expected loss of family income is most to blame for the barrier between the worker and the university; both seek to solve the problem of whether to start with scholarships, educational information, new methods of selection, or day schools. Who represents mind in all this and who power? How can one tell, and who cares? One thing is clear: the man of ideas is no longer a mere court jester to the man of action; nor are the many sociologists who stand in a corresponding relation to mayors, personnel managers, town planners, and hospital directors.

Thus Johan Galtung was right; it is not irrelevant whom the sociologist encounters in the middle of the bridge between theory and practice. It was clearly unreasonable to participate in Project Camelot, unreasonable because the goal of developing modern, open societies cannot be either investigated or realized under the auspices of an army, and a foreign army at that. Those who believed it could be had not given sufficient thought to the sociological connections between theory and practice; those who considered the project's goals irrelevant to its purely scientific purpose accepted a separation of theory and practice whose potential dangers the failure of Project Camelot made evident. Those in both categories showed little awareness of the sociologist's role; they may be people who can do good sociology, but good sociologists they are not.

Thus there are bad sociologists. Must I add that there are also bad politicians, men who regard their arbitrary decisions, their personal convictions, or merely their success as an adequate substitute for reasonable decision-making? Much that I have said here in the mood of "is" must be understood in that of "shall." And this brings us to an important question that we have so far failed to ask: By what standard are we to distinguish between a good politician and a bad one, a good sociologist and a bad one? This is a question, but I want to treat it here as a problem. I often think about a society that is at once modern, open, and civilized. Modern—this means that its members not only bear the name of citizens, but can effectively exercise their citizenship. No privilege and no prison of inherited dependence blocks their access to the life chances of the social world. Open—this means that the available life chances themselves grow all the time, and are so manifold in kind and degree that the competition for them offers something for everyone. In an open society, no idiosyncratic plan rations human opportunity. Civilized—this means that respect for men's integrity and men's lives is a principle of institutions as well as of their human incumbents, so that one man's pain is the pain of all. No one pays with his life for speaking out against authority, or is denounced even in death as a disturber of the peace. This society is no utopia, even if it does not exactly correspond to reality; it harbors not only power and resistance, an interest in the status quo and an interest in changing it, but also error and crime, and even bad sociologists.

And yet it is a society in which conceivably one could devote one's strength primarily to the necessary and the beautiful, instead of exhausting it in the struggle against antiquated ideas, narrow-mindedness, force, and inhumanity—or giving up. In my most daring moments I ask myself whether this land of unused opportunities, Germany, might not become such a society, a society worth living in.

It is the sociologist's business to consider what a modern, open, civilized society might look like, and what roads might lead to it. This is the domain of theory. It is also the sociologist's business, once he is equipped with his theories, to take part in the process of changing reality, in making what is reasonable real. This is the domain of practice. To prepare for work in both domains is one of the tasks of a university education. I should be a bad sociologist if I believed that the world could be changed by education; the substance of education may at best be a few steps ahead of the norms of society, and the most excellent education cannot take the place of institutional change. But a good university education can help make sociologists more than people who are competent to do sociology, can help make them forces for unrest in a self-satisfied and inadequate society. The university can also serve as a birthplace and a testing ground of new and better ideas for reconstructing society. For the university, too, theory and practice have come together. Thus beginning within itself, and expanding its influence through its members and graduates in many walks of life, the university can go a long way toward setting in motion the great transformation that will make the society we live in modern, civilized, and free.

References

References

The following references are grouped alphabetically by chapter; titles are numbered consecutively throughout the volume, however, to facilitate citation in the text.

Preface

1. J. Habermas. Theorie und Praxis: Sozialphilosophische Studien. Neuwied-Berlin: Luchterhand, 1963.
2. ———. "Zur Logik der Sozialwissenschaften," Philosophische Rundschau (Beiheft 5). Tübingen: Mohr (Siebeck), 1967.
3. R. König, ed. Soziologie (Fischer-Lexikon 10). Frankfurt: Fischer, 1958.
4. R. K. Merton. Social Theory and Social Structure. Rev. ed. Glencoe, Ill.: Free Press, 1957.
5. H. Popitz. Der Begriff der sozialen Rolle als Element der soziologischen Theorie. Tübingen: Mohr (Siebeck), 1967.

1. Values and Social Science

Originally written in 1957 and presented to the Philosophy Faculty of the University of the Saarland as part of my *Habilitation,* this paper was expanded in 1960. A German version appears in the collection of my essays entitled *Gesellschaft und Freiheit* (Munich: Piper, 1961).

6. F. Boese. Geschichte des Vereins für Sozialpolitik, 1872–1932. Berlin: Duncker & Humblot, 1939.
7. R. Dahrendorf. Class and Class Conflict in Industrial Society. Stanford, Calif.: Stanford University Press (1959), ⁴1965. British edition, London: Routledge & Kegan Paul, ³1963.
8. Deutsche Gesellschaft für Soziologie. Verhandlungen des Ersten Deutschen Soziologentages. Tübingen: Mohr, 1911.
9. ———. Verhandlungen des Zweiten Deutschen Soziologentages. Tübingen: Mohr, 1913.
10. ———. Max Weber und die Soziologie heute (Verhandlungen des Fünfzehnten Deutschen Soziologentages). Tübingen: Mohr (Siebeck), 1965.
11. G. Friedmann. Où va le travail humain? Paris: Gallimard, 1950.

12. T. Geiger. "Kritische Bemerkungen zum Begriffe der Ideologie." *In* Gegenwartsprobleme der Soziologie, ed. G. Eisermann. Potsdam: Potsdamer Verlagsges, 1949.

13. P. Honigsheim. "Max Weber als Soziologe." *Kölner Vierteljahreshefte für Soziologie,* Vol. I, No. 1 (1921).

14. K. Jaspers. Max Weber: Deutsches Wesen im politischen Denken, im Forschen und Philosophieren. Oldenburg: Stalling, 1932.

15. R. Lynd. "Values and the Social Sciences." *In* Knowledge for What? Princeton, N.J.: Princeton University Press, 1946.

16. E. Mayo. The Social Problems of an Industrial Civilization. London: Routledge & Kegan Paul, 1949.

17. K. R. Popper. The Open Society and Its Enemies. London: Routledge & Kegan Paul (1945), ²1952.

18. ———. The Logic of Scientific Discovery. New York: Basic Books, 1959.

19. J. Rumney and J. Maier. Sociology: The Science of Society. London: Duckworth, 1953.

20. H. Schelsky. Ortsbestimmung der deutschen Soziologie. Düsseldorf-Köln: Diederichs, 1959.

21. ———. Auf der Suche nach Wirklichkeit: Gesammelte Aufsätze. Düsseldorf-Köln: Diederichs, 1965.

22. K. Schiller. "Der Ökonom und die Gesellschaft." *Hamburger Jahrbuch für Wirtschafts- und Gesellschaftspolitik,* Vol. I (1956).

23. G. Schmoller. Grundriss der allgemeinen Volkswirtschaftslehre. München-Leipzig: Duncker & Humblot, 1920.

24. M. Weber. Gesammelte Aufsätze zur Wissenschaftslehre. Tübingen: Mohr (Siebeck) (1923), ²1951.

See also *1* above.

2. Homo Sociologicus

This essay was written in 1957, at the Center for Advanced Study in the Behavioral Sciences, Stanford, California, under the influence of discussions with a number of friends, among whom I should like to mention Joseph Ben-David (Jerusalem), Philip Rieff (Philadelphia), and Fritz Stern (New York), as well as Hellmut Geissner, then my colleague at Saarbrücken. This essay was part of a *Festschrift* presented to my philosophy teacher Josef König on the occasion of his sixty-fifth birthday, February 24, 1958. It was first published, in two installments, in the *Kölner Zeitschrift für Soziologie* (Vol. X, Nos. 2–3) in 1958. A year later Westdeutsche Verlag published a separate edition, which has since gone through five printings. (An Italian edition of the essay appeared in 1966.) The essay is included in this collection with the permission of the publisher.

The Preface gives some indication of the lively debate provoked by this essay. Some of the contributions to that debate are listed below, in the references to this essay and to its postscript, "Sociology and Human Nature." To do justice to the large number of publications on the subject of roles that have appeared since "Homo Sociologicus" was written would require a thorough revision; if I have not undertaken this task here, it is because I see the main point of the essay as critical and philosophical rather than strictly sociological. By way of a further exploration of its sociological aspects, I hope soon to publish a short treatise *On Social Roles.*

25. M. Banton. Roles: An Introduction to the Study of Social Relations. London: Tavistock, 1965.
26. B. Barber. Social Stratification. New York: Harcourt, Brace, 1965.
27. C. I. Barnard. "The Functions and Pathology of Status Systems in Formal Organizations." *In* Industry and Society, ed. W. F. Whyte. New York: McGraw-Hill, 1946.
28. J. Ben-David. "Professionals and Unions in Israel." *Industrial Relations,* Vol. V, No. 1 (1965).
29. J. W. Bennett and M. M. Tumin. Social Life: Structure and Function. New York: Alfred A. Knopf, 1952.
30. Cicero. De officiis.
31. E. R. Curtius. Europäische Literatur und Lateinisches Mittelalter. Bern: Huber, 1948.
32. K. Davis. Human Society. New York: Macmillan, 1949.
33. E. Durkheim. Règles de la méthode sociologique. Paris: Presses Universitaires de France, 1950.
34. S. N. Eisenstadt. From Generation to Generation: Age Groups and Social Structure. Glencoe, Ill.: Free Press, 1956.
35. H. H. Gerth and C. W. Mills. Character and Social Structure. New York: Harcourt, Brace, 1964. British edition, London: Routledge & Kegan Paul, 1954.
36. N. Gross, W. S. Mason, and A. W. McEachern. Explorations in Role Analysis. New York: John Wiley, 1958.
37. P. R. Hofstätter. Sozialpsychologie. Berlin: De Gruyter, 1956.
38. ———. Gruppendynamik. Reinbek: Rowohlt, 1957.
39. G. Homans. The Human Group. London: Routledge & Kegan Paul, 1951.
40. A. Inkeles and D. J. Levinson. "National Character: The Study of Modal Personality and Sociocultural Systems." *In* Handbook of Social Psychology, ed. G. Lindzey. Cambridge, Mass.: Addison-Wesley, 1954.
41. I. Kant. Kritik der reinen Vernunft. Ed. R. Schmidt. Leipzig: Meiner, ²1932.
42. R. Linton. The Study of Man. New York: Appleton-Century, 1936.
43. ———. "Role and Status." *In* Readings in Social Psychology, ed. T. H. Newcomb and E. L. Hartley. New York: Henry Holt, 1957.
44. T. H. Marshall. "A Note on Status." *In* Professor Ghurye Felicitation Volume, ed. K. M. Kapadia. Bombay, 1954.

45. K. Marx. Das Kapital. New ed. Berlin: Dietz, 1953.
46. M. Mead. Male and Female: A Study of the Sexes in a Changing World. New York: Morrow, 1949.
47. H. A. Murray. "Toward a Classification of Interaction." *In 54.*
48. R. Musil. Der Mann ohne Eigenschaften. Reinbek: Rowohlt, 1952.
49. S. F. Nadel. The Foundations of Social Anthropology. London: Cohen & West, 1950.
50. ———. The Theory of Social Structure. London: Cohen & West (1957), ²1962.
51. L. J. Neiman and J. W. Hughes. "The Problem of the Concept of Role: A Re-Survey of the Literature." *Social Forces,* Vol. XXX (1951).
52. T. Parsons. The Structure of Social Action. New York: McGraw-Hill, 1937.
53. ———. The Social System. Glencoe, Ill.: Free Press, 1951. British edition, London: Routledge & Kegan Paul, 1952.
54. ———, and E. A. Shils, eds. Toward a General Theory of Action. Cambridge, Mass.: Harvard University Press, 1951.
55. Plato. Laws.
55a. Plato. Philebus.
56. A. R. Radcliffe-Brown. Structure and Function in Primitive Society. London: Cohen & West, 1952.
57. B. Russell. Human Knowledge: Its Scope and Limits. London: Allen & Unwin, 1948.
58. T. R. Sarbin. "Role Theory." *In* Handbook of Social Psychology, ed. G. Lindzey. Cambridge, Mass.: Addison-Wesley, 1954.
59. K. F. Schumann. "Zur Theorie und Praxis der Messung sozialer Sanktionen." Tübingen: philosophy dissertation, 1967.
60. Seneca. Epistolae morales.
61. N. J. Smelser. Social Change in the Industrial Revolution. Chicago: University of Chicago Press, 1959. British edition, London: Routledge & Kegan Paul, 1959.
62. F. Stern, ed. The Varieties of History. New York: Doubleday, ²1957.
63. A. Weber. Einführung in die Soziologie. München: Piper, 1955.

See also *4, 5, 7,* and *24* above.

3. Sociology and Human Nature

In 1962, when Andreas Flitner, then my colleague at Tübingen, invited me to contribute to a volume he was editing on philosophical anthropology—*Wege zur pädagogischen Anthropologie* (Heidelberg: Quelle & Meyer [1963], ²1967)—I took the opportunity to answer some of the critics of "Homo Sociologicus." In the fourth printing of that essay, the reply appeared as an appendix. Its shortcomings are obvious: after a brief summary of role analysis, it proceeds rapidly to a somewhat esoteric debate; it does not answer all the charges initially made against

"Homo Sociologicus"; and it does not, of course, deal at all with critical studies published after it was written (some of which are listed below). It seems to me, however, that the main methodological point of this brief rejoinder remains valid.

64. H. P. Bahrdt. "Zur Frage des Menschenbildes in der Soziologie." *European Journal of Sociology,* Vol. II (1961).
65. R. F. Beerling. "Homo Sociologicus: Een kritiek op Dahrendorf." *Mens en Maatschappij,* Vol. XXXVIII (1963).
66. D. Claessens. "Rolle und Verantwortung." *Soziale Welt,* Vol. XIV, No. 1 (1963).
67. A. Cuvillier. Review of "Homo Sociologicus." *Kyklos,* Vol. XII, No. 4 (1959).
68. E. Garczyk. "Der Homo Sociologicus und der Mensch in der Gesellschaft." *In* Mensch, Gesellschaft, Geschichte: F. D. E. Schleiermachers philosophische Soziologie. München: Uni-Druck, 1963.
69. A. Gehlen. Review of "Homo Sociologicus." *Zeitschrift für die gesamte Staatswissenschaft,* Vol. CXVII, No. 2 (1961).
70. H. Geissner. "Soziale Rollen als Sprechrollen." *Allgemeine und angewandte Phonetik* (1960).
71. J. Janoska-Bendl. "Probleme der Freiheit in der Rollenanalyse." *Kölner Zeitschrift für Soziologie,* Vol. XIV, No. 3 (1962).
72. R. König. "Freiheit und Selbstentfremdung in soziologischer Sicht." *In* Freiheit als Problem der Wissenschaft. Berlin: De Gruyter, 1962.
73. L. Phillipps. Zur Ontologie der sozialen Rolle. Frankfurt: Klostermann, 1963.
74. H. Plessner. "Soziale Rollen und menschliche Natur." *In* Erkenntnis und Verantwortung: Festschrift für Th. Litt. Düsseldorf: Diederichs, 1960.
75. ———. "Ungesellige Geselligkeit." *In* Die moderne Demokratie und ihr Recht: Festschrift für Gerhard Leibholz. Tübingen: Mohr (Siebeck), 1966.
76. F. H. Tenbruck. "Zur deutschen Rezeption der Rollentheorie." *Kölner Zeitschrift für Soziologie,* Vol. XIII, No. 1 (1961).

See also *1, 4, 5,* and *20* above.

4. Out of Utopia

Written in 1957 at the Center for Advanced Study in the Behavioral Sciences, this essay originated as a talk to sociology students at the University of California, Berkeley. First published in the *American Journal of Sociology,* Vol. LXIV, No. 2 (1958), it has since appeared in anthologies in the United States, Germany, and Mexico. In 1959 it was awarded the Journal Fund Award for Learned Publication. For an example of the sometimes heated discussion to which it gave rise, see Robert K.

Merton's remarks in his Introduction to *Sociology Today* (New York: Basic Books, 1959).

77. M. Buber. Paths in Utopia. New York: Macmillan, 1950. British edition, London: Routledge & Kegan Paul, 1949.
78. L. A. Coser. The Functions of Social Conflict. Glencoe, Ill.: Free Press, 1956. British edition, London: Routledge & Kegan Paul, 1956.
79. M. Friedman. Essays in Positive Economics. Chicago: University of Chicago Press, 1953.
80. R. Gerber. Utopian Fantasy. London: Routledge & Kegan Paul, 1955.
81. S. M. Lipset and R. Bendix. "Social Status and Social Structure." *British Journal of Sociology*, Vol. II, Nos. 2–3 (1951).
82. K. Mannheim. Ideology and Utopia. New York: Harcourt, Brace, 1936. British edition, London: Routledge & Kegan Paul, 1954.
83. T. H. Marshall. Sociology at the Crossroads and Other Essays. London, 1963.
84. K. Marx. Nationalökonomie und Philosophie. New ed. Köln-Berlin: Kiepenheuer, 1950.
85. L. Mumford. The Story of Utopias. New York: Peter Smith, 1941.
86. Plato. The Republic. Trans. F. M. Cornford. New York: Oxford University Press (1945), [32]1966.
87. H. G. Wells. A Modern Utopia. London: T. Nelson, 1909.

See also *4, 17,* and *53* above.

5. In Praise of Thrasymachus

In somewhat different form, this essay was presented as the Henry Failing Distinguished Lecture at the University of Oregon on April 25, 1966.

88. R. Dahrendorf. Society and Democracy in Germany. New York: Doubleday, 1967.
89. K. Deutsch. The Nerves of Government. New York: Free Press, 1963.
90. A. Downs. An Economic Theory of Democracy. New York: Harper & Row, 1957.
91. D. Easton. A Framework for Political Analysis. Englewood Cliffs, N.J.: Prentice-Hall, 1965.
92. Encyclopédie, ou Dictionnaire raisonné etc. New ed. Lausanne, 1786.
93. J. W. Gough. The Social Contract: A Critical Study of Its Development. Oxford: Clarendon Press, [2]1957.
94. I. L. Horowitz, ed. The New Sociology. New York: Oxford University Press, 1965.
95. J. Locke. Second Treatise of Government. New ed. New York: Liberal Arts Press, 1952.
95a. ———. Essay Concerning Human Understanding.

96. T. Parsons. Essays in Sociological Theory. Rev. ed. Glencoe, Ill.: Free Press, 1954.

See also *4*, *53*, and *86* above.

6. On the Origin of Inequality among Men

This essay is an expanded version of my inaugural lecture at the University of Tübingen, given February 8, 1961. It was subsequently published under the title *Über den Ursprung der Ungleichheit unter den Menschen* (Tübingen: Mohr/Siebeck, 1961). A stimulating debate in a number of journals led to a revised version in 1966. A substantial portion of this essay, in somewhat different form, was published in English under the title "On the Origin of Social Inequality," in *Philosophy, Politics and Society, Second Series,* edited by Peter Laslett and W. G. Runciman (Oxford: Basil Blackwell, 1962).

The bibliography to the second German edition of this essay contains 86 titles; here I have listed only works actually quoted.

97. Aristotle. Politics.
98. W. Buckley. "Social Stratification and the Functional Theory of Social Differentiation." *American Sociological Review,* Vol. XXIII, No. 4 (1958).
99. K. Davis and W. E. Moore. "Some Principles of Stratification." *American Sociological Review,* Vol. X, No. 2 (1945).
100. E. Durkheim. De la division du travail social. Paris: Presses Universitaires de France, ⁷1960.
101. P. Fahlbeck. Die Klassen und die Gesellschaft. Jena: G. Fischer, 1922.
102. A. Ferguson. An Essay on the History of Civil Society. London, ⁵1783.
103. H. H. Joglund. Ursprünge und Grundlagen der Soziologie bei Adam Ferguson. Berlin: Dunker & Humblot, 1959.
104. I. Kant. Populäre Schriften. Ed. P. Menzer. Berlin: Reimer, 1911.
105. W. C. Lehmann. Adam Ferguson and the Beginnings of Modern Sociology. New York: Columbia University Press, 1930.
106. ———. "John Millar, Historical Sociologist." *British Journal of Sociology,* Vol. III, No. 1 (1952).
107. G. Lenski. Power and Privilege: A Theory of Social Stratification. New York: McGraw-Hill, 1966.
108. C. Meiners. Geschichte der Ungleichheit der Stände unter den vornehmsten Europäischen Völkern. Hannover, 1792.
109. J. Millar. The Origin of the Distinction of Ranks. Edinburgh, 1771.
110. T. Parsons. "An Analytical Approach to the Theory of Social Stratification." *American Journal of Sociology,* Vol. XLV (1940).
111. J.-J. Rousseau. Discours sur l'origine de l'inégalité parmi les hommes. *In* Du contrat social etc. New ed. Paris: Garnier Frères, n.d.
112. F. von Schiller. "Etwas über die erste Menschengesellschaft nach dem

Leitfaden der mosaischen Urkunde." *In* Sämmtliche Werke, Vol. VI. Ed. Goedeke. Stuttgart: Cotta, 1872.

113. G. Schmoller. "Die Tatsachen der Arbeitsteilung." *Jahrbuch für Gesetz-gebung, Verwaltung, und Volkswirtschaft,* Vol. XIII (1889).

114. ———. "Das Wesen der Arbeitsteilung und die soziale Klassenbildung." *Jahrbuch für Gesetzgebung, Verwaltung, und Volkswirtschaft,* Vol. XIV (1890).

115. R. Schwartz. "Functional Alternatives to Inequality." *American Sociological Review,* Vol. XX, No. 4 (1955).

116. W. Sombart. "Die Anfänge der Soziologie." *In* Erinnerungsgabe für Max Weber, ed. M. Palyi. München-Leipzig, 1923.

117. O. Spann. Der wahre Staat. Leipzig: Quelle & Meyer, 1921.

118. L. von Stein. Die Gesellschaftslehre. 1852.

119. M. M. Tumin. "Some Principles of Stratification: A Critical Analysis." *American Sociological Review,* Vol. XVIII, No. 4 (1953).

120. ———. "On Inequality." *American Sociological Review,* Vol. XXVIII, No. 1 (1963).

121. M. Weber. Wirtschaft und Gesellschaft. Tübingen: Mohr (Siebeck), 41956.

122. D. Wrong. "The Functional Theory of Stratification: Some Neglected Considerations." *American Sociological Review,* Vol. XXIV, No. 6 (1959).

See also *23, 26, 92,* and *96* above.

7. *Liberty and Equality*

This essay was written in 1958. An abridged version was published in Volume IV (1959) of the *Hamburger Jahrbuch für Wirtschafts- und Gesellschaftspolitik,* which brought together contributions in honor of Eduard Heimann on the occasion of his seventieth birthday. A complete version of the essay appeared in my *Gesellschaft und Freiheit* (Munich: Piper, 1961).

123. Lord Acton. Lectures on Modern History. New ed. London: Macmillan, 1956.

124. E. Heimann. Reason and Faith in Modern Society: Liberalism, Marxism, and Democracy. Middletown, Conn.: Wesleyan University Press, 1961.

125. D. Jacobson. "Everything Without Tears." *Encounter,* No. 57 (June 1958).

126. F. Kluge and A. Götze. Etymologisches Wörtesbuch der deutschen Sprache. Berlin: De Gruyter, 1948.

127. H. Laski. A Grammar of Politics. London: Allen & Unwin, 31934.

128. T. H. Marshall. Citizenship and Social Class. Cambridge, Eng.: Cambridge University Press, 1950.

129. K. Marx. Kritik des Gothaer Programms. New ed. Berlin: Neue Weg, 1946.

130. ———, and F. Engels. Die deutsche Ideologie. New ed. Berlin: Dietz, 1943.

131. J. S. Mill. On Liberty. Ed. R. Kirk. Chicago: Regnery, n.d.

132. D. Riesman. The Lonely Crowd. New York: Doubleday, 1953.
133. B. S. Rowntree. The Human Needs of Labour. New ed. London: Longmans, 1937.
134. ———, and G. R. Lavers. Poverty and the Welfare State. London: Longmans, Green, 1951.
135. A. de Tocqueville. Democracy in America. Ed. P. Bradley. New ed. New York: Vintage Books, 1956.
136. P. Townsend. "Measuring Poverty." In Needs and Standards in the Social Services. London: British Sociological Association, 1953.
137. M. Young. On the Rise of the Meritocracy. New York: Random House, 1959.

See also 45, 97, and 104 above.

8. Market and Plan

Written in 1966, this essay originated as a lecture at the University of Freiburg, sponsored by the Walter Eucken Institute. It was published for the Institute under the title Markt und Plan: Zwei Typen der Rationalität (Tübingen: Mohr/Siebeck, 1966). For this volume the text has been modified and notes have been added.

138. H. Arendt. The Origins of Totalitarianism. New York: Meridian Books, 1958.
139. ———. Eichmann in Jerusalem. Rev. ed. New York: Viking, 1965.
140. R. Aron. La Définition libérale de la liberté. European Journal of Sociology, Vol. II, No. 2 (1961) and Vol. V, No. 2 (1964).
141. Club Jean Moulin. L'Etat et le citoyen. Paris, 1964.
142. R. Dahrendorf. Bildung ist Bürgerrecht. Hamburg: Nannen, 1965.
143. ———. Conflict after Class. London: Longmans, Green, 1967.
144. Deutsche Gesellschaft für Soziologie. Max Weber und die Soziologie heute (Verhandlungen des Fünfzehnten. Deutschen Soziologentages). Tübingen: Mohr (Siebeck), 1965.
145. F. Ferrarotti. Max Weber e il destino della ragione. Bari: Laterza, 1965.
146. M. Friedman. Capitalism and Freedom. Chicago: University of Chicago Press, 1962.
147. C. J. Friedrich. Demokratie als Herrschafts- und Lebensform. Heidelberg: Quelle & Meyer, 1959.
148. M. J. Grab. Der Begriff des Rationalen in der Soziologie Max Webers. Karlsruhe: Fischer, 1927.
149. F. A. Hayek. The Constitution of Liberty. London: Hutchinson, 1961.
150. ———. "Two Kinds of Rationalism." In K. Popper, Conjectures and Refutations. London: Routledge & Kegan Paul, 1963.
151. Kölner Zeitschrift für Soziologie, Vol. XIII (1961). [Discussion of 154 by R. Bendix, K. Löwenstein, and others.]
152. E. Kogon. Der SS-Staat. Stockholm: Bermann-Fischer, 1947.

153. K. Mannheim. Man and Society in an Age of Reconstruction. London: Routledge & Kegan Paul, 1940.
154. W. Mommsen. Max Weber und die deutsche Politik. Tübingen: Mohr (Siebeck), 1955.
155. K. R. Popper. The Poverty of Historicism. London: Routledge & Kegan Paul, 1957.

See also 7, *17*, *21*, *24*, *79*, *89*, and *121* above.

9. Uncertainty, Science, and Democracy

This essay was written in 1962, for a *Festschrift* presented to my teacher Josef König on the occasion of his seventieth birthday. The *Festschrift* was later published under the title *Argumentationen,* edited by Hans Delius and Günther Patzig (Göttingen: Vandenhoeck & Ruprecht, 1963).

156. K. Arrow. Social Choice and Individual Values. New York: John Wiley, 1951.
157. J. B. Conant. Zwei Denkweisen (Hamburger Universitätsreden 21). Hamburg, 1957.
158. R. Dahrendorf. Marx in Perspektive. Hannover: Dietz, 1953.
159. ———. "Conflict and Liberty: Some Remarks on the Social Structure of German Politics." *British Journal of Sociology,* Vol. XIV, No. 3 (1963).
160. W. R. Garner. Uncertainty and Structure as Psychological Concepts. New York: John Wiley, 1962.
161. H. Giersch. Allgemeine Wirtschaftspolitik. Wiesbaden: Gabler, 1960.
162. G. W. F. Hegel. Grundlinien der Philosophie des Rechts. Hamburg: Meiner, ⁴1955.
163. J. M. Keynes. A Treatise on Probability. London, 1957.
164. P. Laslett, ed. Philosophy, Politics and Society. Oxford: Basil Blackwell, 1956.
165. ———, and W. G. Runciman, eds. Philosophy, Politics and Society, Second Series. Oxford: Basil Blackwell, 1962.
166. F. Lassalle. Arbeiterprogramm. *In* Ausgewählte Texte. Ed. T. Ramm. Stuttgart: Kröner, 1962.
167. E. Liefmann-Keil. Ökonomische Theorie der Sozialpolitik. Berlin: De Gruyter, 1965.
168. K. R. Popper. On the Sources of Knowledge and of Ignorance (Proceedings of the British Academy, Vol. XLVI). London: Oxford University Press, 1960.
169. F. von Schiller. "Über die notwendigen Grenzen beim Gebrauch schöner Formen." *In* Sämmtliche Werke, Vol. VI. Ed. Goedeke. Stuttgart: Cotta, 1872.
170. J. W. N. Watkins. "Epistemology and Politics." Paper delivered before the Aristotelian Society, December 9, 1957.

See also *19*, *79*, *90*, *104*, *140*, *146*, and *149* above.

10. Sociology and the Sociologist

Written in 1967, this was my inaugural lecture at the University of Constance, delivered on June 21, 1967, and published by the University under the title *Die Soziologie und der Soziologe: Zur Frage von Theorie und Praxis.*

171. T. W. Adorno and M. Horkheimer. Dialektik der Aufklärung. Amsterdam: Querido, 1947.
172. H. Albert. Theorie und Realität. Tübingen: Mohr (Siebeck) 1964.
173. R. Bendix. Social Science and the Distrust of Reason. Berkeley, Calif., 1951.
174. J. Bernard. "Letter to the Editor." *The American Sociologist.* Vol. I, No. 1 (1965).
175. L. Bramson. The Political Context of Sociology. Princeton, N.J.: Princeton University Press, 1961.
176. R. Dahrendorf. "Die drei Soziologien." *Kölner Zeitschrift für Soziologie.* Vol. XII, No. 1 (1960).
177. M. S. Edmonson, et al. "Letter to the Editor." *The American Sociologist.* Vol. I, No. 4 (1966).
178. T. Geiger. Arbeiten zur Soziologie. Neuwied: Luchterhand, 1962.
179. W. J. Goode. "Letter to the Editor." *The American Sociologist.* Vol. I, No. 5 (1966).
180. A. de Grazia. "Project Camelot." *Behavioral Scientist* (Sept. 1965).
181. J. Habermas. Strukturwandel der Öffentlichkeit. Neuwied: Luchterhand, 1962.
182. I. L. Horowitz. "The Life and Death of Project Camelot." *Trans-Action.* Vol. III, No. 4 (1965).
183. D. L. Johnson. "Letter to the Editor." *The American Sociologist.* Vol. I, No. 4. (1965).
184. F. Kambartel. Was ist und soll Philosophie? Constance: Universitätsverlag, 1967.
185. R. Kurtz. "Letter to the Editor." *The American Sociologist.* Vol. I, No. 2 (1965).
186. C. W. Mills. The Sociological Imagination. New York: Oxford, 1959.
187. T. Parsons. "Editor's Introduction." *The American Sociologist.* Vol. II, No. 2 (1967).
188. R. Robinson. Landscape With Dead Dons. Harmondsworth: Penguin, 1963.
189. K. H. Silvert. "American Academic Ethics and Social Research Abroad." *West Coast South America Series.* Vol. XII, No. 3 (1966).
190. C. Tilly. "Letter to the Editor." *The American Sociologist.* Vol. I, No. 2 (1966).
191. J. Walsh. "Cancellation of Project Camelot." *Science* (Sept. 10, 1965).
192. W. Zapf. Materialien zur Theorie des sozialen Wandels. Uupub. dissertation, University of Constance.

See also *1, 9, 17, 20, 21, 94, 106, 130, 150, 153, 154,* and *164* above.

Index

Index

and social roles, 25–74; equilibrium theory of, 113–28 *passim*; constraint theory of (conflict model), 126–28; equilibrium theory vs. constraint theory, 137–50 *passim*; and inequality, 151–78 *passim*; tyranny of, 207–10

Sociology: para-theory in, vi–viii, x; social role of the sociologist, ix, 16, 86–87, 98, 100ff, 119, 256–78 *passim*; and value judgments, 1–18 *passim*, 77n, 84–87; and politics, 18, 85n, 87, 99f, 123, 217–31 *passim*, 256–78 *passim*; problems of defining, 22–25, 94–97; and psychology, 29, 46, 56f, 61, 64, 66; and philosophy, 74–82, 106; historical development of, 76–77, 84–85, 101, 152–65 *passim*, 273; and philosophical anthropology, 95–100; and problem-consciousness, 121–23

Sociology, American, v, vi, 17, 23, 53n, 89ff, 120, 163–65, 176. *See also individual sociologists by name*

Sociology, European, v, vi, 63, 89, 91, 96. *See also individual sociologists by name*

Socrates, 107, 113f, 129–37 *passim*, 150, 232

Sombart, Werner, 2, 157

Spann, Othmar, 3, 167n

Spranger, Eduard, 3

Stein, Lorenz von, 158ff

Stouffer, Samuel A., 46

Strauss, David Friedrich, 76n

Structural-functional theory, *see* Equilibrium theory

Tacitus, 142

Tenbruck, F. H., 94f, 95n, 99, 103ff

Theory and practice, in sociology, 14–16, 256–78 *passim*

Thomas Aquinas, St., 184

Thrasymachus, x, 129–35 *passim*, 137f, 146, 148ff

Tilly, Charles, 265

Tocqueville, Alexis de, 147, 180–81, 182, 193, 206

Treitschke, Heinrich von, 160

Tumin, Melvin M., 62, 154n, 164f, 167n

Uncertainty, 128, 137, 148f, 220, 227, 229; three types, 234–36; and science, 236n, 240–46; in economics, 237–38; and ethics, 239n, 253; and politics, 247–55 *passim*. *See also* Certainty

Utopia, viii, 107–28 *passim*, 176, 178, 226. *See also* Equilibrium theory

Vallance, Theodore, 260n

Values, in social science, vii, 1–18 *passim*, 77n, 84–87, 99f, 123, 134, 264, 266f. *See also* Objectivity; social role of the sociologist *under* Sociology; *and under* Weber, Max

Value Dispute, 1–5 *passim*, 11, 14, 16f, 85n

Verein für Sozialpolitik, 1ff, 85, 266

Watkins, J. W. N., 233, 239n, 249, 254

Webb, Sidney and Beatrice, 77n, 159

Weber, Alfred, 77

Weber, Max: on science and values, 2–11 *passim*, 15–16, 17–18, 85f, 99f, 123, 134, 233, 242, 266, 275n; concept of social action, 24; concept of life chances, 155n; on power, 173, 201; on social rationality, 215–18 *passim*

Wells, H. G., 107n

Wiese, Leopold von, 3, 24

Wisdom, John, 19n

Wrong, Dennis, 138n, 165

Young, Michael, 175, 199n

Zapf, Wolfgang, 265

Znaniecki, Florian, 23

050478